1,000,000 Books

are available to read at

---◆---

www.ForgottenBooks.com

---◆---

**Read online
Download PDF
Purchase in print**

ISBN 978-1-5279-3070-4
PIBN 10930904

English
Français
Deutsche
Italiano
Español
Português

www.forgottenbooks.com

Mythology Photography **Fiction**
Fishing Christianity **Art** Cooking
Essays Buddhism Freemasonry
Medicine **Biology** Music **Ancient
Egypt** Evolution Carpentry Physics
Dance Geology **Mathematics** Fitness
Shakespeare **Folklore** Yoga Marketing
Confidence Immortality Biographies
Poetry **Psychology** Witchcraft
Electronics Chemistry History **Law**
Accounting **Philosophy** Anthropology
Alchemy Drama Quantum Mechanics
Atheism Sexual Health **Ancient History**
Entrepreneurship Languages Sport
Paleontology Needlework Islam
Metaphysics Investment Archaeology
Parenting Statistics Criminology
Motivational

GENERAL AND SPECIAL LAWS

PASSED AT THE

SIXTEENTH SESSION

OF THE

LEGISLATIVE ASSEMBLY

OF THE

TERRITORY OF DAKOTA.

BEGUN AND HELD AT BISMARCK, IN SAID TERRITORY, ON TUESDAY, THE 13th DAY OF JANUARY, A. D. 1885, AND CON- CLUDED MARCH 13th, A. D. 1885.

YANKTON, D. T.
Bowen & Kingsbury, Public Printers.
Press and Dakotaian,
1885.

PUBLIC LAWS.

THE ORGANIC LAW.

BOUNDARIES OF DAKOTA.

All that part of the territory of the United States included within the following limits, namely : Commencing at a point in the main channel of the Red River of the North, where the forty-ninth degree of north latitude crosses the same ; thence up the main channel of the same, and along the boundary of the State of Minnesota to Big Stone lake; thence along the boundary line of the State of Minnesota to the Iowa line; thence along the boundary line of the State of Iowa to the point of intersection between the Big Sioux and Missouri rivers; thence up the Missouri river, and along the boundary line of the State of Nebraska to the mouth of the Niobrara or Running Water river; thence following up the same, in the middle of the main channel thereof, to the mouth of the Keha Paha or Turtle Hill river; thence up that river to the forty-third parallel of north latitude; thence due west to the twenty-seventh meridian of longitude west from Washington; thence due north on that meridian to the forty-ninth degree of north latitude; thence east along the forty-ninth degree of north latitude to the place of beginning, is organized into a temporary government by the name of the Territory of Dakota. [*Section 1900 of the Revised Statutes of the United States.*]

***

Be it enacted, etc., That the northern boundary of the state of Nebraska shall be, and hereby is, subject to the provisions hereinafter contained, extended so as to include all that portion of the Territory of Dakota lying south of the forty-third parallel of north latitude, and east of the Keya Paha river, and west of the main channel of the Missouri river; and when the Indian title to the lands thus described shall be extinguished, the jurisdiction over said land shall be, and hereby is, ceded to the state of Nebraska, and subject to all the conditions and limitations provided in the act of congress admitting Nebraska into the Union, and the northern boundary of the state shall be extended to said forty-third parallel as fully and effectually as if said lands had been included in the boundaries of said state at the time of its admission into the Union ; reserving to the United States the original right of soil in said lands, and of disposing of the same ; *Provided*, That this act, so far as jurisdiction is concerned, shall not take effect until the President shall, by proclamation, declare that the Indian title to said lands has been extinguished, nor shall it take effect until the state of Nebraska shall have assented to the provisions of this act, and if the state of Nebraska shall not by an act of its legislature consent to the provisions of this act within two years next after the passage hereof, this act shall cease and be of no effect. [*Approved, March* 28, 1882.

THE FOLLOWING SECTIONS OF THE REVISED STATUTES OF THE UNITED STATES, OF 1874, AND EXTRACTS FROM SUBSEQUENT STATUTES AT LARGE, INCLUDE ALL EXISTING UNITED STATES LAWS RELATING TO DAKOTA.

§ 1839.   Nothing in this title shall be construed to impair the rights of person or property pertaining to the Indians in any territory, so long as such rights remain unextinguished by treaty between the United States and such Indians, or to include any territory which, by treaty with any Indian tribe, is not, without the consent of such tribe, embraced within the territorial limits or jurisdiction of any state or territory; but all such territory shall be excepted out of the boundaries, and constitute no part of any territory now or hereafter organized, until such tribe signifies its assent to the president to be embraced within a particular territory.

§ 1840.   Nor shall anything in this title be construed to affect the authority of the United States to make any regulations respecting the Indians of any territory, their lands, property, or rights, by treaty, law, or otherwise, in the same manner as might be if no temporary government existed, or is hereafter established in any such territory.

§ 1841.   The executive power of each territory shall be vested in a governor, who shall hold his office for four years, and until his successor is appointed and qualified, unless sooner removed by the president.   He shall reside in the territory for which he is appointed, and shall be commander in chief of the militia thereof. He may grant pardons and reprieves, and remit fines and forfeitures for offenses against the laws of the territory for which he is appointed, and respites for offenses against the laws of the United States, till the decision of the president can be made known thereon.   He shall commission all officers who are appointed under the laws of such territory, and shall take care that the laws thereof be faithfully executed.

§ 1842.   Every bill which has passed the legislative assembly of any territory shall, before it becomes a law, be presented to the Governor.   If he approve, he shall sign it, but if not, he shall return it, with his objections, to that House in which it originated, and that House shall enter the objections at large on its journal, and proceed to reconsider. If, after such reconsideration, two-thirds of that House agree to pass the bill, it shall be sent, together with the objections, to the other House, by which it shall likewise be reconsidered; and, if approved by two-thirds of that House, it shall become a law. But in all such cases the votes of both Houses shall be determined by yeas and nays, and the names of the persons voting for or against the bill shall be entered upon the journal of each House. If any bill is not returned by the Governor within three days, Sundays excluded, after it has been presented to him, the same shall be a law, in like manner as if he had signed it, unless the Legislative Assembly, by adjournment *sine die*, prevent its return, in which case it shall not be a law.

§ 1843. There shall be appointed a Secretary for each territory, who shall reside within the territory for which he is appointed, and shall hold his office for four years, and until his successor is appointed and qualified, unless sooner removed by the President. In case of the death, removal, resignation, or absence of the Governor from the territory, the Secretary shall execute all the powers and perform all the duties of Governor during such vacancy or absence, or until another Governor is appointed and qualified.

§ 1844. The Secretary shall record and preserve all the laws and proceedings of the Legislative Assembly, and all the acts and proceedings of the Governor in the executive department; he shall transmit one copy of the laws and journals of the Legislative Assembly, within thirty days after the end of each session thereof, to the President, and two copies of the laws within like time, to the President of the Senate, and to the Speaker of the House of Representatives, for the use of Congress. He shall transmit one copy of the executive proceedings and official correspondence semi-annually, on the first day of January and July in each year, to the President. He shall prepare the acts passed by the Legislative Assembly for publication, and furnish a copy thereof to the public printer of the Territory, within ten days after the passage of each act.

**

And hereafter it shall be the duty of the Secretary of each Territory to furnish estimates in detail for the lawful expenses thereof, to be presented to the Secretary of the Treasury on or before the first day of October of every year. [*Part of act approved June* 20, 1874.

**

And it shall be the duty of the Secretary of each of the Territories of the United States to furnish the Surveyor-General of the Territory for the use of the United States, a copy duly certified of every act of the Legislature of the Territory, incorporating any city or town, the same to be forwarded by such Secretary to the Surveyor-General within one month from the date of its approval. [*Part of act approved March* 3, 1877.

***

§ 1845. From and after the first day of July, eighteen hundred and seventy-three, the annual salaries of the Governors of the several Territories, shall be three thousand five hundred dollars, and the salaries of the Secretaries shall be two thousand five hundred dollars each.

§ 1846. The Legislative power in each Territory shall be vested in the Governor and a Legislative Assembly. The Legislative Assembly shall consist of a Council and House of Representatives The members of both branches of the Legislative Assembly shall have the qualifications of voters as herein prescribed. They shall be chosen for the term of two years, and the sessions of the respective Legislative Assemblies shall be biennial. Each Legislative Assembly shall fix by law the day of commencement of its regular session. The members of the Council and House of Representatives shall reside in the district or county for which they are respectively elected.

§ 1847. Previous to the first election for members of the Legislative Assembly of a Territory in which Congress may hereafter provide a temporary government, the Governor shall cause a census of the inhabitants and qualified voters of the several counties and districts of the Territory to be taken by such persons and in such mode as he may designate and appoint, and the persons so appointed shall receive a reasonable compensation for their services. And the first election shall be held at such time and places, and be conducted in such manner, both as to the persons who superintend such election and the returns thereof, as the Governor may direct, and he shall, at the same time, declare the number of members of the Council and House of Representatives to which each of the counties and districts is entitled under the act providing such temporary government for the particular Territory. The persons having the highest number of legal votes in each of the districts for members of the Council shall be declared by the Governor to be duly elected to the Council, and the persons having the highest number of legal votes for the House of Representatives shall be declared by the Governor to be duly elected members of that House; but in case two or more persons voted for have an equal number of votes, and in case a vacancy otherwise occurs in either branch of the Legislative Assembly, the Governor shall order a new election, and the persons thus elected to the Legislative Assembly shall meet at such place and on such day as the Governor appoints.

§ 1848. After such first election, however, the time, place and manner of holding elections by the people in any newly created territory, as well as of holding all such elections in territories now organized, shall be prescribed by the laws of each territory.

§ 1849. The apportionment of representation which the Governor is authorized to make by section 1847, in case of a territory hereafter erected by Congress, shall be as nearly equal as practicable among the several districts and counties for such first election of the Council and House of Representatives, giving to each section of the territory representation in the ratio of its population, except Indians not taxed; and thereafter in such new territory, as well as in all territories now organized, the legislative assemblies respectively may readjust and apportion the representation to the two houses thereof, among the several counties and districts, in such manner, from time to time, as they deem just and proper, but the members of either house, as authorized by law, shall not be increased.

§ 1851. The legislative power of every territory shall extend to all rightful subjects of legislation not inconsistent with the constitution and laws of the United States. But no law shall be passed interfering with the primary disposal of the soil; no tax shall be imposed upon the property of the United States, nor shall the lands or other property of non-residents be taxed higher than the lands or other property of residents.

§ 1925. In addition to the restrictions upon the legislative power of the territories, contained in the preceding chapter, section eighteen hundred and fifty-one, the legislative assemblies of Colorado, Dakota and Wyoming shall not pass any law impairing the rights of private property, nor make any discrimination in taxing different kinds of property; but all property subject to taxation shall be taxed in proportion to its value

⁎

Be it enacted, etc., That section eighteen hundred and fifty-two be, and the same hereby is, so amended as to read as follows: " § 1852. The sessions of the legislative assemblies of the several territories of the United States shall be limited to sixty days' duration." [*Approved, December* 23, 1880.

⁎

Hereafter no extraordinary session of the Legislature of any Territory, wherever the same is now authorized by law, shall be called until the reasons for the same have been presented to the President of the United States, and his approval thereof has been duly given. [*Part of act approved June* 22, 1874.

⁎

That from and after the adjournment of the next session of the several territorial legislatures the Council of each of the territories of the United States shall not exceed twelve members, and the House of Representatives of each shall not exceed twenty-four members, and the members of each branch of the said several legislatures shall receive a compensation of four dollars per day each during the sessions provided by law, and shall receive such mileage as the law provides; and the President of the Council and the Speaker of the House of Representatives shall each receive six dollars per day for the same time.

And the several legislatures at their next sessions are directed to divide their respective territories into as many Council and representative districts as they desire, which districts shall be as nearly equal as practicable, taking into consideration population, except "Indians not taxed;" *Provided,* The number of Council districts shall not exceed twenty-four in any one of said territories, and all parts of sections eighteen hundred and forty-seven, eighteen hundred and forty-nine, eighteen hundred and fifty-three, and nineteen hundred and twenty-two of the Revised Statutes of the United States in conflict with the provisions herein are repealed.

That the subordinate officers of each branch of said territorial legislatures shall consist of one chief clerk, who shall receive a compensation of six dollars per day ; one enrolling and engrossing clerk at five dollars per day; sergeant-at-arms and doorkeeper at five dollars per day; one messenger and watchman at four dollars per day each ; and one chaplain at one dollar and fifty cents per day.

Said sums shall be paid only during the sessions of said legislatures, and no greater number of officers or charges per diem shall be paid or allowed by the United States to any territory. [*Part of act approved June* 19, 1878.

*

Be it enacted by the Senate and House of Representatives of the United States of America in Congress Assembled,. That the Legislature of the Territory of Dakota shall hereafter consist of twenty-four members of the Council and forty-eight members of the House of Representatives, and that there shall be elected at the next general election in said territory two members of the Council and four members of the House of Representatives in each of the twelve legislative districts provided for in chapter seven of the territorial statutes of eighteen hundred and eighty-three of said territory. [*Approved, June* 12, 1884.

*

And the Legislature of Dakota may divide said territory into as many Council and Representative districts as they desire, which districts shall be as nearly equal as practicable taking into consideration population (except Indians not taxed); *Provided,* That the number of Council districts shall not exceed twenty-four, and the number of Representative districts shall not exceed forty-eight. [*Part of act approved March* 3, 1885.

§ 1942. The members of the legislative assemblies of New Mexico, Utah, Washington, Colorado, Dakota, Arizona and Wyoming territori.s shall each receive three dollars for every twenty miles' tiavel in going to and returning from the sessions of their respective bodies, estimated according to the nearest usually traveled route.

§ 1854 No member of the legislative assembly of any territory now organized shall hold or be appointed to any office which has been created, or the salary or emoluments of which have been increased while he was a member, during the term for which he was elected, and for one year after the expiration of such term; but this restriction shall not be applicable to members of the first legislative assembly in any territory hereafter organized; and no person holding a commission or appointment under the United States, except postmasters, shall be a member of the legislative assembly, or shall hold any office under the government of any territory. The exception of postmasters shall not apply in the territory of Washington.

§ 1855. No law of any territorial legislature shall be made or enforced by which the Governor or Secretary of a territory, or the members or officers of any territorial legislature, are paid any compensation other than that provided by the laws of the United States.

And section eighteen hundred and sixty-one of the Revised Statutes is hereby repeal.d, and this substituted in lieu thereof: *Provided,* That for the performance of all official duties imposed by the territorial legislatures, and not provided for in the organic act, the secretaries of the territories respectively shall be allowed such fees as may be fixed by the territorial legislatures. And in no case shall the expenditure for public printing in any of the territores exceed the sum of two thousand five hundred dollars for any one year.

§ 1856. Justices of the peace and all general officers of the militia in the several territories shall be elected by the people in such manner as the respective legislatures may provide by law.

Be it enacted, etc., § 1. That when from any cause there shall be a vacancy in the office of justice of the peace in any of the territories of the United States, it shall be lawful to fill such vacancy by appointment or election, in such manner as has been or may be provided by the Governor and legislative assembly of

such Territory; *Provided,* That such appointee, or person
elected to fill such vacancy, shall hold office only until his successor shall be regularly elected and qualified as provided by law.

§ 2.   That all laws and parts of laws in conflict with the provisions of this act be and the same are hereby repealed. [*Approved, April* 16, 1880.

..

§ 1857.   All township, district and county officers except justices
of the peace and general officers of the militia, shall be appointed
or elected in such manner as may be provided by the Governor
and legislative assembly of each Territory; and all other officers
not herein otherwise provided for, the Governor shall nominate,
and by and with the advice and consent of the legislative Council of
each territory, shall appoint; but, in the first instance, where a
new territory is hereafter created by Congress, the Governor alone
may appoint all the officers referred to in this and the preceding
section, and assign them to their respective townships, districts
and counties, and the officers so appointed shall hold their offices
until the end of the first session of the legislative assembly.

§ 1858.   In any of the territories, whenever a vacancy happens
from resignation or death, during the recess of the legislative
Council, in any office which, under the organic act of any territory, is to be filled by appointment of the Governor, by and with
the advice and consent of the Council, the Governor shall fill
such vacancy by granting a commission, which shall expire at the
end of the next session of the legislative Council.

§ 1859.   Every male citizen above the age of twenty-one, including persons who have legally declared their intention to become citizens, in any territory hereafter organized, and who are
actual residents of such territory at the time of the organization
thereof, shall be entitled to vote at the first election in such territory, and to hold any office therein, subject, nevertheless, to the
limitations specified in the next section.

§ 1860.   At all subsequent elections, however, in any territory
hereafter organized by congress, as well as at all elections in territories already organized, the qualifications of voters and of holding office shall be such as may be prescribed by the legislative assembly of each territory; subject, nevertheless, to the following
restrictions on the power of the legislative assembly, namely:

First.   The right of suffrage and of holding office shall be exercised only by citizens of the United States above the age of
twenty-one years, and by those above that age who have declared
on oath, before a competent court of record, their intention to become such, and have taken an oath to support the Constitution
and government of the United States.

Second. There shall be no denial of the elective franchise, or of holding office, to a citizen on account of race, color, or previous condition of servitude.

Third. No officer, soldier, seaman, mariner, or other person in the army or navy, or attached to troops in the service of the United States, shall be allowed to vote in any territory, by reason of being on service therein, unless such territory is, and has been for the period of six months, his permanent domicile.

Fourth. No person belonging to the army or navy shall be elected to or hold any civil office or appointment in any territory.

§ 1862. Every territory shall have the right to send a delegate to the house of representatives of the United States, to serve during each congress, who shall be elected by the voters in the territory qualified to elect members of the Legislative Assembly thereof. The person having the greatest number of votes shall be declared by the Governor duly elected, and a certificate shall be given accordingly. Every such delegate shall have a seat in the House of Representatives, with the right of debating, but not of voting,

§ 1863. The first election of a delegate in any territory for which a temporary government is hereafter provided by congress, shall be held at the time and places, and the manner the Governor of such territory may direct, after at least sixty days' notice, to be given by proclamation; but at all subsequent elections therein, as well as at all elections for a delegate in organized territories, such time, places and manner of holding the election, shall be prescribed by the law of each territory.

**

Be it enacted by the Senate and House of Representatives of the United States of America in Congress Assembled: That hereafter the Supreme Court of the Territory of Dakota shall consist of a chief justice and five associate justices, any five of whom shall constitute a quorum.

§ 2. That it shall be the duty of the President to appoint two additional associate justices of said supreme court, in a manner now provide by law, who shall hold their office for the term of four years, and until their successors are appointed and qualified.

§ 3. That the said territory shall be divided into six judicial districts, and a district court shall be held in each district by one of the justices of the supreme court, at such time and place as may be prescribed by law. Each judge after assignment, shall reside in the district to which he is assigned.

§ 4. That until changed by the Legislative Assembly of said territory, the fifth district of said territory, shall consist of the following counties, namely: Brookings, Kingsbury, Beadle, Deuel, Hamlin, Grant, Codington, Clark, Day, Spink, Brown, Hand, Hyde, Hughes, Sully, Edmunds, Faulk, McPherson Potter,

Campbell, Roberts and Walworth, and the Sisseton and Wahpeton Indian reservation. And the second district and fourth district shall consist of the remainder of the Territory which now constitutes said second district and the fourth district, respectively, as defined by the statutes of said Territory.

§ 5. That until changed by the Legislature of said Territory, the sixth district shall consist of the following counties, namely: Bowman, Villard, Billings, Dunn, McKenzie, Allred, Buford, Flannery, Wallace, Mountraille, Williams, Stark, Hettinger, Morton, Mercer, McLean, Stevens, Renville, Wynn, Bottineau, McHenry, Sheridan, Burleigh, Emmons, McIntosh, Logan, Kidder, Wells, DeSmet, Rolette, Towner, Benson, Foster, Stutsman, Lamoure, Dickey, Griggs, Steele and Barnes.

§ 6. That temporal, and until otherwise ordered by law, the additional associate justices to be appointed under this act are hereby assigned to said fifth and sixth districts, and the time and place as now fixed by the statutes of said Territory for holding court therein shall remain until changed by law.

§ 7. That the district court for said fifth judicial district shall have no jurisdiction to try, hear or determine any matter or cause wherein the United States is a party, and no United States grand or petit jury shall be summoned in said court, but said fifth district is hereby attached to and made a part of the second judicial district for the purpose of hearing and determining all matters and causes arising within said fifth district in which the United States is a party.

§ 8. That the district court for said sixth judicial district shall have and possess jurisdiction to try, hear and determine all matters and causes that the court of any district in said Territory now possesses. And for such purposes two terms of said court shall be held annually in the city of Bismarck, in the county of Burleigh, and a grand and petit jury shall be summoned thereon in the manner now required by law in the United States Courts in said Territory.

§ 14. That all offenses committed before the passage of this act shall be prosecuted, tried and determined, in the same manner and with the same effect, (except as to number of judges) as if this act had not been passed. [*Approved, July 4, 1884.*

And all suits or proceedings pending in the district courts of Dakota and Washington Territories at the time of the passage of said act (*July 4, 1884,*) and which would, if instituted after the passage of said act, be required to be brought in the new districts created and provided for in said act, may be transferred by consent of parties to said new district courts, and there disposed of in like manner and with like effect as if the same had there been instituted; and all writs and recognizances relating to such suits and proceedings so transferred shall be considered as belonging to the courts of the said new districts, respectively, in the same manner and with like effect as if they had issued or had been taken in reference thereto originally. [*Part of act approved March 3, 1885.*

***

§ 1866. The jurisdiction both appellate and original, of the courts provided for in sections 1907 and 1908, shall be limited by law.

***

§ 1907. The judicial power in New Mexico, Utah, Washington, Colorado, Dakota, Idaho, Montana and Wyoming, shall be vested in a supreme court, district courts, probate courts, and in justices of the peace.

***

§ 1867. No justices of the peace in any territory shall have jurisdiction of any case in which the title to land, or the boundary thereof, in any wise comes in question.

§ 1926. Justices of the peace in the territories of New Mexico, Utah, Washington, Dakota, Idaho, Montana, and Wyoming shall not have jurisdiction of any matter in controversy where the debt or sum claimed exceeds one hundred dollars.

§ 1868. The supreme court and the district courts, respectively, of every territory, shall possess chancery, as well as common law jurisdiction.

***

Be it enacted, etc, That it shall not be necessary in any of the courts of the several territories of the United States to exercise separately the common law and chancery jurisdictions vested in said courts; and that the several codes and rules of practice adopted in said territories, respectively, in so far as they authorize a mingling of said jurisdictions or a uniform course of proceeding in all cases whether legal or equitable, be confirmed; and that all proceedings heretofore had or taken in said courts in conformity with said respective codes and rules of practice, so far as relates to the form and mode of proceeding be, and the same are hereby validated and confirmed; *Provided*, That no party has been or shall be deprived of the right of trial by jury in cases cognizable at common law.

§ 2. That the appellate jurisdiction of the supreme court of the United States over the judgments and decrees of said territorial courts in cases of trial by jury, shall be exercised by writ of error, and in all other cases by appeal according to such rules and regulations as to form and modes of proceedings as the said supreme court have prescribed or may hereafter prescribe; *Provided*, That an appeal instead of the evidence at large, a statement of the facts of the case in the nature of a special verdict, and also the rulings of

the court on the admission or rejection of evidence when excepted
to, shall b made and certified by the court below, and transmitted to the supreme court together with the transcript of the proceedings and judgment or decree; but no appellate proceedings in
said supreme court, heretofore taken upon any judgment or decree, shall be invalidated by reason of being instituted by writ of
error or by appeal; and *provided, further,* That the appellate court
may make any orde in any case heretofore appealed, which may
be necessary to save the rights of t! e parties, and that this act
shall not apply to cases now pending in the supreme court of the
United States, where the record has already been filed. [*Approved
April 7,* 1874.

§ 1869. Writs of error, bills of exception, and appeals, shall be
allowed, in all cases, from the final decisions of the district courts
to the supreme court, of all the territories, respectively, under
such regulation as may be prescribed by law; but in no case removed to the supreme court shall trial by jury be allowed in that
court.

§ 1909. Writs of error and appeal from the final decisions of
the supreme court of either of the Territories of New Mexico,
Utah, Colorado, Dakota, Arizona, Idaho, Montana and Wyoming,
shall be allowed to the Supreme Court of the United States, in the
same manner and under the same regulations as from the circuit
courts of the United States, where the value of the property or the
amount in controversy, to be ascertained by the oath of either
party, or of other competent witnesses, exceeds one thousand dollars, except that a writ of error or appeal shall be allowed to the
Supreme Court of the United States from the decision of the supreme courts created by this Title, or of any judge thereof, or of the
district courts created by this Title, or of any judge thereof, upon
writs of *habeas corpus* involving the question of personal freedom.

§ 1910. Each of the district courts in the Territories mentioned
in the preceding section shall have and exercise the same jurisdiction, in all cases arising under the Constitution and laws of the
United States, as is vested in the circuit and district courts of the
United States; and the first six days of every term of the respective district courts, or so much thereof as is necessary, shall
be appropriated to the trial of causes arising under such Constitution and laws, but writs of error and appeals in all such cases
may be had to the supreme court of each territory, as in other
cases.

§ 1870. The supreme court of each territory shall appoint its
own clerk, who shall hold his office at the pleasure of the court
for which he is appointed.

§ 1871. Each judge of the supreme court of the respective territories shall designate and appoint one person as clerk of the district over which he presides, where one is not already appointed, and shall designate and retain but one such clerk where more than one is already appointed, and only such district clerk shall be entitled to a compensation from the United States.

§ 1918. The legislative assembles of New Mexico, Washington, Colorado, Dakota, Arizona, and Wyoming Territories, may assign the judges appointed for such territories, respectively, to the several judicial districts thereof, in such manner as each legislative assembly deems proper and convenient.

§ 1919. The legislative assemblies of Colorado, Dakota and Wyoming Territories may fix or alter the times and places of holding the district courts for such territories, respectively, in such manner as such legislative assembly deems proper and convenient.

§ 1874. The judges of the supreme court of each territory are authorized to hold court within their respective districts, in the counties wherein, by the laws of the territory, courts have been or may be established, for the purpose of hearing and determining all matters and causes, except those in which the United States is a party; but the expense of holding such courts shall be paid by the territory or by the counties in which the courts are held, and the United States shall in no case be chargeable therewith.

§ 1875. There shall be appointed in each territory a person learned in the law, to act as attorney for the United States. He shall continue in office for four years, and until his successor is appointed and qualified, unless sooner removed by the president.

§ 1876. There shall be appointed a marshal for each territory. He shall execute all process issuing from the territorial courts when exercising their jurisdiction as circuit and district courts of the United States. He shall have the power and perform the duties, and be subject to the regulations and penalties imposed by law on the marshals for the several judicial districts of the United States. He shall hold his office for four years, and until his successor is appointed and qualified, unless sooner removed by the president.

§ 1877. The governor, secretary, chief justice and asssociate justices, attorney and marshal, of every territory, shall be nominated, and by and with the advice and consent of the senate, appointed by the president.

§ 1878. The governor and secretary for each territory shall, before they act as such, respectively take an oath before the district judge, or some justice of the peace in the limits of the territory for which they are appointed, duly authorized to administer oaths by the laws in force therein, or before the chief justice or some associate justice of the supreme court of the United States, to support the constitution of the United States and faithfully to discharge the duties of their respective offices; and such oaths shall be certified by the person before whom the same are taken, and such certificates shall be received and recorded by the secretary among the executive proceedings; and the chief justice and associate justices, and all other civil officers appointed for any territory, before they act as such, shall take a like oath before the governor or secretary, or some judge or justice of the peace of the territory, who may be duly commissioned and qualified, and such oath shall be certified and transmitted by the person taking the same, to the secretary, to be by him recorded as above directed; but after the first qualification of the officers herein specified in the case of a new territory, as well as in all organized territories, the like oath shall be taken, certified and recorded in such manner and form as may be prescribed by the law of each territory.

***

Hereafter payment of salaries of all officers of the territories of the United States appointed by the president shall commence only when the person appointed to any such office shall take the proper oath and shall enter upon the duties of such office in such territory: And said oath shall hereafter be administered in the territory in which such office is held. [*Part of act approved May 1, 1876.*

***

§ 1879. The annual salary of the Chief Justice and Associate Justices of all the territories now organized, shall be three thousand dollars each.

§ 1880. The salary of the attorney of the United States for each territory shall be at the rate of two hundred and fifty dollars annually.

§ 1881. The salary of the Marshal of the United States for each territory shall be at the rate of two hundred dollars a year.

§ 1882. The salaries provided for in this title, to be paid to the Governor, Secretary, Chief Justices and Associate Justices, District Attorney, and Marshal of the several territories, shall be paid quarter-yearly at the treasury of the United States.

§ 1935. There shall be appropriated annually one thousand dollars, to be expended by the respective Governors, to defray the contingent expenses of New Mexico, Utah, Colorado, Dakota, Arizona, Idaho, Montana and Wyoming, including the salary of the clerk in the executive departments of those territories.

§ 1883. The fees and costs to be allowed to the United States Attorneys and Marshals, to the clerks of the Supreme and District Courts, and to jurors, witnesses, commissioners, and printers, in the territories of the United States shall be the same for similar services by such persons as prescribed in chapter 16, title "The Judiciary," and no other compensation shall be taxed or allowed.

§ 1884. When any officer of a territory is absent therefrom, and from the duties of his office, no salary shall be paid him during the year in which such absence occurs, unless good cause therefor be shown to the President, who shall officially certify his opinion of such cause to the proper accounting officer of the treasury, to be filed in his office.

§ 1886. All accounts for disbursements in the territories of the United States, of money appropriated by Congress for the support of government therein, shall be settled and adjusted at the treasury department; and no act, resolution, or order of the Legislature of any territory, directing the expenditure of the sum, shall be deemed a sufficient authority for such disbursement, but sufficient vouchers and proof for the same shall be required by the accounting officers of the treasury. No payment shall be made or allowed, unless the Secretary of the Treasury has estimated therefor and the object been approved by Congress. No session of the Legislature of a territory shall be held until the appropriation for its expenses has been made.

§ 1939. There shall be appropriated respectively for the territories of New Mexico, Utah, Colorado, Dakota, Arizona, and Wyoming annually a sufficient sum, to be expended by the Secretary of each territory herein named, upon an estimate to be made by the Secretary of the Treasury, to defray the expenses of the Legislative Assembly and other incidental expenses; and the Secretary of each territory above specified shall annually account to the Secretary of the Treasury for the manner in which such sum has been expended.

§ 1888. No Legislative Assembly of a territory shall in any instance or under any pretext, exceed the amount appropriated by Congress for its annual expenses

§ 1889. The legislative assemblies of the several territories shall not grant private charters or especial privileges; but they may, by general incorporation acts, permit persons to associate themselves together as bodies corporate, for mining, manufacturing, and other industrial pursuits, or the construction or operation of railroads, wagon roads, irrigating ditches, and the colonization and improvement of lands in connection therewith, or for colleges, seminaries, churches, libraries, or any benevolent, charitable or scientific association.

**

Be it enacted, etc., That the words "the legislative assemblies of the several territories shall not grant private charters or especial privileges" in section eighteen hundred and eighty-nine of the

Revised Statutes of the United States, shall not be construed as prohibiting the legislative assemblies of the several territories of the United States from creating towns, cities, or other municipal corporations, and providing for the government of the same, and conferring upon them the corporate powers and privileges necessary to their local administration, by either general or special acts; and that all general and special acts of such legislative assemblies heretofore passed creating and providing for the government of towns, cities, or other municipal corporations, and conferring such rights, powers and privileges upon the same as were necessary to their local administration, be and the same are hereby ratified and confirmed and declared to be valid, any law to the contrary notwithstanding, subject however to amendment or repeal hereafter by such territorial assemblies. But nothing herein shall have the effect to create any private right, except that of holding and executing municipal offices, or to divest any such right, or to make valid or invalid any contract or obligation heretofore made by or on behalf of any such town, city, or other municipal corporation, or to authorize any such corporation to incur hereafter any debt or obligation other than such as shall be necessary to the administration of its internal affairs. [*Approved, June 8, 1878.*]

***

§ 1890. No corporation or association for religious or charitable purposes shall acquire or hold real estate in any territory, during the existence of the territorial government, of a greater value than fifty thousand dollars; and all real estate acquired or held by such corporation or association contrary hereto, shall be forfeited and escheat to the United States; but existing vested rights in real estate shall not be impaired by the provisions of this section.

§ 1891. The constitution and all laws of the United States which are not locally inapplicable, shall have the same force and effect within all the organized territories, and in every territory hereafter organized, as elsewhere within the United States.

§ 1892. Any penitentiary which has been, or may hereafter be erected by the United States in an organized territory shall, when the same is ready for the reception of convicts, be placed under the care and control of the Marshal of the United States for the territory or district in which such penitentiary is situated, except as otherwise provided in the case of the penitentiaries in Montana, Idaho, Wyoming and Colorado.

§ 1893. The attorney general of the United States shall prescribe all needful rules and regulations for the government of such penitentiary, and the Marshal having charge thereof shall cause them to be duly and faithfully executed and obeyed, and the reasonable compensation of the Marshal and of his deputies for their services under such regulations as shall be fixed by the Attorney General.

§ 1894.   The compensation, as well as the expense incident to the subsistence and employment of offenders against the laws of the United States, who have been, or may hereafter be, sentenced to imprisonment in such penitentiary, shall be chargeable on, and payable out of, the fund for defraying the expenses of suits in which the United States are concerned, and of prosecutions for offenses committed against the United States ; but nothing herein shall be construed to increase the maximum compensation now allowed by law to those officers.

§ 1895.   Any person convicted by a court of competent jurisdiction in a territory for a violation of the laws thereof, and sentenced to imprisonment may, at the cost of such territory, on such terms and conditions as may be prescribed by such rules anb regulations, be received, subsisted and employed in such penitentiary during the term of his imprisonment, in the same manner as if he had been convicted of an offense against the laws of the United States.

***

That the legislative assemblies of the several territories of the United States may make such provision for the care and custody of such persons as may be convicted of crime under the laws of such territory as they shall deem proper, and for that purpose may authorize and contract for the care and custody of such convicts in any other territory or state, and provide that such person or persons may be sentenced to confinement accordingly in such other territory or state, and all existing legislative enactments of any of the territories for that purpose are hereby legalized; *Provided*, That the expense of keeping such prisoners shall be borne by the respective territories, and no part thereof shall be borne by the United States.   [*Part of act approved June* 16, 1880.

***

§ 1944.   The seat of goverament of the territories of New Mexico, Utah, Washington, Colorado, Dakota, Arizona and Wyoming, may be changed by the Governors and Legislative Assemblies thereof respectively.

§ 1946.   Sections numbered 16 and 36 in each township of the territories of New Mexico, Utah, Colorado, Dakota, Arizona, Idaho, Montana, and Wyoming, shall be reserved for the purpose of being applied to schools in the several territories herein named, and in the states and territories hereafter to be erected out of the same.

***

That if any timber cut on the public lands shall be exported from the territories of the United States, it shall be liable to seizure by United States authority wherever found. [*Part of act approved April* 30, 1878.

Resolved, etc, That the Secretary of War is hereby authorized to cause to be issued to the territories, and the states bordering thereon, such arms as he may deem necessary for their protection, not to exceed one thousand to said states each ; *Provided*, That such issues shall only be from arms owned by the government, which have been superseded and no longer issued to the army ; *Provided, however*, That said arms shall be issued only in the following manner, and upon the following conditions, namely : Upon the requisition of the Governors of said states or territories, showing the absolute necessity of arms for the protection of the citizens and their property against Indian raids into said states or territories; also that militia companies are regularly organized and under the control of the Governors of said states or territories, to whom said arms are to be issued, and that said Governor or Governors shall give a good and sufficient bond for the return of said arms or the payment of the same at such time as the Secretary of War may designate. [*Resolution approved July* 3, 1876.

Resolved, etc., That the joint resolution approved July third, eighteen hundred and seventy-six, authorizing the Secretary of War to issue arms to the territories and the states bordering thereon, be and the same is hereby amended by inserting after the words, "each of said territories," the words, "and ammunition for the same, not to exceed fifty ball-cartridges for each arm." [*Approved, March* 3, 1877.

Be it enacted, etc., That a joint resolution, approved July third, eighteen hundred and seventy-six, entitled "Joint resolution authorizing the Secretary of War to issue arms," be amended as follows: By inserting in the fifth line, after the word "states," and before the word "each," the words "and territories," and by striking out after the word " each," in said fifth line, and before the word "provided," in sixth line, the words " and not more than five hundred to each of said territories." *Provided*, That the quota to the states now authorized by law shall not hereby be diminished. [*Approved, May* 16, 1878.

Be it resolved, etc., That the Secretary of War is hereby authorized to cause to be issued to each of the territories of the United States, (in addition to arms and ammunition the issue of which has been heretofore provided for), such arms, not to exceed one thousand in number, as he may deem necessary, and ammunition for the same, not to exceed fifty ball-cartridges for each arm ; *Provided*, That such issue shall be only from arms owned by the Government of the United States, which have been superseded and no longer issued to the army ; *And provided, further*, That said arms shall be issued only in the following manner, and upon the following conditions, namely: Upon the requisition of the Governors of said territories, showing the absolute necessity for arms for the protection of citizens and their property against hostile Indians within or of Indian raids into such territories; *And provided further*, That the said Governor or Governors of said territories to whom the said arms may be issued, shall give good and sufficient bond or bonds for the return of said arms, or payment therefor, at such time as the Secretary of War may designate, as now provided for by law. [*Approved, June* 7, 1878.

TABLE OF CONTENTS.

CENSUS.

CHANGE OF NAMES.

CHATTEL MORTGAGES.

CONSTITUTIONAL CONVENTION.

CORPORATIONS.

COSTS IN CIVIL ACTIONS.

COUNTY ORGANIZATION.

COUNTY OFFICES.

DAMAGES.

DENTAL SURGERY.

DEPOSITIONS.

DISTRICT ATTORNEYS.

DISTRIBUTION OF LAWS.

DRAINAGE.

EDUCATION.

ELECTIONS.

EXEMPTIONS

FEES.

FISH.

FUEL.

GRAND JURIES.

HEALTH.

HOMESTEAD.

IMMIGRATION.

IMPRISONMENT.

INSANE.

INSURANCE.

JUDICIAL DISTRICTS.

JURIES.

JUSTICES OF THE PEACE.

JUSTICES PRACTICE.

LEGAL HOLIDAYS.

LEGISLATIVE ASSEMBLIES.

MILITIA.

NEW TRIALS.

NORMAL SCHOOL

NOTICE OF PENDENCY OF ACTION.

NOTICE OF MOTION.

OFFICIAL BONDS.

OPIUM.

PASSAGE TICKETS

PENITENTIARY.

PROOF OF SERVICE.

RAILROAD COMMISSION.

SPECIAL LAWS.

COUNTIES.

DIVISION AND ADMISSION.

IROQUOIS.

TOWNSHIPS.

AUTHENTICATION.

GENERAL LAWS.

Acknowledgments.

CHAPTER 1.

AN ACT to Amend Section 656, of the Civil Code, Territory of Dakota

Be it enacted by the Legislative Assembly of the Territory of Dakota:

§ 1. BEFORE WHOM MADE.] That section 656 of the Civil Code of the Territory of Dakota, be and the same is hereby amended so as to read as follows:

§ 656: The proof or acknowledgment of an instrument may be made in this Territory within the judicial district, county, subdivision or city, for which the officer was elected or appointed, before either:

1. A judge or clerk of a court of record ; or
2. A mayor of a city ; or
3. A register of deeds ; or
4. A justice of the peace ; or
5. A United States circuit or district court commissioner ; or
6. A county clerk ; or
7. A county auditor.

§ 2. This act shall take effect and be in force from and after its passage and approval.

Approved, March 12, 1885.

1885—1

Affidavits.

BEFORE WHOM MADE.

CHAPTER 2.

AN ACT to amend Section 468 of Code of Civil Procedure.

Be it enacted by the Legislative Assembly of the Territory of Dakota:

§ 1. BY ANY PERSON AUTHORIZED.] That section 468 of the Code of Civil Procedure be amended so as to read as follows : "An affidavit may be made in and out of this Territory before any person authorized to administer an oath."

Approved, February 19, 1885.

Agriculture.

CHAPTER 3.

AN ACT to create a Territorial Department of Agriculture, and Relating to Agricultural Societies and Agricultural Fairs, and Providing for Reports of the same.

Be it enacted by the Legislative Assembly of the Territory of Dakota:

§ 1. DEPARTMENT OF AGRICULTURE CREATED—ANNUAL MEETINGS.] That a Department of Agriculture for the promotion of agriculture and horticulture, manufactures and domestic arts, is hereby created and shall be managed by a board styled the Territorial Board of Agriculture, to consist of one president, and one vice president from each legislative district of the Territory. The first election of officers is to be held in the city of Mitchell, in the Territory of Dakota, on the 17th day of June, 1885, and thereafter on the fair grounds on the Wednesday of the week of the annual territorial fair, and every two years thereafter, by delegates or alternates or their written proxies, chosen by the several agricultural societies in counties where such societies exist, in the following manner, to-wit: In counties having one agricultural society such county may appoint three delegates; in counties having two agricultural societies each society may appoint one delegate who shall be entitled to one and one-half votes; in counties having three agricultural societies each society may appoint one delegate, and if either society shall neglect or refuse to appoint such delegate the delegate or delegates appointed shall be entitled to cast the full vote of the county; and in counties where no agricultural society exists the delegates may be appointed by the board of supervisors or county board, as the case may be: each county to be entitled to three votes and no more, and each union or district agricultural society shall be accredited to that county in which its fair grounds or the greater part thereof shall be located. The members of the territorial board of agriculture shall enter upon the duties of their office on the second Tuesday of January succeeding their election, and hold their office for two years and until their successors are elected and enter upon their duties. The territorial board of agriculture may fill any vacancy arising from any cause by appointment from the district in which the vacancy occurs.

§ 2. SECRETARY.] The territorial board shall appoint some person not a member of the board, secretary, and fix his compensation, said compensation not to exceed two hundred dollars per annum, who shall hold his office during the term for which the members of the board appointing him are elected, unless for good cause he shall sooner be removed by the board, and who shall perform such duties as usually pertain to the office of secretary or as shall be required of him by the board.

§ 3. TREASURER.] They shall also appoint some person not a member of the board as treasurer and fix his compensation, said compensation not to exceed one hundred dollars, per annum, who shall give bond in such sum and with such security as the board shall direct, conditioned for the faithful discharge of the duties of his office. He shall hold his office during the term for which the members of the board appointing him are elected, unless for good cause he shall sooner be removed by the board. He shall keep an accurate itemized account of all money received by him and paid out, and make an annual report thereof to the territorial board, and make full settlement with the board.

§ 4. TERRITORIAL OFFICE.] The territorial board of agriculture shall keep an office for the transaction of business at the city of Huron, in the Territory of Dakota, providing said city of Huron shall provide a suitable room for such purposes, free of cost to the Territory, to be under the control of said board.

§ 5. POWERS OF BOARD.] The territorial board of agriculture in that name may contract and be contracted with ; may purchase, hold or sell property ; may sue or be sued in all courts or places ; may hold territorial fairs and fat stock shows at such times and places as the board may determine ; but this Territory shall never be liable for any debt or contract of said board.

§ 6. BOARD MAY HAVE CONTROL.] The territorial board of agriculture shall have the sole control of the affairs of the Depart ment of Agriculture, of all territorial fairs and fat stock shows, and may make such by-laws, rules and regulations in relation to the Department of Agriculture and the management of the business of such department and territorial fairs and fat stock shows and offering of premiums, as a majority of said board shall from time to time determine, not inconsistent with the constitution and laws of the Territory or of the United States.

§ 7. MONEYS APPROPRIATED, HOW EXPENDED.] Whatever money shall be appropriated to the Department of Agriculture shall be paid to the territorial board of agriculture, and may be expended by them as in the opinion of said board will best ad-vance the interests of agriculture and horticulture, manufactures and domestic arts in this Territory ; *Provided,*When any appro-priation is made for the benefit of county or other agricultural societies, the same shall be actually divided between such agri-cultural societies as shall have given satisfactory evidence to' said territorial board of having held an annual fair and paid as pre-miums not less than three hundred dollars ($300), and made their annual report on or before the 15th day of November to the terri-torial board of agriculture; *Provided,* That in counties having more than one agricultural society only one of them shall be en-titled to receive a share of the money appropriated for county or district fairs, and the territorial board shall have full power to determine which one shall receive such appropriation.

§ 8. ANNUAL REPORT.] The territorial board of agriculture shall after their annual meeting in January in each year, make and deliver to the governor a report of their acts and doings as required by law, and no other annual report shall be made by said board.

§ 9. REPORTS OF KINDRED ASSOCIATIONS.] Said territorial board of agriculture shall append to and publish with their said report the annual report of the territorial entomologist and such other reports or essays connected with agriculture, horticulture, manu-factures or the domestic arts as in the judgment of said board the interests of the Territory require; said annual report and ap-pended essays not to exceed seven hundred printed pages, and one thousand copies of said reports shall be published annually, in pamphlet form, by the public printer of the Territory at the contract rates, and the same shall be distributed jointly by the president of the agricultural society and the president of the territorial horticultural and forestry association, and a sufficient amount of money is hereby appropriated out of the territorial treasury to pay for the publishing of the same.

§ 10. ANNUAL FAIR—SPECIAL POLICE.] It shall be lawful for the territorial board of agriculture or other agricultural society, at or before the time for holding its annual fair, to select and appoint as many persons to act in the capacity of special police as are by said society deemed requisite to insure peace and good order on or about the grounds or place of holding such fair for and during the holding of the same; *Provided.* That such person before entering upon the duties of special police shall receive his authority from and take the oath of office before any judge or justice of the peace or other officer authorized to administer oaths, residing or holding his office in the town or municipal corporation most contiguous to the fair grounds or place of holding such fair, and shall receive from such judge or justice of the peace a certificate, under seal, of his appointment and authority to act as such special police, which shall be indicated by some appropriate badge of office, and when so authorized he shall be clothed with full police powers.

§ 11. TRESPASSING UPON FAIR GROUNDS.] Whoever trespasses upon any fair grounds to commit any depredations upon the property of any agricultural society by cutting or destroying any timber or trees, breaking or carrying away any box, trough, stall, bench, fence, lock, door, gate, lumber or other appurtenances to any fair grounds, whether within or without the enclosure thereof, shall be fined not less than five nor exceeding two hundred dollars and shall be liable civilly for all damages sustained by such wrongful act.

§ 12. SALE OF LIQUORS PROHIBITED.] Whoever shall keep any shop, booth, tent, wagon, vessel, boat or other place for the sale of spirituous liquors, or expose for sale, sell or otherwise dispose of any spirituous liquors, or engages in gaming at or within one-half mile of the place where any agricultural, horticultural or mechanical fair is being held under the auspices of the territorial board of agriculture, shall for each offense be fined not less than five nor more than one hundred dollars; *Provided,* This section shall not affect tavern keepers, distillers or others exercising their calling at their usual place of business.

§ 13. ARREST OF VIOLATORS.] Any person violating the provisions of the preceding section may be arrested upon view or upon warrant by any sheriff, coroner, constable or other officer authorized to make arrest, and such officer may also seize the booth, tent, wagon, vessel or boat and articles to be sold, and upon a judgment being rendered against the offender the same may be sold upon the execution issued upon such judgment; and if sufficient property is not found to satisfy such fine, the offender may be committed to the county jail until the fine and costs are paid, or the prisoner discharged according to law.

§ 14. DEFINITION OF FAIR.] Wherever the word "fair" occurs in this act, it shall be held to mean a *bona fide* exhibition of the four principal classes of live stock, together with agricultural and horticultural products and mechanical arts.

§ 15. COMPENSATION.] The officers of the territorial board of agriculture, except the secretary and treasurer, shall serve without pay, but shall receive mileage at the rate of ten cents per mile one way from their home to the place of meeting of the society, which shall be paid by the territorial treasurer upon a warrant issued and certified to by the president of the territorial board of agriculture.

Approved, March 10, 1885.

Agricultural College.

NORTH DAKOTA.

CHAPTER 4.

AN ACT to Revive and Re enact Chapter Four of the Session Laws of 1883, entitled "An Act to Locate and Establish the North Dakota Territorial Agricultural College," Approved March 9, 1883.

Be it enacted by the Legislative Assembly of the Territory of Dakota:

§ 1. ACT REVIVED.] That chapter four of the session laws of 1883 of the Territory of Dakota, entitled "An act to locate and establish The North Dakota Territorial Agricultural College," be and the same is hereby revived, re-enacted and continued in force.

§ 2 TIME EXTENDED.] The time provided in section 1 of said act for donating and securing to the Territory the land mentioned in section 1 of said act is hereby extended for one year from the taking effect of this act.

§ 3. This act shall take effect and be in force from and after its passage and approval.

Approved, February 27, 1885.

SOUTH DAKOTA.

CHAPTER 5.

JOINT RESOLUTION Providing for the Printing of the Report of the Regents of Brookings Agricultural College.

Be it resolved by the Council and House of Representatives of the Territory of Dakota:

PROVIDING FOR PRINTING REPORTS.] That the regents of Brookings Agricultural College, be and they are hereby authorized to procure the printing of five hundred copies of the report of said regents, and that a sufficient sum of money is hereby appropriated to pay for the same out of any money in the territorial treasury not otherwise appropriated.

Approved, February 5, 1885.

Aid to Sufferers by Storms.

CHAPTER 6.

AN ACT to Authorize the County Commissioners of Minnehaha, Lake, Miner and Kingsbury, Faulk, Hyde, Richland, Beadle, Sully, Aurora and Potter Counties to aid certain Persons whose Crops were Destroyed by Storms.

Be it enacted by the Legislative Assembly of the Territory of Dakota:

§ 1. COMMISSIONERS OF CERTAIN COUNTIES EMPOWERED TO EXTEND AID.] That the board of county commissioners of Minnehaha, Miner, Lake, Kingsbury, Faulk, Hyde, Richland, Beadle Sully, Aurora and Potter counties are hereby authorized to lend the credit of said counties, or aid by donation in money or seed grain, to such persons as had their crops destroyed by storms in the year eighteen hundred and eighty-four. Said board of commissioners shall use their discretion, and after a careful investigation extend such aid only to such persons as are in great need of assistance.

§ 2. This act shall take effect and be in force from and after its passage and approval.

Approved, March 12, 1885.

Appeals in Civil Actions.

WHEN BOND NOT REQUIRED.

CHAPTER 7.

AN ACT to amend Section (414) Four Hundred and Fourteen of Chapter (XVI) Sixteen of the Code of Civil Procedure of Dakota Territory.

Be it enacted by the Legislative Assembly of the Territory of Dakota:

§ 1. BOND NOT REQUIRED IN CERTAIN CASES.] That section (414) four hundred and fourteen of chapter (XVI) sixteen of the Code of Civil Procedure of Dakota Territory, be and the same is hereby amended by adding thereto after the word "respondent," the following words: "*Provided,* That this section shall not apply to the Territory of Dakota, or any county thereof, and no bond shall in any action or proceeding be required of the Territory of Dakota, or any county thereof, on any appeal to any court of the Territory of Dakota, or to the Supreme Court of the United States, when the Territory or any county shall be the party directly interested therein."

Approved, March 12, 1885.

Apportionment.

CHAPTER 8.

AN ACT to amend Chapter Seven (7) of the Session Laws of 1883.

Be it enacted by the Legislative Assembly of the Territory of Dakota:

§ 1. FIRST DISTRICT.] That chapter seven (7) of the session laws of 1883 be amended to read as follows: The counties of Union, Clay and Lincoln shall constitute the first council and representative district, and Union county shall be the senior county.

§ 2. SECOND DISTRICT.] The counties of Yankton, Hutchinson, and Turner shall constitute the second council and representative district, and shall be entitled to elect one member of the council and three members of the house of representatives, and Yankton county shall be the senior county.

§ 3. THIRD DISTRICT.] The counties of Bon Homme, Douglas, and Charles Mix shall constitute the third council and representative district, and shall be entitled to elect one member of the council and one member of the house of representatives, and Bon Homme county shall be the senior county.

§ 4. FOURTH DISTRICT.] The counties of Minnehaha, McCook, and Hanson shall constitute the fourth council and representative district and Minnehaha shall be the senior county, and they shall be entitled to elect one member of the council and three members of the house of representatives

§ 5. FIFTH DISTRICT.] The counties of Davidson, Aurora and Brule shall constitute the fifth council and representative district, and the county of Davison shall be the senior county.

§ 6. SIXTH DISTRICT.] The counties of Moody, Lake and Miner shall constitute the sixth council and representative district and Moody county shall be the senior county, and they shall be entitled to one member of the council and two members of the house of representatives.

§ 7. SEVENTH DISTRICT.] The counties of Brookings, Kingsbury, Hamlin and Deuel shall constitute the seventh council and representative district, and Brookings shall be the senior county.

§ 8. EIGHTH DISTRICT.] The counties of Beadle, Sanborn and Jerauld shall constitute the eighth council and representative district, and Beadle county shall be the senior county.

§ 9. NINTH DISTRICT.] The counties of Spink and Clark shall constitute the ninth council and representative district, and Spink county shall be the senior county.

§ 10. TENTH DISTRICT.] The counties of Hand, Faulk, Potter, Walworth and Campbell shall constitute the tenth council and representative district, and Hand county shall be the senior county.

§ 11. ELEVENTH DISTRICT.] The counties of Hyde, Hughes, Sully and Buffalo shall constitute the eleventh council and representative district, and Hughes county shall be the senior county.

§ 12. TWELFTH DISTRICT.] The counties of Coddington, Grant, Roberts and Day shall constitute the twelfth council and representative district, and Grant shall be the senior county.

§ 13. THIRTEENTH DISTRICT.] The counties of Marshall, Brown, Edmunds and McPherson shall constitute the thirteenth council and representative district, and Brown shall be the senior county.

§ 14. FOURTEENTH DISTRICT.] The counties of Fall River, Custer, Pennington, Lawrence and Butte shall constitute the fourteenth council and representative district, and shall be entitled to elect two councilmen and three representatives, and the county of Lawrence shall be the senior county.

§ 15. FIFTEENTH DISTRICT.] The counties of Dickey, Sargeant, McIntosh and Richland shall constitute the fifteenth council and representative district, and Richland shall be the senior county.

§ 16. SIXTEENTH DISTRICT.] The county of Cass shall constitute the sixteenth council and representative district.

§ 17. SEVENTEENTH DISTRICT.] The counties of Ransom, La Moure, Logan and Barnes shall constitute the seventeenth council and representative district, and Barnes shall be the senior county.

§ 18. EIGHTEENTH DISTRICT.] The counties of Traill, Steele, and Griggs shall constitute the eighteenth council and representative district, and Traill shall be the senior county.

§ 19. NINETEENTH DISTRICT.] The county of Grand Forks shall constitute the nineteenth council and representative district.

§ 20. TWENTIETH DISTRICT.] The counties of Walsh, Blaine, and Ramsey shall constitute the twentieth council and representative district, and Walsh shall be the senior county.

§ 21. TWENTY-FIRST DISTRICT] The counties of Pembina, Cavalier, Towner, Roulette and Bottineau shall constitute the twenty-first council and representative district, and Pembina shall be the senior county.

§ 22. TWENTY-SECOND DISTRICT.] The counties of Stutsman, Foster, Nelson, Wells, Benson, De Smit, Stanton, McHenry and Eddy shall constitute the twenty-second council and representative district, and Stutsman shall be the senior county.

§ 23. TWENTY-THIRD DISTRICT.] The counties of Emmons, Kidder, Burleigh, Sheridan, McLean, Mercer, Norton, Boreman, Hellinger, Bowman, Villard, Billings, Stark, Williams, Dunn, Oliver, McKenzie, Allred, Wallace, Garfield, Ward, Stevens, Wynn, Renville, Mountraille, Flannery and Buford shall constitute the twenty-third council and representative district, and Burleigh shall be the senior county.

§ 24. NUMBER APPORTIONED TO EACH DISTRICT.] Each of the districts, except as otherwise provided for shall be entitled to elect one member of the council and two members of the house of representatives.

§ 25. All acts or parts of acts in conflict with this act are hereby repealed.

Approved, March 13, 1885.

Appropriations and Bonds.

CHARITABLE, PENAL AND EDUCATIONAL INSTITUTIONS.

CHAPTER 9.

AN ACT making Appropriations for the Maintenance of Charitable, Penal and Educational Institutions of this Territory, and for other Purposes.

Be it enacted by the Legislative Assembly of the Territory of Dakota:

§ 1. DAKOTA HOSPITAL FOR INSANE.] That there is hereby appropriated the following sums of money, or so much thereof as may be necessary, for the maintenance of the Dakota Hospital for the Insane at Yankton, Dakota Territory, for the ensuing two years:

For the maintenance of patients, necessary clothing, board of employes and officers residing in the hospital, the sum of $35,000

For necessary wages of the employes, the sum of 22,000

For necessary fuel and lights, the sum of 12,500

For incidental expenses, the sum of............ 1,500

For drugs, medicines, medical books, miscellaneous, periodicals and amusements for patients, the sum of 2,500

For necessary repairs and improvements for hospital, the sum of........................ 2,500

For necessary improvements of hospital farm, the sum of................................. 3,000

For improving hospital grounds, the sum of..... 2,500

For completing and furnishing the main building, the sum of............................. 3,250

For building ice house, extension of barn, slaughter house, root and hen house, fitting the basement for the amusement of patients, the sum of... 4,000

For purchasing team and conveyance for patients, 700

For improving the sewerage,................. 1,500

For deficiency, amount for fuel for the past two years 5,000

For return of patients and burial of the dead,.... 1,000

Amount due contractors for building west wing of Dakota Hospital for the Insane,........... 520

§ 2. NORTH DAKOTA HOSPITAL FOR INSANE.]   There is hereby appropriated for the maintenance of the North Dakota Hospital for the Insane, near Jamestown, Dakota, the following sums of money, or so much thereof as may be necessary, out of any funds in the territorial treasury not otherwise appropriated, for the ensuing two years :

For the maintenance of patients of the North Dakota Hospital for the Insane, near Jamestown,
   for their necessary clothing and for the board
   of employes and officers residing in the hospital, the sum of.......................$22,000
Wages of employes,... 12,000
Fuel and lights,............................. 6,000
Incidental expenses,......................... 2,000
For the necessary drugs, medicines, medical books,
   miscellaneous periodicals and amusements for
   patients,................................. 3,000
For the necessary repairs and improvements of
   such hospital,............... 2,500
For the necessary improvements of hospital farm, 3,000
For improving hospital grounds,.............. 1,000
For stocking the farm with horses, cows, hogs and
   fowl,........... 2,000
Farm implements,............................. 1,000
Moving North Dakota patients from Yankton,
   under the direction of the board of trustees
   of the North Dakota Hospital,............. 2,000
For return of patients and burial of dead,....... 800
For purchasing team and conveyance for patients, 700

§ 3. UNIVERSITY OF DAKOTA, VERMILLION.]   There is hereby appropriated out of the money in the territorial treasury, not otherwise appropriated, or so much thereof as may be necessary for the purpose of paying the current and contingent expenses of the University of Dakota, at Vermillion, for the ensuing two years :

For the salary of president,....................$ 4,000
For the salaries of teachers and professors,...... 13,750
For salary of secretary, ... 1,000
For lights and fuel,......................... 3,000
For anitor and engineer,..................... 1,200
For library, ... 1,000
For apparatus,..... 1,000
For contingent expenses,..................... 1,000
For dormitory and water works,.............. 10,000

§ 4. UNIVERSITY OF NORTH DAKOTA.]   There is hereby appropriated out of any money in the territorial treasury not otherwise appropriated, the following sums of money, or so much thereof as may be necessary, for the purpose of paying the current and contingent expenses of the University of North Dakota for the ensuing two years:

For salaries of teachers and professors,	$20,000
For salary of secretary,	1,000
For fuel and lights,	4,000
For janitor and engineers,	2,400
For incidental expenses,	1,000
For laying water mains to connect with the water works of the city of Grand Forks, and for plumbing,	10,000

§ 5. PENITENTIARY, SIOUX FALLS.] The following sums of money are hereby appropriated, or so much thereof as may be necessary, out of any money in the territorial treasury not otherwise appropriated for the purpose of paying the current and contingent expenses of the territorial penitentiary at Sioux Falls, Dakota, for the ensuing two years:

For warden's salary,	$ 4,000
For deputy warden's salary,	1,800
For pay of physicians and medicines,	1,500
For pay of officers, guards, overseers and watchman	20,000
For maintenance of prisoners, board of officers and employes,	23,000
For necessary lights, fuel, pay of directors and clothing for prisoners,	12,300
For clothing, cash and transportation of discharged convicts,	2,600
For incidental expenses,	2,000

Provided, That all sums of money now due said penitentiary from any source for labor or material, and all money received for the services of convicts under contract, which may be made by the directors of said penitentiary, shall be paid into the territorial treasury.

§ 6. MADISON NORMAL SCHOOL] That there is hereby appropriated the following sums of money, or so much thereof as may be necessary, out of any funds in the territorial treasury not otherwise appropriated, for the purpose of paying the current and contingent expenses for the Normal School of Madison, Dakota, for the ensuing two years:

For salaries of teachers and professors,	$10,000
Fuel and lights,	2,000
Janitor, incidental expenses and library,	2,000

§ 7. SCHOOL OF MINES.] The following sums of money, or so much thereof as may be necessary, are hereby appropriated out of any funds in the territorial treasury not otherwise appropriated, for the current and contingent expenses of the School of Mines at Rapid City, Dakota, for the ensuing two years :

For the pay of teachers and assistants,..........$ 5,000

For fuel and lights, apparatus and furniture,....   .',500

§ 8. AGRICULTURAL COLLEGE, BROOKINGS.] The following sums of money, or so much thereof as may be necessary, are hereby appropriated out of any funds in the territorial treasury not otherwise appropriated, for the current and contingent expenses of the Agricultural College at Brookings for the ensuing two years :

Salary of president, professors and teachers,.....$18,000

For secretary,............................ 1,000

For janitor,................................ 1,000

For stationery, printing, postage and incidentals, 1,500

For fuel and lights,.......................... 2,000

Teachers salary for 1884,.................... 2,000·

Provided, That all bonds remaining unsold,which may have been issued under chapter 3 of laws of 1883, shall be cancelled and destroyed by the treasurer, and no additional bonds shall be issued by virtue of that act.

§ 9. TERRITORIAL LIBRARY—PURCHASE OF CODES AND SESSION LAWS—FOR BLANKS FOR GOVERNOR—PRINTING REPORT OF THE GRAIN COMMISSION.]   There is hereby appropriated out of any money in the territorial treasury not otherwise appropriated, to be expended by the secretary of the Territory, for the care and custody of the territorial library, $400.

To print report of board of regents, directors or trustees, and to purchase two hundred copies of the laws of 1881 and 200 copies of the laws of 1883 ; one hundred and fifty copies of the laws of the codes of 1877 ; four hundred copies of the session laws of 1885 ; all printing to be let to the lowest bidder residing in the Territory, after giving four weeks notice by publication in at least four newspapers of general circulation, two of which newspapers are published in North and two in South Dakota ; the notice so published to state the time and place of opening such bids by the secretary of the Territory, or so much thereof as may be necessary, $4,000.

For blanks for the governor's office and for printing, to be expended by the governor, $400.

Printing report of grain commissioners, $265.

§ 10: PENITENTIARY AT BISMARCK.] ·The following sums be and they are hereby appropriated out of any money in the territorial treasury not otherwise appropriated, or so much thereof as may be necessary, for the purpose of paying the current and contingent expenses for two years of the territorial penitentiary of Dakota at Bismarck, namely :

For pay of the warden (two years),.............$ 3,000
Pay of officers, guards and employes,......... 12,000
Pay of physicians and for medicine,........... 750
For maintenance of prisoners and board of officers
    and employes,........................ 11,964
For necessary lights, fuel, clothing and bedding, 4,500
For clothing, cash and transportation of discharged
    prisoners,............................... 750
Team and tools,.............................$ 1,214
Incidentals, including repairs (two years)........ 2,250

It is made the duty of the warden, and he is hereby required, to make out and present to the directors of the penitentiary a detailed estimate of the amount of money necessary to meet the current expenses of the penitentiary for the next ensuing month, and upon presentation of the said estimate to the territorial auditor, after being duly approved and certified by the president of the board of directors of said penitentiary, the said territorial auditor shall draw a warrant upon the territorial treasurer for the amount of said estimate or estimates so certified and approved in favor of the said warden of the said penitentiary.

§ 11. BONDS FOR BISMARCK PENITENTIARY.] For the purpose of providing funds to pay the costs of making necessary improvements at the Dakota penitentiary at Bismarck, and for other purposes, to-wit:

Constructing a building for boiler house,.......$ 1,000
Laundry and hospital,.....................,..... 1,500
Steam heating and plumbing,................. 4,000
Temporary yard walls,......:............... 1,500
Sewerage,................................. 1,500
Fixtures for cells,........................... 800
Fixtures for chapel,......................... 300
Fixtures for office,.......................... 300
Furniture and fixtures for guard rooms,........ 765.15
Kitchen and dining room furniture,........... 600
Amount due contractors,.................... 2,334.85
Stables,.................................. 600

The territorial treasurer is hereby authorized and empowered and it is made his duty to prepare for issue fourteen thousand and six hundred dollars of territorial bonds, running for a period of twenty years, and payable at the option of the Territory at any time after ten years from the date of the same, and bearing interest at the rate of six per cent. per annum, with coupons attached, made payable semi-annually on the first day of July and January of each year, in denominations of not less than five hundred dollars each; such bonds shall be executed for the Territory, and under the seal thereof by the governor and treasurer, and shall be attested by the secretary, and shall be negotiated by the treasurer of the Territory. It shall be the duty of the treasurer to receive sealed proposals for the purchase of said bonds, by giving notice for thirty days in two newspapers of general circulation, one of which shall be published in the Territory and the other in the city of New York, and the bonds shall be sold to the highest bidder for cash ; *Provided, however,* That no bond shall be disposed of for less than par. For the purpose of prompt payment of principal and interest of the bonds herein provided, there shall be levied by the territorial board of equalization at the time the other taxes are levied and collected, in the same manner as other territorial taxes are collected, such sums as shall be sufficient to pay such interest and exchange thereon, and after ten years from the first day of May, 1885, in addition thereto a sinking fund tax shall be annually levied sufficient to retire and pay said bonds at their maturity ; and it shall be the duty of the territorial treasurer to pay promptly on the first day of July and January in each year such interest as shall then be due, and to purchase said bonds at not more than their par value, and retire and cancel the same with the sinking fund tax as fast as the same shall be received ; and no tax or fund provided for the payment of such bonds, either principal or interest, shall at any time be used for any other purpose. If for any reason the territorial treasurer shall not have in his hands sufficient of the funds herein provided to pay either principal or interest upon such bonds when due, he shall pay such interest or principal out of any other unappropriated funds belonging to the Territory; and there is hereby appropriated and set apart out of the general fund belonging to the Territory, a sum sufficient to pay said interest on said [such] bonds as may become due before the funds and tax herein provided can be available; and it shall be the duty of said treasurer to pay said interest promptly at the time it falls due out of said funds. All moneys belonging to the general territorial fund applied by said treasurer in payment of either principal or interest of said bonds, shall be replaced from the special tax levied to pay the same. It shall be the duty of the territorial auditor to issue his warrant upon the territorial treasurer for such sums as may be required in the progress of the work or maintenance of the penitentiary, upon vouchers issued by order of the board of directors, attested by the secretary or warden, and approved by the chairman of the said board of directors of the territorial penitentiary of Dakota at Bismarck ; *Provided,* That in the event of the division of the Territory of Dakota, that portion of the Territory in which said penitentiary is situated, shall pay the bonds issued under this act. The governor may by proclamation provide for the opening of the said territorial penitentiary at Bismarck as a temporary reform school, and the board of directors of said penitentiary are hereby authorized to make such rules and regulations to govern the same as may be necessary, subject to revision of the governor, and so much of the foregoing appropriations (mentioned in sections 10 and 11) as is necessary may be used for the purpose of carrying out these provisions.

§ 12. LIMIT OF TERRITORIAL TAX.] That the territorial board of equalization is hereby prohibited from levying a tax to exceed three mills on the dollar of the assessed valuation in any one year.

§ 13. NO INSURANCE.] The property of this Territory shall not be insured.

§ 14. SALARIES, ETC., OF R. R. COMMISSION.] That the sums of money hereinafter named, or so much thereof as may be necessary, are hereby appropriated out of any funds in the territorial treasury not otherwise appropriated for the purpose hereafter named :

For salary of railroad commissioners for the next
two years,.............................$12,000
For salary of secretary of the railroad commission
for two years,........................... 3,000
For traveling expenses, printing, postage and rent
for railroad commissioners,.............. 2,500
For the purpose of assisting and encouraging
county agricultural societies, to be distributed
by the territorial agricultural society under
such rules and regulations as they may adopt, 5,000

§ 15. LEGISLATIVE FURNITURE.] There is hereby appropriated the sum of five thousand two hundred and fifty-eight dollars and eighty-nine cents ($5,258.89) to A. H. Andrews & Co. of Chicago, Ills., for legislative furniture and for furniture in the territorial offices, etc., the same to be the property of the Territory, and to be under the care and custody of the auditor of the Territory of Dakota.

§ 16. CHICAGO CARPET COMPANY.] There is hereby appropriated the sum of four thousand one hundred and ninety-eight dollars and forty-five cents ($4,198.45) to the Chicago Carpet Company of Chicago, Ills., for carpets for the legislative halls and territorial offices, etc., the same to be the property of the Territory and to be under the care and custody of the auditor of the Territory of Dakota.

§ 17. HEATING APPARATUS—PROVISO.] There is hereby appropriated to Samuel I. Pope & Co. ten thousand five hundred and sixty-one dollars and forty-six cents ($10,561.46) for steam heating apparatus and tools; *Provided*, That no appropriation provided for in this act for furniture, labor, steam-heating appa-

1885—3

ratus, or otherwise, shall in any way be construed as an endorsement by the Territory of the acts of the Capital Commission, or be construed in any manner as a ratification or endorsement of the acts of said commission in locating the capital of the Territory at Bismarck in said Territory, but such appropriations are hereby declared to be made to discharge a moral rather than a legal obligation of the Territory.

There is hereby appropriated $1,415 to Thomas Hennesy for plumbing.

Approved, March 13, 1885.

TO PURCHASE CODES AND SESSION LAWS.

CHAPTER 10.

JOINT RESOLUTION to Purchase Codes and Session Laws for the use of the Legislature.

Be it resolved by the House, the Council concurring:

AUTHORITY TO PURCHASE.] That the secretary of the Territory be authorized to purchase forty copies of the Code of 1877, and seventy-two copies each of all such session laws as have been published since said Code; and that said secretary also be authorized to purchase thirty-two copies of Levisee's Code, such codes to be distributed to the members of this Legislature, and that the sum of seven hundred dollars, or so much thereof as may be necessary, is hereby appropriated out of any funds in the Territory not otherwise appropriated, to pay for such codes and session laws.

Approved, January 26, 1885.

CONTESTED SEAT.

CHAPTER 11.

AN ACT to Appropriate Funds for Certain Purposes.

Be it enacted by the Legislative Assembly of the Territory of Dakota:

§ 1. APPROPRIATION TO PAY EXPENSE OF CONTEST.] That there is hereby appropriated out of the general funds of the Territory not otherwise appropriated the sum of three hundred and seventy dollars ($370) for the payment of the following expenses incurred in the contest cases of Anderson vs. Hutchinson and Bechtel vs. Stong, and the Auditor of the Territory is hereby authorized to draw his warrant upon the territorial treasury for the amount herein stipulated in favor of the parties thereto entitled, to-wit:

Jno. A. Munro (serving subpœnas),	$70 00
Iver Larson (witness' fees and mileage),	60 00
T. G. Anderson, " " "	60 00
Dr. E. M. Faulk, " " "	40 00
M. M. Sullivan, " " "	30 00
E O. Faulkner for Bechtel vs. Stong,	60 00
M. M. Sullivan, cash advanced, Dr. E. M. Faulk, for witness' fees,	50 00

§ 2. This act shall be in force and effect from and after its passage and approval.

Approved, March 13, 1885.

DEFRAYING EXPENSE OF SENDING MILITIA TO SPINK COUNTY

CHAPTER 12.

AN ACT to Provide for the Payment of the Expenses of Sending Militia to Spink County.

Be it enacted by the Legislative Assembly of the Territory of Dakota:

§ 1. MONEY APPROPRIATED.] There is hereby appropriated out of any monies in the territorial treasury not otherwise appropriated the sum of twenty-six hundred dollars ($2600), or so much thereof as may be necessary for the purpose of paying the expenses incurred by the Governor of said Territory in sending militia to Redfield, Spink county, Dakota, on December twelfth, 1884; and the territorial Auditor is hereby authorized and directed to draw his warrant upon the territorial treasury for the payment of the said expenses, said expenses to be audited and approved by the Governor.

§ 2. This act shall take effect and be in force from and after its passage and approval.

Approved, February 27, 1885.

PRINTING AUDITOR AND TREASURER'S REPORT.

CHAPTER 13.

JOINT RESOLUTION Authorizing the Printing of the Biennial Reports of the Territorial Treasurer and Auditor, and Making an Appropriation to Pay for the Same.

Be it resolved by the Council and House of Representatives of the Legislative Assembly of the Territory of Dakota:

AMOUNT APPROPRIATED.] That there is hereby appropriated out of the funds in the territorial treasury not otherwise appropriated the sum of eleven hundred and twenty-five dollars and sixty cents (1125.60, or so much thereof as may be necessary, to defray the expenses of printing and binding six hundred copies each of the biennial reports of the territorial Treasurer and territorial Auditor; and that each member of the Council and House of Representatives be entitled to four copies each of said reports, the balance to be used by said Treasurer and Auditor for exchanges with states and territories and for general distribution; and the Auditor of the Territory is hereby directed to audit and allow the above amount, upon a correct and duly certified voucher filed in his office.

Approved, February 6, 1885.

FOR RENT OF OFFICES FOR TERRITORIAL OFFICERS.

CHAPTER 14

AN ACT to Provide for the Maintenance of the Public Offices of the Territory of Dakota.

Be it enacted by the Legislative Assembly of the Territory of Dakota:

§ 1. APPROPRIATIONS.] That there is hereby appropriated out of the general funds of the Territory the sum of three thousand dollars, or so much thereof as may be necessary, to be expended in providing offices and suitable furnishings therefor for the use of the Governor, Secretary, Treasurer and Auditor of the Territory for the ensuing two years.

§ 2. AUDITOR TO ISSUE WARRANTS.] That the territorial Auditor be directed to draw warrants upon the treasury for payment of claims, for the purposes specified in section one, upon verification thereof as the same may become due.

§ 3. This act shall take effect and be in force from and after its passage and approval.

Approved, March 13, 1885.

SPEARFISH NORMAL SCHOOL

CHAPTER 15.

AN ACT Making Appropriations for the Normal School at Spearfish.

Be it enacted by the Legislative Assembly of the Territory of Dakota:

§ 1. APPROPRIATIONS.] That there is hereby appropriated out of the funds of the territorial treasury, not otherwise appropriated, the sum of five thousand dollars, for the purpose of teachers' salaries, fuel, furniture and for the maintenance of the territorial Normal School at Spearfish, Dakota, for the ensuing two years from the passage and approval of this act.

§ 2. AUDITOR TO DRAW WARRANTS.] It shall be the duty of the Auditor of the Territory, upon the application of the board of education of said Normal School, or a majority thereof, to draw warrants on the territorial Treasurer, for the purpose of carrying out the provisions of this act.

§ 3. NINE MONTHS SCHOOL.] It shall be the duty of the board of education to have at least nine months school in each year for two years after the passage and approval of this act.

§ 4. This act shall take effect and be in force from and after its passage and approval.

Approved, March 7, 1885.

NEW ORLEANS EXPOSITION.

CHAPTER 16.

AN ACT relating to the World's Industrial and Cotton Centennial Exposition at New Orleans, Louisiana.

Be it enacted by the Legislative Assembly of the Territory of Dakota :

§ 1. APPROPRIATION.] That the sum of twenty-five thousand dollars or so much thereof as may be necessary, be, and the same is hereby appropriated out of any money in the territorial treasury, not otherwise appropriated, for the purpose of paying for the Dakota exhibit at the World's Industrial and Cotton Centennial exposition at New Orleans, in the State of Louisiana and for maintaining the same until the close of said exposition.

§ 2. COMMISSIONER TO RECEIVE WARRANT AND GIVE BOND.] That Alexander McKenzie, United States Commissioner for the Territory of Dakota at said exposition, or his successor in office, shall receive a warrant from the territorial Auditor, drawn upon the territorial treasurer, for the said sum of twenty-five thousand dollars, whenever he shall file his bond with the said auditor duly examined and approved, as provided by this act.

§ 3. BOND.] That before receiving said warrant, said United States Commissioner, or his successor in office, shall execute a bond, in the penal sum of twenty-five thousand dollars, with good and sufficient sureties to be approved by one of the Justices of the Supreme Court of this Territory, conditioned for the faithful performance of his duties as such commissioner and rendering a true and correct account of all moneys received and expenditures made by him for or on account of said exhibit.

§ 4. RETURN OF COUNTY WARRANTS, &C.] It shall be the duty of said Commissioner, or his successor in office, immediately after receiving the said sum of twenty-five thousand dollars, to return to each county in this Territory any warrant or warrants heretofore issued by the county commissioners of such county, in aid of or as a loan of credit to such commissioner or his deputies for the purpose of making said exhibit; and it shall be the duty of said commissioner to immediately deliver to any citizen or citizens of this Territory any note or notes that such citizen or citizens may have made and delivered to said commissioner or his deputies to aid in raising funds for said exhibit; and if any such warrants have been paid by any county treasurer, it shall be the duty of said commissioner, to immediately return to said treasurer the amount of said warrant or warrants; and if any such notes have been paid by said makers, said commissioner shall immediately pay over to said maker or makers the amount or amounts so paid on said notes. And it shall be the duty of said commissioner, or his successor in office, at the close of said exposition to dispose of, for the benefit of the Territory, the products and other articles of which said exhibit is composed, and it shall be the duty of said commissioner to account for all moneys received from the sale of said exhibit.

§ 5. EXAMINING BOARD.] That the Governor of this Territory, the territorial Treasurer and the territorial Auditor are hereby constituted and appointed an examining board, whose duty it shall be to examine and approve the accounts of said commissioner.

§ 6. REPORT OF COMMISSIONER.] That within thirty days after the close of said exposition, the said commissioner shall render to said examining board, a true and correct statement of all moneys received by him, and expenditures made on account of such exhibit, which statement shall be made under oath and accompanied by proper vouchers and all moneys so received and remaining in the hands of such commissioner, after deducting the sum total of expenditures, approved by said board of examiners, or a majority of them, the said commissioner shall forthwith pay over to the territorial Treasurer.

§ 7. REPEALED.] Chapter one hundred and forty-one (141) of the Session Laws of 1881 in relation to the World's Fair, is hereby repealed

§ 8. This act shall take effect and be in force from and after its passage and approval.

Approved, January 28, 1885.

SUPREME COURT REPORTS—THIRD VOLUMES.

CHAPTER 17.

AN ACT to authorize the Purchase and Distribution of Two Hundred and Fifty Copies of the Third Volume of Dakota Supreme Court Reports.

Be it enacted by the Legislative Assembly of the Territory of Dakota :

§ 1. AUTHORITY TO PURCHASE.] That the Territorial Librarian of the Territory of Dakota is hereby authorized to purchase of the publishers of the third volume of Dakota Supreme Court Reports, two hundred and fifty volumes thereof, at a price not exceeding five dollars per volume; *Provided, however*, That if he cannot obtain two hundred and fifty volumes of said reports at the price herein stated, then he shall not purchase any of said reports.

§ 2. ACCOUNT TO BE APPROVED.] That said books shall be well bound in law sheep, and shall be delivered to the said librarian, who shall thereupon approve the publisher's account for said two hundred and fifty volumes at the price agreed upon, not exceeding the amount named in section 1. And when said account so approved shall be presented to the territorial Auditor, he is authorized, and it is made his [duty] to audit said account, and to issue to said publishers a territorial warrant for said account, and the territorial Treasurer is authorized to pay said warrant the same as other warrants drawn upon the territorial treasury.

§ 3. APPROPRIATION.] There is hereby appropriated out of any moneys in the territorial treasury the sum of twelve hundred and fifty dollars to defray the expense of such purchase.

§ 4. WHO TO RECEIVE COPYS OF REPORT.] That it is hereby made the duty of the Librarian of the Territory upon receiving books to distribute them as follows:

One copy to each of the Judges of the supreme court ;

One copy to the district attorney of each county in the Territory ;

One copy to the United States Attorney for Dakota ;

Also, to transmit one copy by mail to the public library of each state and organized territory that has exchanged, or will exchange reports with this Territory ;

One copy to the library of Congress ;

One copy to the library of the Supreme Court of the United States ;

Five copies to the Clerk of the supreme court of this Territory for the use of the supreme court when in session;

One copy to the Attorney General of the United States;

One copy to the Governor of this Territory, and the remaining copies, if any, shall be disposed of as provided by law, and all the officers of the Territory when he receives such volume shall forthwith give the official receipt therefor, on a form furnished by said librarian, and it is hereby made the duty of such officer receiving such volume, to forthwith deliver the same to his successor in office at the expiration of such term of office;

§ 5 This act shall take effect and be in force from and after its passage and approval.

Approved February 19, 1885.

———

Attachments.

CHAPTER 18.

AN ACT to Amend Section 218 of the Code of Civil Procedure.

Be it enacted by the Legislative Assembly of the Territory of Dakota:

§ 1. SECTION AMENDED.] That section two hundred and eighteen of the Code of Civil Procedure be amended by striking out the following words in the last paragraph thereof: " But judgment must not be rendered in the action under the debt or claim upon which such attachment is made and shall become due and payable," and inserting instead thereof the following: " But judgment must not be rendered in the action until the debt or claim upon which such attachment is made shall become due and payable."

§ 2. This act shall take effect and be in force from and after its passage and approval.

Approved, February 10, 1885.

1885—4

Bail.

WHEN TO BE TAKEN IN CAPITAL CASES.

CHAPTER 19.

AN ACT to Amend Section Five Hundred and Fifty-three of the Code of Criminal Procedure of the Territory of Dakota.

Be it enacted by the Legislative Assembly of the Territory of Dakota:

§ 1. WHEN BAIL MAY BE ADMITTED.] That section five hundred and fifty-three of the Code of Criminal Procedure of the Territory of Dakota, be and the same is hereby amended to read as follows: § 553. Bail, by sufficient sureties, may be admitted upon all arrests in criminal cases where the punishment may be death, unless the proof is evident or the presumption great; and in such cases it shall be taken only by the supreme court or a district court, or by a justice or judge thereof, who shall exercise their discretion therein, having regard to the nature and circumstances of the offense, and of the evidence and to the usages of law; but if the case has been tried by jury, and the jury have disagreed on their verdict, then the above presumption is removed and the defendant shall thereupon be entitled to bail, unless it shall appear to the court or judge thereof, by due proof, that such disagreement was occasioned by the misconduct of the jury.

COUNCIL CHAMBER, BISMARCK, DAKOTA,
March 13, 1885.

I hereby certify that on the 7th day of March, 1885, the within bill—Council bill No. 178—was returned to the Council, the house in which it originated, without the approval of his excellency, Governor Gilbert A. Pierce, with his objections to said bill in writing. His objections were entered at large upon the journal of the Council, and on the 13th day of March, 1885, the Council proceeded to reconsider the bill, and after such reconsideration two-thirds of the Council voted to pass the bill, the objections of the Governor to the contrary notwithstanding.
J. H. WESTOVER,
President of the Council.

Attest:
A. W. HOWARD,
Chief Clerk of the Council.

HOUSE OF REPRESENTATIVES,
BISMARCK, March 13, 1885.

I hereby certify that the within bill—Council bill No. 178—was received from the Council, together with the Governor's objections thereto March 13, 1885; that the objections of the Governor were read at length, and the ques-

tion stated by the Speaker: "Shall the bill pass notwithstanding the objections of the Governor," and that the bill did pass, more than two-thirds of the House voting in the affirmative.   GEO. RICE.
Attest: *Speaker of the House.*
   O. M. REED,
       Chief Clerk of the House.

Bill of Exceptions.

CHAPTER 20.

AN ACT to Amend Section Four Hundred and Sixteen of the Code of Criminal Procedure of the Territory of Dakota.

Be it enacted by the Legislative Assembly of the Territory of Dakota:

§ 1. WHERE JUDGE REFUSES TO ALLOW.] That section four hundred and sixteen of chapter five of the Code of Criminal Procedure of Dakota Territory, be, and the same is hereby amended by adding thereto the following proviso:

Provided, however, if the judge in any case refuse to allow an exception in accordance with the facts, the party desiring the bill settled, may apply by petition to the Supreme Court, to prove the same. The application may be made in the mode and manner and under such regulations as the court may prescribe, and the bill, when proven, must be certified by a justice thereof as correct and filed with the clerk of the court in which the action was tried; and when so filed, it has the same force and effect as if settled by the judge who tried the cause.

§ 2. This act shall take effect from and after its passage and approval.

Approved, February 27, 1885.

Blind Asylum.

PROVIDING FOR INSTRUCTION.

CHAPTER 21.

AN ACT to Amend Section 5 of Chapter 13 of the laws of 1879, Concerning the Blind.

Be it enacted by the Legislative Assembly of the Territory of Dakota:

§ 1. WHO MAY BE EDUCATED—PROVISO:] That section five of chapter thirteen of the laws of eighteen hundred and seventy-nine, entitled, an act to provide for the instruction and education of deaf, dumb and blind persons, be, and the same is hereby amended so as to read as follows: "That every blind person of this territory, and all such as may be too blind to acquire an education in the common schools, of suitable capacity, between the ages of five and twenty one years, shall be entitled to receive an education for at least eight years, at the expense of the Territory of Dakota at the said institution for the support and education of the blind." *Provided,* That the time that any pupil or pupils have spent in any institution for the education of the blind, shall be deducted from the eight years above specified, and provided further, that whenever the parent, guardian or other person, responsible for the support of such blind person shall be able so to do, such parent, guardian or other person shall defray the expense of the support and education of such blind person at such institution, and the board of county commissioners shall be the judges of the ability of the person responsible for such support.

§ 2. That all acts or parts of acts in conflict with this are hereby repealed.

§ 3. This act shall be in force from and after its passage and approval.

Approved March 12th, 1885.

Bonds.

AGRICULTURAL COLLEGE, BROOKINGS.

CHAPTER 22.

AN ACT to Provide Funds for Completing the Agricultural College at Brookings, Dakota, and to Repeal Section two of Chapter two and Section six of Chapter three of the Session Laws of 1883.

Be it Enacted by the Legislative Assembly of the Territory of Dakota:

§ 1. CONTROL OF COLLEGE AFFAIRS.] That chapter two of the laws of 1883, is hereby amended by striking out section two and inserting the following: § 2. "Said Agricultural College shall be under the direction of the board of directors, consisting of five members, who shall be appointed by the Governor by and with the consent of the Legislative Council." Said directors shall hold their offices for two years or until their successors are appointed and qualified. All vacancies shall be filled by the remaining members of the board. They shall elect a Treasurer and Secretary from their own number. The Treasurer shall execute to the Territory sufficient sureties in such sum as the board may direct. Said Board of Directors shall have charge of the building and repairing of the building and have the government and control of said Agricultural College. The office of Regents of the college is hereby abolished and the duties and powers of said Regents shall be performed and enjoyed by the directors provided for in this act.

§ 2. REPEALED.] That section six of chapter three (3) of the Session Laws of 1883, is hereby repealed, and the duties and powers of the directors provided for by said section shall be performed by the directors provided for by this act.

§ 3. BONDS TO BE ISSUED.] For the purpose of providing funds to finish the Agricultural College at Brookings, Dakota, and build a Boarding House, and furnish the same, and put in steam heating, the territorial Treasurer is hereby authorized and empowered and it is made his duty to prepare for issue $20,000 of territorial bonds.

§ 4. DESCRIPTION OF BONDS.] Said bonds shall be dated on the day of the execution and delivery thereof; shall be due in twenty years from and after their date, and shall be payable at

the option of the Territory at any time after ten years from their
date. Said bonds shall bear interest at the rate of six (6) per
cent. per annum which interest shall be expressed by coupons
attached to said bonds, and be made payable semi-annually on
the first day of January and July of each year. Said bonds shall
be drawn in denominations of $500.00 each, and shall be num-
bered in the order of their issue; and shall be made payable at
the Chemical National Bank in the City of New York. Said
bonds shall be executed for the Territory, under the seal thereof,
by the Governor and the Treasurer, attested by the Secretary
and negotiated by the Treasurer.

§ 5. NAME OF BOND.] Said bonds, and the money arising
from the sale of the same shall be known and designated as the
" Brookings Agricultural College Fund," and shall be kept as
a separate fund on the books of the Treasurer.

§ 6. WHEN TO BE SOLD.] Said bonds shall be sold by the
Treasurer whenever the directors herein provided for shall request him to do so, and the Treasurer shall offer said bonds for
sale by such public advertisement as he may deem expedient,
at such price, not less than par, as he shall be able to obtain for
the same.

§ 7. PAYMENT OF INTEREST, &C.] For the purpose of the
prompt payment of the principal and interest of the bonds
herein provided for, there shall be levied annually by the territorial Board of Equalization, at the time other taxes are levied,
and collected in the same manner as other territorial taxes are
collected, such a tax as shall be sufficient to pay such interest,
and the exchange thereon, and after nine years from the date of
said bonds, if no other provisions shall have been made for the
payment of the principal of the same, the Board of Equalization
or any other officer or officers then empowered to perform the
duties now performed by the territorial Board of Equalization,
shall levy such sinking fund tax annually as shall be sufficient
to retire and pay said bonds at their maturity. It shall be the
duty of the territorial Treasurer to pay promptly on the first day
of July and January of each year such interest as shall be due
on said bonds, and at the end of twenty years, if a sinking fund
tax is raised as herein provided, to pay, retire and cancel said
bonds in the order of their issue with the sinking fund, as fast as
the same shall be received in sufficient amounts to pay a bond.
The tax and fund herein provided for, for the payment of the
principal or interest of said bonds, shall not be used for any other
purpose.

§ 8. INTEREST PROVIDED FOR.] If at any time the territorial
Treasurer shall not have in his hands sufficient funds, as hereinafter provided, to pay the interest on said bonds when the same

is due, he shall pay such interest out of any funds in the territorial treasury, not otherwise appropriated, and all money belonging to the general territorial fund applied by the said treasurer to the payment of such interest on said bonds, shall be replaced, from time to time, by special tax levied to pay the same.

§ 9. APPROPRIATION.] There is hereby appropriated out of the territorial treasury all the funds realized by the sale of the bonds provided for in this act, for the following purposes:

For furnishing the Agricultural College at Brookings, Dakota,...............................$ 8,000
For steam heating appliances,.................. 2,000
For furnishing,............................... 2,000
For farm additions and improvements,......... 800
For dormitory and boarding house,............ 6,000
For furnishing the same,...................... 1,200

And it shall be the duty of the Auditor of the Territory, upon the application of the Board of Directors, or a majority thereof, to draw on the Territorial Treasurer for the purpose of carrying out the provisions of this act.

Approved March 7, 1885.

- - - - - - - - - -

DEAF MUTE SCHOOL.

CHAPTER 23.

AN ACT to Provide Funds for the Construction of a Dormitory and the Completion of the Buildings for the Dakota School for Deaf Mutes, and for other Purposes.

Be it enacted by the Legislative Assembly of the Territory of Dakota:

§ 1. BONDS TO BE ISSUED.] That for the purpose of providing funds to pay the cost of erecting a dormitory, and furnishing the building and grounds of the Dakota school for deaf mutes at Sioux Falls, Dakota Territory, the territorial Treasurer is hereby authorized and empowered and it is made his duty to prepare for issue sixteen thousand dollars of territorial bonds, running for a term of twenty years and payable at the option of the Territory after ten years, and bearing interest at the rate of six per cent. per annum, with coupons attached, made payable semi-annually on

the first day of July and January, each year; such bonds shall
be executed under the seal of the Territory by the Governor and
Treasurer of the Territory.

§ 2. SALE OF BONDS.] It shall be the duty of the Treasurer to
receive sealed proposals for the purchase of said bonds, and upon
the request of the board of trustees of said school, he shall give
public notice for thirty days in two newspapers of general circulation, one of which shall be published in the city of New York,
and said bonds shall be sold to the highest bidder for cash; *Provided*, That said bonds shall not be sold at less than par value.

§ 3. PAYMENT OF INTEREST, ETC.] For the purpose of the
prompt payment of principal and interest of the bonds herein
provided for, there shall be levied by the territorial board of
equalization, at the time the other taxes are levied and collected,
in the same manner as other territorial taxes are collected, such
sums as shall be sufficient to pay such interest and exchange
thereon, and after nine years from the first day of May, 1885, in
addition thereto a sinking fund tax shall be annually levied,
sufficient to retire and pay such bonds at their maturity; and it
shall be the duty of the territorial Treasurer to pay promptly on
the first days of July and January of each year, such interest as
shall be due, and to purchase said bonds at their market value,
and retire and cancel the same with the sinking fund tax as fast
as the same be received, and no tax or fund provided for the payment of such bonds, either principal or interest, shall at any time
be used for any other purpose.

§ 4. INTEREST PROVIDED FOR.] If for any reason the territorial
Treasurer shall not have in his hands sufficient funds herein provided, to pay the interest upon such bonds when due, he shall
pay such interest out of any other unappropriated funds belonging to the Territory; and there is hereby appropriated and set
apart out of the general funds belonging to the Territory, a sum
sufficient to pay such interest on said bonds as may become due
before the funds and taxes therein provided for can be made
available; and it shall be the duty of said Treasurer to pay said
interest promptly at the time it falls due out of said funds.

§ 5. FUNDS TO BE REPLACED.] All moneys belonging to the
general territorial fund, applied by said treasurer in payment of
the interest of said bonds, shall be replaced from the special tax
levied to pay the same.

§ 6. DUTY OF TRUSTEES.] And the board of trustees of said
school are hereby empowered and directed to commence the construction of said building, and after the same is completed to furnish the same; said building to be of stone; said board of trustees shall make a full and detailed report of their expenditures
and action under this act, to the next territorial Legislative Assem
bly.

§ 7. APPROPRIATION.] There is hereby appropriated out of the territorial treasury all the funds realized by the sale of the bonds provided for in this act ; said funds to be expended for the following purposes :

For building a dormitory and furnishing the same, twelve thousand dollars.

For deficiency, amount due on main building, two hundred dollars.

For steam heating and plumbing, twenty-five hundred dollars.

For sewerage, eight hundred dollars.

For fencing and improving grounds, five hundred dollars.

And it shall be the duty of the Auditor of the Territory, upon the application of the board of trustees, or a majority thereof, of said school for deaf mutes, to draw on the territorial Treasurer for the purpose of constructing said dormitory and carrying out the other provisions of this act.

§ 8. IN CASE OF DIVISION.] In case of division of the Territory of Dakota, that part of said Territory in which said Deaf Mute school is situated, shall assume and pay said bonds and coupons which are issued by virtue of this act.

§ 9. This act shall take effect and be in force from and after its passage and approval.

Approved, March 7, 1885.

NORTH DAKOTA INSANE HOSPITAL.

CHAPTER 24.

AN ACT for the Erection of Additional Buildings for the North Dakota Hospital for the Insane, making Appropriation for the same, and for other purposes:

Be it enacted by the Legislative Assembly of the Territory of Dakota :

§ 1. APPROPRIATED.] There is hereby appropriated out of the funds provided for in this act, the sums hereinafter mentioned for the erection of buildings on the grounds of the North Dakota Hospital for the Insane near Jamestown, Dakota, as follows : For ward building, kitchen, bakery, dining room, laundry, boiler

1885—5

house, boiler, fixtures, machinery, furniture, steam heating, offices and residence, the sum of sixty-three thousand ($63,000.) dollars. Officers' residences not to exceed in cost, four thousand dollars. Section of officers building not to exceed in cost, five thousand dollars. Laundry not to exceed three thousand dollars. Barn not to exceed in cost, three thousand dollars. Sewerage two thousand dollars. Water supply, four thousand dollars. Gas, two thousad dollars.

§ 2. BONDS TO BE ISSUED.] To provide such funds, bonds of this Territory shall be issued to the amount of not to exceed sixty-three thousand ($63,000) dollars, in denominations of five hundred ($500) dollars each, bearing date the first day of May, 1885, with interest payable semi-annually, at some place in New York City, to be specified in said bonds, on the first day of July and January of each year, at the rate of six per cent. per annum, running twenty years, and payable at the option of the Territory at any time after five years from the date of the same.

§ 3. BONDS HOW EXECUTED.] Such bonds shall be executed for the Territory, and under the seal thereof by the Governor and Treasurer and shall be attested by the Secretary and shall be negotiated by the Treasurer of the Territory.

§ 4. PROPOSALS FOR BONDS.] It shall be the duty of the Treasurer to receive sealed proposals for the purchase of said bonds, after giving notice for thirty days in two newspapers of general circulation, one of which shall be published in the Territory, and the other in the city of New York, and said bonds shall be sold to the highest bidder for cash at not less than par.

§ 5. TAX FOR PAYMENT OF BONDS] For the purpose of prompt payment of principal and interest of the bonds herein provided there shall be levied by the Territorial Board of Equalization at the time the other taxes are levied and collected, in the same manner as other territorial taxes are collected, such sums as shall be sufficient to pay such interest and the exchange thereon, and after ten years from the first day of May, 1885, in addition thereto, a sinking fund tax shall be annually levied sufficient to retire and pay said bonds at their maturity. And it shall be the duty of the territorial Treasurer to pay promptly on the first days of January and July of each year, such interest as shall be due and to purchase said bonds at not more than their par value, and retire and cancel the same with the sinking fund tax as fast as the same shall be received. And no tax or fund provided for the payment of such bonds, either principal or interest shall at any time be used for any other purpose.

§ 6. PAYMENT OF INTEREST.] If for any reason the territorial Treasurer shall not have in his hands sufficient of the funds herein provided to pay either principal or interest upon such bonds, when due, he shall pay such interest or principal out of any other unappropriated fund belonging to the Territory; and there is hereby appropriated and set apart out of the general fund belonging to the Territory, a sum sufficient to pay such interest on said bonds, as may become due before the funds and tax herein provided can be made available, and it shall be the duty of said Treasurer to pay said interest, promptly, at the time it falls due out of said funds.

§ 7. REPLACING FUNDS] All moneys belonging to the general territorial fund, applied by said Treasurer in payment of either principal or interest of said bonds, shall be replaced from the special tax levied to pay the same.

§ 8. PLANS AND SPECIFICATIONS.] The board of trustees of the Northern Dakota Hospital for the Insane near Jamestown, shall immediately after passage and approval of this act, prepare, or cause to be prepared, plans and specifications for building the additions and improvements enumerated in section one of this act, and after the same shall have been adopted and approved by them and the Governor of the Territory, the said board of trustees shall cause said plans and specifications to be filed with their secretary, and it shall be the duty of said board, within twenty days thereafter, to give public notice, which notice shall be inserted for thirty days in two newspapers published in the Territory, and of general circulation therein, and in two newspapers published in other states, and that on a day specified in such notice they will receive sealed proposals at the office of the Hospital, near Jamestown, for the building of the said additions and improvements to the Northern Dakota Hospital for the Insane near Jamestown, Dakota, according to plans and specifications aforesaid, which shall be open for inspection of bidders at the office of the Hospital for the Insane, or at such place in the city of Jamestown as the board may designate.

§ 9 TOTAL COST.] The total cost of said buildings and improvements shall not exceed sixty-three thousand ($53,000.) dollars.

§ 10. AWARDING CONTRACT.] On the day advertised for the opening of said proposals for erecting and completing the said additions and improvements, the board of trustees shall proceed to award the contract or contracts, reserving the right to reject any or all bids, if in their judgment they are too high, and may again advertise for proposals, or to accept such bids as in their judgment may be for the best interests of the institution.

§ 11. How BUILT.] The walls of said buildings shall be constructed of good brick or stone, and said building shall be made as nearly fire-proof as practicable.

§ 12.　PARTIAL PAYMENTS.] The board of trustees, as the work progresses, shall, on application of the contractor or contractors, certify to the territorial Auditor the value of the work done on the additions and improvements at the time, and on such certified statement the Auditor shall issue a warrant on the territorial Treasurer for a sum not exceeding eighty-five per cent. of the value of the work so certified to have been done on said additions and improvements at the time of making such application, including amount of all warrants previously issued in part payment of such work; *Provided,* That no part of the funds herein appropriated for the construction of said additions or improvements shall be paid, or value of work certified by the trustees, until at least one-fourth of the work has been completed by the contractor or contractors.

§ 13.　MATERIAL TO BE OF GOOD QUALITY.] The contract or contracts aforesaid shall stipulate that all material shall be of good quality, and that the work shall be performed in a good workmanlike manner, and these stipulations shall be enforced.

§ 14.　FINAL PAYMENT.] The balance due the contractor or contractors, under the contract or contracts, shall be paid on the completion of the additions or improvements, and their acceptance and approval by the board of trustees.

§ 15.　IN CASE OF DIVISION.] In case of division of [the] Territory, that part of the Territory of Dakota in which said Hospital for the Insane is located, shall, on the division of the Territory, assume and pay all bonds and coupons issued and then existing on account of the construction of the said Hospital building.

§ 16.　This act shall take effect and be in force from and after its passage and approval.

Approved, March :, 1885.

NORMAL SCHOOL, MADISON.

CHAPTER 25.

AN ACT entitled an act for the completion of the Territorial Normal School at Madison, Lake County, Dakota.

Be it enacted by the Legislative Assembly of the Territory of Dakota:

§ 1. BONDS TO BE SOLD.] That for the purpose of providing a fund to complete a Normal School, the territorial Treasurer is hereby authorized and empowered, and it is made his duty to prepare for issue, thirteen thousand six hundred dollars ($13,600.) of territorial bonds, ten thousand ($10,000) dollars to be used for completing the building, sixteen hundred dollars for steam heating apparatus; two thousand dollars for school furniture, including model. Said bonds shall be dated on the day of execution and delivery thereof, shall be due in twenty years from and after their date, and shall be payable at the option of the Territory at any time, after ten years from their date. Said bonds shall draw interest at the rate of six (6) per cent. per annum, which interest shall be expressed in coupons attached to said bonds, and be made payable semi-annually on the first days of July and January of each year. Said bonds shall be drawn in denominations of five hundred dollars each, and shall be. numbered in the order of their issue, and shall be made payable at the office of the treasurer of the Territory. Said bonds shall be executed for the Territory and under seal thereof by the Governor and Treasurer, attested by the Secretary and negotiated by the Treasurer.

§ 2. FUND HOW DESIGNATED.] Said bonds and the money arising from the sale of the same, shall be known and designated as the "Madison Normal School Fund," and shall be kept as a separate fund on the books of the Treasurer.

§ 3. BONDS HOW SOLD.] Said bonds shall be sold in the fol. lowing manner. Whenever the directors appointed to superin. tend the completion of said Normal School as hereinafter pro.

vided, shall certify to the Treasurer, that contracts for the completion of said Normal School have been entered into, according to provisions of this act, it shall be the duty of the said Treasurer to offer for sale by such public advertisements as he shall deem expedient, to the person or persons paying par, or the highest premium above par, the whole amount of bonds as herein provided for.

§ 4. TAX.] For the purpose of the prompt payment of the principal and interest of the bonds herein provided for, there shall be levied annually by the Territorial Board of Equalization at the time the other taxes are levied and collected in the same manner as other territorial taxes are collected. Such a tax as shall be sufficient to pay such interest, and the exchange thereon. And after *nineteen* [nine] years from the date of said bonds,if no other provisions shall have been made for the payment of the principal of the same, the said board of equalization or any other officer empowered to perform the duties now performed by said territorial board of equalization shall levy such sinking fund tax annually as shall be sufficient to retire and pay such bonds at their maturity. It shall be the duty of the territorial Treasurer to pay promptly on the first days of July and January of each year such interest as shall then be due on said bonds, and at the end of twenty years if a sinking fund tax is raised as herein provided, to pay, retire and cancel said bonds in the order of their issue with the sinking fund as fast as the same shall be received in sufficient amounts to pay a bond. The tax and fund herein provided for, for the payment of the principal or interest of said bonds, shall not be used for any other purpose.

§ 5. PAYMENT OF INTEREST.] If at any time the territorial Treasurer shall not have in his hands sufficient funds as hereinbefore provided to pay the interest on said bonds, when the same is due, he shall pay such interest out of any funds in the territorial treasury not otherwise appropriated, and all money belonging to the general territorial fund applied by the said Treasurer to the payment of such interest on said bonds, shall be replace! from the special tax levy to pay the same.

§ 6. IN CASE OF DIVISION.] In case of division of Territory, that part of the Territory of Dakota in which said Normal School is located, shall on the division of the Territory, assume and pay all bonds and coupons issued, existing on account of the construction of said Normal School building.

§ 7. That this act shall take effect and be in force from and after its passage and approval.

Approved March 7th, 1885.

NORTH DAKOTA UNIVERSITY.

CHAPTER 26.

AN ACT to Provide Funds to Pay the Deficiency Caused by the Construction of the Main Building of the University of North Dakota, and for other Purposes.

Be it enacted by the Legislative Assembly of the Territory of Dakota:

§ 1. BONDS TO BE ISSUED.] That for the purpose of providing funds to pay the deficiency caused by the erection of a main building, and improve the grounds and out buildings, purchase apparatus and water supply for the University of North Dakota, at Grand Forks, Dakota Territory, the territorial Treasurer is hereby authorized and empowered, and it is made his duty, to prepare for issue twenty-four thousand dollars of territorial bonds, running for a term or period of twenty years, and payable at the option of the Territory after a term of ten years, and bearing interest at the rate of six per cent. per annum, with coupons attached, made payable semi-annually on the first days of July and January, each year; such bonds shall be executed under the seal of the Territory by the Governor and Treasurer, and shall be attested by the Secretary, and shall be negotiated by the Treasurer of the Territory.

§ 2. PROPOSALS FOR BONDS.] It shall be the duty of the Treasurer to receive sealed proposals for the purchase of said bonds, and upon request of the board of regents he shall give public notice for thirty days in two newspapers of general circulation, one of which shall be published in the city of New York, and said bonds shall be sold to the highest bidder for cash; *Provided,* That said bonds shall not be sold for less than their par value.

§ 3. TAX TO MEET PAYMENT.] For the purpose of prompt payment of principal and interest of the bonds herein provided, there shall be levied by the territorial board of equalization at the time the other taxes are levied, and collected in the same manner as other territorial taxes are collected, such sum as shall be sufficient to pay such interest and exchange thereon; and after ten years from the first day of May, 1885, and in addition thereto, a sinking fund tax shall be annually levied, sufficient to retire and pay said bonds at their maturity; and it shall be the duty of the territorial Treasurer to pay promptly on the first days of July and January of each year, such interest as shall then be due, and to purchase said bonds at their market value, and retire and cancel the same with the sinking fund tax as fast as the same shall be received, and no tax or bonds, either principal or interest, shall at any time be used for any other purpose.

§ 4. INTEREST TO BE PAID FROM ANY FUND.] If for any reason the territorial Treasurer shall not have in his hands sufficient funds herein provided to pay the interest upon such bonds when due, he shall pay such interest out of any other unappropriated fund belonging to the Territory; and there is hereby appropriated and set apart out of the general funds belonging to the Territory, a sum sufficient to pay such interest on said bonds as may become due before the funds and tax herein provided can be made available; and it shall be the duty of said Treasurer to pay said interest promptly at the time it falls due out of said funds.

§ 5. REPLACED FUND.] All moneys belonging to the general territorial fund, applied by said Treasurer in payment of the interest on said bonds, shall be replaced from the special tax levied to pay the same.

§ 6. APPROPRIATION.] There is hereby appropriated out of the territorial treasury, all the funds realized by the sale of the bonds provided for in this act, for deficiency in construction of building as now built, twenty thousand three hundred and sixty-two dollars.

For library, one thousand dollars.

For improving grounds, five hundred dollars.

For water closets, five hundred dollars.

For apparatus for laboratory, etc., one thousand dollars.

For water supply, six hundred and thirty-eight dollars.

§ 7. WARRANTS TO BE DRAWN.] It shall be the duty of the Auditor of the Territory, upon the application of the board of regents, or a majority thereof, to draw warrants on the territorial Treasurer for the purpose of carrying out the provisions of the aforesaid act.

§ 8. IN CASE OF DIVISION.] In case the Territory of Dakota is divided the bonds issued under the provisions of this act, shall be paid by that portion of the Territory within which said University is situated.

§ 9. This act shall take effect and be in force from and after its passage and approval.

Approved, March 7, 1885.

DAKOTA UNIVERSITY.

CHAPTER 27.

AN ACT to provide for furnishing the Main Building of the University of Dakota, and other purposes.

Be it enacted by the Legislative Assembly of the Territory of Dakota:

§ 1. APPROPRIATIONS.] There is hereby appropriated out of the funds provided for in this act the sums hereinafter mentioned for the erection of buildings on the grounds of the University of Dakota and other necessary expenses, as follows, namely:

First, for heating, plumbing and sewerage, Five Thousand ($5,000) dollars.

Second, completing and deficiency in constructing main building and furnishing the main building of the University of Dakota, Ten Thousand ($10,000) dollars.

§ 2. BONDS TO BE ISSUED.] To provide such funds, bonds of this Territory shall be issued to the amount of fifteen thousand ($15,000) dollars in denominations of five hundred ($500) dollars bearing date the first day of May, 1885, with interest payable semi-annually, at some place in New York city, to be specified in said bonds, on the first day of July and January of each year, at the rate of six per cent. per annum, running twenty years, and payable at the option of the Territory at any time after five years from date of the same.

§ 3. BONDS HOW EXECUTED.] Such bonds shall be executed for the Territory and under the seal thereof by the Governor and Treasurer and shall be attested by the Secretary and shall be negotiated by the Treasurer of the Territory.

§ 4. PROPOSALS FOR BONDS.] It shall be the duty of the territorial Treasurer to receive sealed proposals for the purchase of said bonds, after giving notice for thirty days in two newspapers of general circulation, one of which shall be published in the Territory and the other in the city of New York, and said bonds shall be sold to the highest and best bidder for cash, and said bonds shall not be sold for less than par.

§ 5. TAX FOR THE PAYMENT OF BONDS.] For the purpose of prompt payment of the principal and interest of the bonds herein provided, there shall be levied by the territorial Board of Equalization, at the time the other taxes are levied and collected in the same manner as other territorial taxes are collected, such sums as shall be sufficient to pay such interest and the exchange thereon. And after ten years from the first day of May, 1885, in addition thereto a sinking fund tax shall be annually levied sufficient to retire and pay said bonds, at their maturity, and it shall be the duty of the territorial Treasurer to pay promptly on the first days of July and January of each year at the Chemical National Bank in the city of New York such interest as shall then be due, and to purchase said bonds at not more than their par value, and retire and cancel the same with the sinking fund tax as fast as the same shall be received, and no tax or fund provided for the payment of such bonds, either principal or interest, shall at any time be used for any other purpose.

§ 6. PAYMENT OF INTEREST.] If for any reason the territorial Treasurer shall not have in his hands sufficient of the funds herein provided to pay either principal or interest upon such bonds when due, he shall pay such interest or principal out of any other unappropriated fund belonging to the Territory, and there is hereby appropriated and set apart out of the general fund belonging to the Territory, a sum sufficient to pay such interest on said bonds as may become due before the funds and tax herein provided can be available, and it shall be the duty of said Treasurer to pay said interest promptly at the time it falls due out of said funds.

§ 7. REPLACING FUNDS.] All moneys belonging to the general territorial fund applied by said Treasurer in payment of either principal or interest of said bonds shall be replaced from the special tax levied to pay the same.

§ 8. PLANS AND SPECIFICATIONS.] The board of Regents of the University of Dakota, shall immediately after the passage and approval of this act prepare or cause to be prepared plans and specifications for building the additions and improvements enumerated in section one of this act, and after the same shall have been adopted and approved by them and the Governor of the Territory. Said board of Regents shall cause said plans and specifications to be filed with their Secretary, and it shall be the duty of said board within twenty days thereafter to give public notice, which notice shall be inserted for thirty days in two newspapers published in the Territory and of general circulation therein, and in two newspapers published in other States, and that on a day specified in such notice, they will receive sealed proposals at the office of the Secretary of the board of Regents of the University of Dakota, according to plans and specifications aforesaid, which shall be open for inspection of bidders at the office of the Secretary of the board of Regents of the University of Dakota, or at such place as the board may designate.

§ 9 TOTAL COST.] The cost of said buildings and improvements shall not exceed the sum of fifteen thousand ($15,000) dollars, and shall be used in the manner provided in section one of this act.

§ 10. AWARDING CONTRACTS.] On the day advertised for the opening of said proposals for erecting and completing the said additions and improvements, the board of Regents shall proceed to award the contract or contracts, reserving the right to reject any or all bids if in their judgment they are too high, and may again advertise for proposals, or accept such bids as in their judgment may be for the best interest of the institution.

§ 11. How BUILT.] The walls of said building shall be constructed of good brick or stone, and shall be made as near fire proof as practicable and at a proper and safe distance from the main building.

§ 12. PARTIAL PAYMENTS.] The board of Regents as the work progresses, shall on application of the contractor or contractors, certify to the territorial Auditor the value of the work done on the said additions and improvements at the time, and on such certified statement the Auditor shall issue a warrant on the territorial Treasurer for a sum not exceeding seventy-five per cent. of the value of the work so certified to have been done on said additions and improvements at the time of making such application including amount of all warrants previously issued in part payment of such work; *Provided*, that no part of the funds herein appropriated for the construction of said additions and improvements shall be paid, or value of work certified by the Regents, until and least one fourth of the work has been completed by the contractor or contractors.

§ 13. MATERIALS TO BE OF GOOD QUALITY.] The contract or contracts aforesaid shall stipulate that all material shall be of good quality, and that the work shall be performed in a good workmanlike manner and these stipulations shall be enforced.

§ 14. FINAL PAYMENT.] The balance due the contractor or contractors under the contract or contracts, shall be paid on the completion of the additions and improvements and their acceptance and approval by the board of Regents.

§ 15. IN CASE OF DIVISION.] In case of the division of the Territory that part of the Territory of Dakota in which said University is located shall on the division of the Territory assume and pay all bonds and coupons outstanding on account of the construction of said University.

§ 16. REGENTS ABOLISHED.] The university of Dakota shall

be governed by a board of five directors to be appointed by the
Governor, by and with the consent of the Legislative Council,
who shall hold their office for two years, or until their successors
are elected and qualified, and the office of Regents is hereby abolished, and the powers and duties conferred upon the Regents
provided for in section three of chapter thirty-eight of the laws
of 1883, are hereby conferred upon the board of directors hereby
authorized to be appointed, and said section is hereby repealed.

§ 17.   All acts and parts of acts in conflict with this act are
hereby repealed.

§ 18.   This act shall take effect and be in force from and after
its passage and approval.

Approved, March 7, 1885.

Caucuses.

CHAPTER 28.

AN ACT to regulate Caucuses or Primary Meetings in this Territory.

Be it enacted by the Legislative Assembly of the Territory of Dakota:

§ 1.   WHO MAY VOTE AT PRIMARY MEETINGS.]   It shall be unlawful for any person not a qualified elector of the ward or election precinct in which any Caucus or Primary meeting is held,
having for its object either immediately or ultimately, the nomi-
nation or selection of any delegate or candidate for any public
office to be voted on at any election in this Territory, to vote in
any manner or on any question which may come before such caucus or primary meeting.   Any person who shall violate the provisions of this act shall be deemed guilty of a misdemeanor, and
shall be punished according to law.

§ 2.   This act shall take effect and be in force from and after
its passage and approval.

Approved, March 13, 1885.

Capital Punishment.

CHAPTER 29.

AN ACT to Amend Section Two of Chapter Nine of the Laws of 1883, entitled "Capital Punishment."

Be it enacted by the Legislative Assembly of the Territory of Dakota :

§ 1. DESIGNATION OF PENALTY.] That section two of chapter nine of the laws of 1883, be and the same is hereby amended by adding thereto at the close thereof the following: "But upon a plea of guilty the court shall determine the same."

§ 2. All acts or parts of acts conflicting with the provisions of this act are hereby repealed.

§ 3. This act shall take effect and be in force from and after its passage and approval.

Approved, March 13, 1885.

Census.

CHAPTER 30

AN ACT to Provide for taking the Census of the Territory of Dakota.

Be it enacted by the Legislative Assembly of the Territory of Dakota :

§ 1. SUPERINTENDENT.] The Governor of this Territory is hereby designated as the Superintendent of Census and is hereby empowered to employ one clerk, who shall receive such compensation for his services as the Governor shall deem adequate.

§ 2. BLANKS.] The Superintendent of Census shall cause to be prepared such blanks as are necessary for taking the census of the Territory of Dakota for the year 1885.

§ 3. SUPERVISORS OF CENSUS.] The Governor shall nominate,

and by and with the advice and consent of the Legislative Council, shall appoint two Supervisors of the Census, one of whom shall be Supervisor of the Census for North Dakota, and the other Supervisor of the Census of South Dakota. The Supervisors of Census, shall, upon entering upon the duties of their office respectively take and subscribe the following oath or affirmation: "I, ..., Supervisor of Census, do solemnly swear, (or affirm) that I will support the Constitution of the United States, and the Organic Act of this Territory, and perform and discharge the duties of Supervisor of Census according to law, honestly and correctly, to the best of my ability." Which oath shall be filed in the office of the Governor.

§ 4. ENUMERATORS.] Each Supervisor of Census shall divide his district into subdivisions most convenient for the purpose of enumeration, and designate and employ suitable persons as enumerators within his district, one for each subdivision, a resident therein, to transmit to the enumerators printed forms and schedules prepared by the superintendent in quantities suited to the requirements of such subdivision, to communicate to the enumerators information, instructions and directions, relative to their duties, and the methods relative to taking the census, and to advise with and counsel enumerators, in person and by letter, as fully as may be required to fulfill the purposes of this act: To provide for the early and safe transmission to his office of the returns of the enumerators, embracing all the schedules filled by them in the course of enumeration, and for the due receipt and custody of such returns, and for their transmission to the superintendent, to examine and scrutinize the returns of the enumerators in order to ascertain whether or not the work has been performed in all respects in compliance with the provisions of law, and whether any city, village or integral portion of the district has been omitted from the enumeration: To forward to the Superintendent of Census the complete returns of his district, in such time and manner as shall be prescribed by such superintendent, and in case of any error in the returns, to use all diligence in causing the same to be corrected or supplied: To make up returns to the superintendent of accounts required for ascertaining the amount due under the provisions of this act, to each enumerator in his district.

§ 5. COMPENSATION OF SUPERVISORS.] The Supervisor of Census for South Dakota, shall, upon the completion of his duties, receive the sum of eight hundred dollars, and the Supervisor of Census for North Dakota shall receive the sum of six hundred dollars, in full compensation for all services rendered and expenses incurred by them, except an allowance for clerk hire may be made, in the discretion of the Superintendent of Census.

§ 6. OATH OF ENUMERATOR.] Each enumerator, upon receiving his appointment, shall take and subscribe the following oath : "I ......, an enumerator for taking the census of the Territory of Dakota, do solemnly swear, that I will make a true and exact enumeration of all the inhabitants within the subdivision assigned to me, and will also faithfully collect all other statistics therein, as provided for in the act for taking the census, and in conformity with all lawful instructions which I may receive, and will make due and correct returns. thereof as required by this act: and will not disclose any information contained in the schedules, lists or statements, obtained by me, to any person or persons, except to my superior officers." Which oath may be administered by any person authorized to administer oaths under the laws of this Territory, and shall be forwarded to the Supervisor of Census before the date herein fixed for the commencement of the enumeration And the duties of the enumerators shall be the same as provided by chapter 195, of the United States statutes at large, approved March 3rd, 1879, entitled, "an act for taking the tenth and subsequent censuses." And their compensation shall be the same as provided for the compensation of enumerator's under said act, and they shall be subject to the same penalties for neglect of duty as in said act provided.

§ 7. FORMS.] The blanks and forms used in taking such census shall be the same as those required by the laws of the United States for taking the tenth census, and the Superintendent of Census shall obtain such facts and information relative to railroads, express, telegraph and insurance companies within this Territory as were required to be obtained by the Superintendent of Census under the act of Congress of March 3, 1879, in relation to the tenth census.

§ 8. WHEN TO BE TAKEN—COMPENSATION.] The enumeration required by this act shall commence on the first Monday of June, and shall be taken after that date, and each enumerator shall prosecute the canvass of his subdivision from that day forward, on each week day, without intermission, except from sickness or other urgent cause ; and any unnecessary cessation of his work shall be sufficient ground for his removal, and the appointment of another person in his place ; and any person so appointed shall take the oath required of enumerators, and shall receive compensation at the same rate, and it shall be the duty of each enumerator to complete the enumeration of his district on or before the first day of July, 1885.

§ 9. REMOVALS.] The Supervisor of Census may remove any enumerator in his district, and fill any vacancy thereby caused, or otherwise occurring ; and in such case but one compensation shall be allowed for the entire service, to be apportioned among the persons performing the same, in the discretion of the Supervisor of the Census.

§ 10. APPROPRIATION.] There is hereby appropriated out of the territorial treasury a sum of money sufficient to carry out the provisions of this act; and upon the approval of any amount by the Governor, on filing the proper voucher therefor, the territorial Auditor is hereby authorized to draw his warrant upon the territorial Treasurer for the payment of the same.

§ 11. BLANKS.] The Governor, or Superintendent of Census, is hereby authorized and required to cause to be printed the necessary blanks for carrying out the provisions of this act; which printing shall be done by the lowest responsible bidder.

§ 12. GENERAL GOVERNMENT FUNDS.] The sums of money received by the Governor for taking the census as herein provided, from the United States, as provided by section 22, of chapter 195, of the Statutes at Large of the United States, approved March 5, 1879, shall be paid into the territorial treasury for the benefit of the general fund.

Approved, March 13, 1885.

Change of Names.

TOWNS AND VILLAGES.

CHAPTER 31.

AN ACT Providing a Method for Changing the Names of Towns and Villages.

Be it enacted by the Legislative Assembly of the Territory of Dakota:

§ 1. PETITION.] When any number of the inhabitants of any town or village shall desire to change the name thereof, there shall be filed in the office of the county clerk, or county auditor, a petition for that purpose which must be signed by at least two-thirds of the qualified electors of said town or village, setting forth the name by which said town or village is known; its location, as near as practicable, and giving the name which they desire the town shall thereafter be known by.

§ 2. NOTICE.] Notice of the filing of said petition, and the

time and place when the same shall be heard, and the objects and
purposes thereof shall be given by posting up a written or printed
notice, in at least five public places in the town or village, the
name of which is sought to be changed, at least four weeks before
the meeting of the board of county commissioners.

§ 3. DUTY OF COUNTY BOARD.] At the next regular meeting
of the board of county commissioners, after said notices shall have
been posted as aforesaid, said board shall proceed to hear and determine said petition, unless said hearing is for good cause continued until the next meeting; and said board shall on the hearing of said petition, also hear any remonstrance against the
proposed change; and if on the hearing it shall appear to the
said board that two-thirds of the qualified electors of said town or
village in good faith signed said petition for change of name and
desired the same, then the said board shall order said name to be
changed as prayed for.

§ 4. RECORD.] Said order of the board shall thereupon be
entered of record, giving the name of said town or village as set
forth in said petition; the new name given; the time when the
change shall take effect, which shall not be less than thirty days
thereafter, and directing that notice of said change shall be published in at least one newspaper published in said county, if any;
and if there is no newspaper published in said county, then said
notice shall be published by posting the same for four weeks on
the front door of the court house where the last term of the District
Court of said county was held.

§ 5. FILING PROOF.] The ordinary proof of such publications
shall be filed in the office of the county clerk or county auditor,
and shall be by him filed for preservation; and on the day fixed
by the board as aforesaid, the change shall be complete; *Provided*,
That whenever the name of any town or village shall be changed
by order of the provisions of this act, the county clerk or county
auditor shall immediately notify the register of deeds, who shall
note the change of name upon the plat of said town or village
with the date thereof.

§ 6. COSTS.] In all cases arising under the provisions of this
act, where there is no remonstrance or opposition to said petition,
the petitioners shall pay all costs; but in all other cases costs shall
abide the result of the proceeding, and be taxed to either party,
in the discretion of the board, or divided equitably between the
parties.

§ 7. All acts and parts of acts in conflict with the provisions
of this act are hereby repealed.

Approved, March 12, 1885.

1885—7

Chattel Mortgages.

CHAPTER 32.

AN ACT Relating to the Foreclosure of Chattel Mortgages.

Be it enacted by the Legislative Assembly of the Territory of Dakota:

§ 1　MANNER OF FORECLOSING.] A chattel mortgage, when the conditions of the same have been broken, may be foreclosed by a sale of the property mortgaged, upon the notice and in the manner following. The notice shall contain:

1. The names of the mortgagor and mortgagee, and the assignor, if any.

2. The date of the mortgage.

3. The nature of the default and the amount claimed to be due thereon at the date of the notice.

4. A description of the mortgaged property conforming substantially to that contained in the mortgage.

5- The time and place of sale.

6. The name of the party, agent or attorney foreclosing such mortgage.

§ 2.　POSTING NOTICE.] Such notice shall be posted in five (5) public places in the county where the property is to be sold, at least ten (10) days before the time therein specified for such sale.

§ 3.　PURCHASER.] The mortgagee, his assigns or any other person may in good faith become a purchaser of the property sold.

§ 4.　ATTORNEY'S FEES.] Such attorney fee as shall be specified in the mortgage may be taxed and made a part of the costs of foreclosure; *Provided*, Such mortgage is foreclosed by an attorney of record of this Territory, and the name of such attorney appears as attorney on the notice of sale, and in no other cases shall an attorney fee be allowed.

§ 5.　ACT, HOW CONSTRUED] This act shall not be construed to affect the provisions relating to foreclosures of chattel mortgages by action.

§ 6.　This act shall take effect and be in force from and after its passage and approval.

Approved, March 13, 1885.

Constitutional Convention.

CHAPTER 33.

AN ACT providing for a Constitutional Convention and the Formation of a State Constitution preparatory to the Admission of Dakota into the Union, and for other purposes.

PREAMBLE:—Whereas, experience has abundantly demonstrated that the welfare of the people is promoted by the establishment among them of a permanent government, sovereign in character and republican in form; and

WHEREAS, The territorial system of government has no stability, is temporary in character, possessing no sovereign powers, and meets neither the requirements of the people, nor, in the case of Dakota, the rapidly increasing demands of its various and growing interests; and

WHEREAS, It has ever been and still remains the wise policy of the parent government to foster and encourage the development and settlement of the Territories until such time as their population shall be sufficiently numerous to entitle the people to be admitted into and become a part of the United States, on an equal footing with the States which compose the Union; and

WHEREAS, That part of the Territory of Dakota south of the 46th parallel of latitude now contains a population sufficient to entitle it to admission into the Union, and such population now being desirous of being fully enfranchised and enjoying all the privileges of American Citizenship; and

WHEREAS, Public opinion in the United States has decided and the Congress of the United States by their action upon the bill for the admission of such part of Dakota into the Union, has admitted that that portion of Dakota south of the 46th parallel does possess the requisite population and all other qualifications necessary to entitle it to admission into the Union as a State; therefore:

Be it enacted by the Legislative Assembly of the Territory of Dakota:

§ 1. CONVENTION PROVIDED FOR.] That for the purpose of enabling the people of that part of Dakota south of the 46th parallel, to organize and form a State Government and make application for admission into the Union of States, a delegate convention is hereby called to meet at the city of Sioux Falls in the county of Minnehaha, in said Territory of Dakota, on Tuesday the eighth day of September, A. D. 1885, at twelve o'clock, meridian, for the purpose of framing a Constitution, republican in form, and performing all other things essential to the preparation of the Territory for making application to the general government for the admission of such part of Dakota into the Union of States.

§ 2. APPORTIONMENT.] The said convention shall be composed of one hundred and eleven delegates, who shall be apportioned among the several counties of that part of the Territory south of the 46th parallel, as follows:

County		County	
Aurora	2	Lincoln	2
Bon Homme	3	McPherson	1
Buffalo	1	Beadle	5
Brule	3	Brookings	3
Campbell	1	Brown	4
Charles Mix	1	Turner	4
Clay	2	Walworth	1
Custer	1	Moody	2
Day	2	Potter	1
Douglas	2	Sanborn	2
Fall River	1	Sully	2
Lawrence	8	Union	3
McCook	2	Yankton	4
Miner	2	Butte	1
Minnehaha	6	Clark	2
Pennington	2	Codington	2
Roberts	1	Davison	2
Spink	6	Deuel	1
Grant	2	Edmunds	1
Hand	3	Faulk	1
Hughes	3	Hamlin	1
Hyde	1	Hanson	2
Kingsbury	2	Hutchinson	3
Lake	2	Jerauld	2

Provided, That all organized counties in the Territory south of the 46th parallel, at the time the election hereinafter provided for is held to choose members to said convention, and which counties are not above named, shall be entitled to one delegate, who shall be given a seat, and have a vote in said convention, as other members thereof, and said delegates shall be in addition to the one hundred and eleven heretofore provided for.

§ 3. TIME OF ELECTION AND CONVENTION.] An election for the purpose of choosing said delegates is hereby appointed to be held on the thirtieth day of June, ('1 uesday) 1885; at which time the delegates to the said Constitutional Convention shall be chosen; said election shall be conducted in all respects as elections under the general laws of this Territory. And the several county clerks of the several counties of the Territory, are hereby required to issue notice of such election, at least twenty days prior thereto, stating the object of such election, and the number and character of the officers to be chosen. and shall deliver the same to the sheriff, who is required to post the same, as the law now requires; and the several boards of county commissioners are required to establish precincts for such election, and to appoint polling places and judges of such election, and to do and perform all things that are now required of them by law in the case of general elections; and the canvass and return of the votes shall be as now required by law in the case of county officers. And it is hereby made the duty of the several county clerks to issue certificates of election to all persons who shall be declared elected; *Provided*, That the persons receiving the highest number of votes at such election shall be elected as such delegates. It shall be the further duty of such county clerks, within ten days after such election, to certify to the Secretary of the Territory the names of all persons chosen as such delegates from their respective counties, and to transmit the same to said Secretary by mail.

§ 4. SECRETARY TO RECEIVE RETURNS.] The Secretary of the Territory shall receive all certificates so transmitted to him by the several county clerks, and shall preserve the same, and it is hereby made his duty to enter the names of all persons so certified to him as such delegates in a book which he shall provide for that purpose.

§ 5. ORGANIZATION OF CONVENTION.] The delegates so elected at such election shall meet at the time and place appointed by this act, and in such room as the Secretary of the Territory, or the convention, have provided; and at the hour heretofore named, the Secretary of the Territory, or some member elect of said convention, shall call the convention to order, and shall call the roll of the members from the book heretofore provided, if such book can be obtained, and if not, from the official returns of said election, and the certificate of election of each member, in such manner as the convention shall prescribe, and the several delegates as their names are called, shall take their seats in said convention. When the calling of the roll of members shall be completed the several delegates shall be required to take and subscribe an oath to support the constitution of the United States, and to faithfully and impartially discharge their duties as delegates to said convention; said oath may be administered by said Secretary or by any judicial officer of the Territory. The convention shall then proceed to organize by the election of a president who shall be chosen from among the delegates, and the other officers herein provided for. Said convention shall adopt such rules and regulations for their government as are provided in the case of legislative bodies. It may adjourn from time to time, and shall be the sole judge of the election an ! qualifications of its members. The president and all officers of said convention shall take and subscribe an oath to faithfully and impartially discharge the duties of their respective offices.

§ 6. DUTY OF CONVENTION.] Said convention after its organization shall proceed to draft a constitution for that portion of Dakota south of the 46th parallel, republican in form, in which shall be defined the boundaries of the proposed State south of the 46th parallel. It shall be the further duty of said convention to provide for an election by the people of the proposed State, at which election the said constitution shall be submitted to the people for ratification ; and at which election the State officers, member of Congress, members of the Legislature, and all other officers provided for in said constitution shall be elected : and the said convention shall have power to provide all necessary means for holding said election, and for reassembling said Legislature when elected, and for carrying into effect all the purposes of said constitution ; *Provided*, That the expenses of all special elections under the provisions of this act, and of any ordinance of said convention shall be paid by each county in said Territory respectively.

§ 7. PER DIEM.] The delegates to the said Constitutional Convention shall each receive a *per diem* of two dollars and fifty cents (2.50) for each day's attendance upon said convention, and five cents per mile for each mile necessarily traveled in going to and returning from said convention ; said *per diem* and mileage to be paid by the territorial Treasurer upon the warrant of the territorial Auditor.

§ 8. ACCOUNTS TO BE AUDITED.] The territorial Auditor is hereby authorized to audit and allow the accounts of the several delegates to said convention, upon certificates of the presiding officer of said convention, countersigned by the secretary thereof.

§ 9. OFFICERS OF CONVENTION—PROVISO.] Said convention shall have power to elect a secretary, assistant secretary, employ stenographers, a chaplain, sergeant-at-arms, messengers and clerks, and janitor, each of whom shall receive such compensation as the said convention shall determine, to be audited and paid in the same manner as the accounts of the members of said convention are audited and paid ; *Provided,* That said convention before its adjournment shall ascertain the entire expense of holding the same, including the *per diem* and mileage of its members, compensation of its officers and all necessary expenses, and shall certify the same under the hand of the presiding officer of said convention and attested by the secretary thereof to the Secretary of Territory, and which shall be filed by said Secretary of the Territory in his office, and be kept as a record thereof; and it is hereby made the duty of the several boards of county commissioners of the counties named herein or represented in said convention, to cause to be levied and collected in the same manner as other taxes are levied and collected, a special tax sufficient to pay all of said expenses, which tax shall be apportioned among the said counties in proportion to the assessed valuation; and when said tax is collected in each of said counties, the same shall be paid by said counties into the territorial treasury; *Provided*, That in case of the division of the Territory of Dakota, or the admission of the southern half as a State before the collection and payment of said tax into the territorial treasury as herein provided, then the Treasurer of said State or Territory formed from that portion of Dakota south of the 46th parallel, as the case may be, shall pay over to the Territory of North Dakota such proportion of said moneys as the assessed valuation of the property in North Dakota bears to the assessed valuation of property in South Dakota, in said new State or Territory.

§ 10. STATE ELECTION.] The laws now in force governing elections, and the canvass and return of the votes cast therein, and the qualifications of voters, shall govern in any election that may be held under this act or under any ordinance of said convention; But said convention shall designate the board of State canvassers, and ordain the method by which the result of the State election shall be promulgated. The said convention shall also provide the manner of presenting the said constitution to the Congress of the United States, and do and ordain all things necessary to be done for the purpose of carrying into effect the government of the State, as soon as it shall be admitted into the union of states.

§ 11. LIMIT OF PAY.] That the members of said convention shall not receive pay for a session of more than thirty days, but said convention may sit for a longer period, and may adjourn from time to time

§ 12. APPROPRIATION.] That for the purpose of defraying the expenses of said convention, there is hereby appropriated out of any money in the territorial treasury, not otherwise appropriated, a sum sufficient to defray the expenses of said convention, not to exceed in the aggregate the sum of twenty thousand dollars.

§ 13. This act shall take effect after its passage and approval.
Approved, March 9, 1885.

Corporations.

BUILDING AND LOAN ASSOCIATIONS.

CHAPTER 34.

AN ACT to Provide for the Incorporation and Regulation of Building and Loan Associations.

Be it enacted by the Legislative Assembly of the Territory of Dakota:

§ 1. CHARTER.] At any time when ten or more persons may desire to form a Building and Loan Association under the provisions of this act, they shall make application to the Secretary of the Territory in the manner prescribed by the 10th section of this act. The said Secretary is hereby fully empowered to grant charters to said associations, provided that no charter granted under or by virtue of the provisions of this act shall be for a longer period than twenty years.

§ 2. CAPITAL STOCK.] The capital stock of any corporation created by virtue of this act shall at no time consist of more than two thousand five hundred shares of two hundred dollars each. The installments on which stock are to be paid at such time and place as the by-laws shall appoint. No periodical payment to be made exceeding two dollars on each share. Every share of stock shall be subject to a lien for the payment of unpaid installments and other charges incurred thereon, under the provisions of the charter and by-laws, and the by-laws may prescribe the form and manner of enforcing such lien. New shares of stock may be issued in lieu of the shares withdrawn or forfeited; the stock may be issued in one or successive series in such amount as the Board of Directors or stock holders may determine, and any stock holder wishing to withdraw from the said corporation shall have power to do so by giving thirty days notice of his or her intention to withdraw when he or she shall be entitled to receive the amount paid in by him or her, and such proportion of the profits as the by-laws may determine, less all fines and other charges; *Provided,* That at no time shall more than one-half of the funds in the treasury of the corporation be applicable to the demands of withdrawing stock holders without the consent of the Board of Directors, and that no stock holder shall be entitled to withdraw, whose stock is held in pledge for security. Upon the death of a stock holder, his or her legal representative shall be entitled to receive the full amount paid in by him or her, and legal interest thereon, first deducting all charges that may be due on the stock. No fines shall be charged to a deceased member's account from or after his or her decease, unless the legal representatives of such decedent assume the future payments on the stock.

§ 3. BY-LAWS TO CONTAIN.] The number, titles, functions and compensation of the officers of any corporation created by virtue of this act, their terms of office, the times of their election, as well as the qualifications of electors and the votes and manner of voting, and the periodical meetings of said corporation, shall be determined by the by-laws.

§ 4. LOANING FUNDS.] The said officers shall hold stated meetings, at which the money in the treasury, if over two hundred dollars, shall be offered for loan in open meeting, and the stock holder who shall bid the highest premium for the preference or priority of loan shall be entitled to receive a loan of two hundred dollars for each share of stock held by such stock holder. *Provided*, that good and ample security shall be given by the borrower to secure the repayment of the loan. In case the borrower shall neglect to offer security or shall offer security that is not approved by the Board of Directors by such time as the by-laws may prescribe, he or she shall be charged with one month's interest at the rate charged by the association on loans, and a fine not to exceed one dollar per share, together with any expenses incurred, and the money shall be re-sold at the next stated meeting. In case of non-payment of installments, or interest or premium by borrowing stock holder for the space of six months, payment of principal, and interest without deducting the premium paid or interest thereon may be enforced by proceeding on their securities according to law.

§ 5. PAYMENT OF LOANS.] A borrower may repay a loan at any time by the payment to the corporation of the principal sum borrowed, together with interest not to exceed twelve per cent. per annum, together with such per cent. of premium per annum as may have been bid for the preference or priority of such loan and any fines or charges that may be imposed upon such stock holder at the time of such repayment, or in case the amount of premium bid for the priority of such loan be deducted in advance, and the repayment thereof is made before the expiration of the eighth year after the organization of the corporation, there shall be refunded to such borrower one eighth of the premium paid for every year of the said eight years unexpired: *Provided*, that when the stock is issued in separate series, the time shall be computed from the date of the issuing of the shares of stock on which the loan was made.

1885—8

§ 6. INTEREST NOT USURIOUS.] No premiums, fines, or interest on such premiums that may accrue to the said corporation according to the provisions of this act shall be deemed usurious ; and the same may be collected as debts of like amount are now by law collected in this Territory.

§ 7. NEGLECT NOT TO AFFECT LIFE OF CORPORATION.] No corporation created under this act shall cease or expire from neglect on the part of the corporation to elect officers at the time mentioned in their charter, or by-laws, and all officers elected by such corporation shall hold their offices until their successors are duly elected and qualified.

§ 8. MAY PURCHASE AT SHERIFF'S SALE.] Any building or Loan Association incorporated by or under the provisions of this act, or any one heretofore incorporated accepting of the provisions of the same, is hereby authorized and empowered to purchase at any sheriff's, or other judicial sale, or at any other sale, public or private, any real estate upon which such association may have or hold any mortgage, judgment, lien or other incumbrance or in which said association may have an interest; and the real estate so purchased, or any other that such association may hold, or be entitled to at the passage of this act, to sell, convey, lease or mortgage at pleasure to any person or persons whatsoever, and all sales of real estate heretofore made by such association to any person or persons not members of the association so selling, are hereby confirmed and made valid.

§ 9. VALIDATING SECURITIES.] All mortgages heretofore given to Building and Loan Associations organized under the laws of this Territory before the passage of this act, but such associations subsequently accepting the provisions hereof, be and the same are hereby declared good and valid to all intents and purposes, as though they had been made to corporations organized under the provisions of this act.

§ 10. MODE OF INCORPORATION.] The charter of an intended corporation under the provisions of this act, must be subscribed by ten or more persons, a majority of whom must be citizens of this Territory, and set forth :
1. The name of the corporation.
2. The purpose for which it is formed.
3. The place where its principal office, or the business to be transacted.
4. The time for which it is to exist.
5. The names and residences of the subscribers, and the number of shares subscribed by each.
6. The number of its directors, and the names and residences of those who are selected as directors, and who shall hold their

office until the next annual election, or until their successors are elected and qualified.

7. The amount of its capital stock, and the number and par value of its shares.

§ 11. PUBLIC NOTICE.] Notice of the intention to apply for any such charter shall be inserted in two news papers of general circulation printed in the proper county for three weeks, setting forth briefly the character and object of the corporation to be formed, and the intention to make application therefor. The certificate for a corporation under the provisions of this act, shall set forth all that is hereinbefore required to be set forth, the same shall be acknowledged by at least five ot the subscribers thereto before a notary public or other officer authorized to administer oaths, and they shall also make and subscribe an oath or affirmation before him, to be endorsed on said certificate that the statements contained therein are true. The said certificate, accompanied with proof of publication of the notice as hereinbefore provided, shall then be produced to the Secretary of the Territory, who shall examine the same and if he find it to be in proper form, as specified in the foregoing sections, he shall approve thereof, and endorse his approval thereon, and issue letters patent in the usual form incorporating the subscribers and their associates and successors into a body politic and corporate in deed and in law, by the manner chosen, and the said certificate shall be recorded in the office of the Secretary of the Territory, in a book to be by him kept for that purpose, and a certified copy of the said certificate shall be recorded in the office of the Register of Deeds of the county where the principal business of the association is transacted. Certified copies of the records thereof shall be competent evidence for all purposes in the several Courts of this Territory.

§ 12. BY-LAWS.] The by-laws of every corporation created under the provisions of this act or of those accepting the provisions of the same, shall be deemed and taken as its law, subordinates to this statute. They shall be made by the stock holders, or the Board of Directors, at their annual meeting or at any stated meeting of the Board of Directors. They shall prescribe the time and place of meeting of the corporation, the power and duty of its officials, the fines and penalties to be imposed upon delinquents and borrowers for the non-payment of dues, interest, and premiums, and such other matters as may be pertinent and necessary for the business to be transacted.

§ 13. BUSINESS—HOW MANAGED.] The business of every corporation created hereunder, or of those accepting the provisions of the same, shall be managed and conducted by a President, a Board of Directors, or Trustees, a Secretary and Treasurer, and such other officers or agents as the by-laws may provide. The Directors or Trustees shall be elected annually by the stock holders, or members, at the time fixed by the by-laws, and shall hold their office until others are chosen and qualified in their stead; the manner of such choice, and of the choice or appointment of all other agents or officers, shall be prescribed by the by-laws. The number of Directors or Trustees shall not be less than five, one of whom shall be chosen President by the Directors, or by the members of the corporation, as the by-laws may direct; the members of said corporation may, at a meeting called for that purpose, determine, fix or change the number of Directors or Trustees that shall thereafter govern its officers, and a majority of the whole number of such Directors or Trustees shall be necessary to constitute a quorum. The Treasurer shall give bond in such sum, and with such sureties, as shall be required by the by-laws, for the faithful discharge of his duties, and he shall keep the moneys of the corporation in a separate bank account, to his credit, as Treasurer, and if he shall neglect or refuse so to do, he shall be liable to a penalty of fifty dollars for every day he should fail so to do, to be recovered at the suit of any informer in an action of debt.

§ 14. STOCK CERTIFICATES.] The directors of such Corporation shall procure certificates or evidences of stock, and shall deliver them signed by the President and Secretary and sealed with the common seal of the Corporation to each person or party entitled to receive the same according to the number of shares by him, her, or them respectively held, which certificate or evidence of stock shall be transferable at the pleasure of the holder in person or by attorney duly authorized as the by laws may prescribe, subject, however, to all payments due or to become due thereon, and the assignee or party to whom the same shall have been so transferred shall be a member of said corporation, and have and enjoy all the immunities, privileges and franchises, and be subject to all the liabilities, conditions and penalties incident thereto, in the same manner as the original subscriber or holder would have been, but no certificate shall be transferred so long as the holder is indebted to said Company unless the Board of Directors shall consent thereto.

§ 15. OATH OF OFFICER.] No person acting as judge or officer for holding an election for any such Corporation shall enter upon the duties of his appointment until he take and subscribe an oath or affirmation before a Notary Public or other person qualified by law to administer oaths, that he will discharge the duties of his office with fidelity, that he will not receive any rate but such as he really believes to be legal, and if any such judge or officer shall knowingly or wilfully violate his oath or affirmation he shall be subject to all the penalties imposed by law upon the officers of the general election of this Territory for violating their duties, and shall be proceeded against in like manner and with like effect.

§ 16. VACANCIES.] In case of the death, removal or resignation of the President, or any of the Directors, Secretary, Treasurer, or other officer of such Company, the remaining Directors may supply the vacancy thus created until the next general election.

§ 17. LAWFUL TO RECEIVE PREMIUMS.] It shall be lawful for any Building and Loan Association now incorporated under the general laws of this Territory and accepting the provisions of this act, or that may hereafter be incorporated, in addition to dues and interest to charge and receive the premiums or bonus bid by a stockholder for preference or priority of right to a loan in periodical installments, and such premium or bonus so paid in installments shall not be deemed usurious but shall be taken to be a payment, as it falls due, in contradistinction to a premium charged and paid in advance, in so far as said premium or bonus so charged and paid. in addition to dues and interest, shall be in excess of two dollars for each periodical payment, the same shall be lawful, any law, usage or custom to the contrary notwithstanding. *Provided*, that the certificate of incorporation of each association hereafter to be incorporated, and the certificate provided in section nineteen of this act for those heretofore incorporated, shall set forth whether the premium or bonus bid for the prior rights to a loan shall be deducted therefrom in advance or paid in periodical installments.

§ 18. WITHDRAWAL OF STOCK.] The by-laws of such association may provide for the voluntary withdrawal and cancellation, at or before maturity of shares of stock not borrowed on. *Provided*, that such withdrawal and cancellation shall be pro rata among the shares of the same series of stock, and, *provided, further*, that not less than twelve per cent. per annum shall be credited and allowed to each share so withdrawn and cancelled.

§ 19. WHEN ENTITLED TO PRIVILEGES OF THIS ACT.] Any Building and Loan Association heretofore incorporated under the provisions of any law of the Territory shall be entitled to all the privileges and immunities, franchises and powers, conferred by this act, upon filing with the Secretary of the Territory a certificate to be by him recorded as provided in section eleven of this act of their acceptance of the same, in writing under the duly authenticated seal of the said association, which certificate shall also prescribe their mode or plan of charging premiums or bonus for priority of loan as set forth in section seventeen of this act, and upon such acceptance and approval thereof by the Secretary of the Territory he shall issue his certificate to said corporation, reciting the same.

§ 20. This act shall take effect and be in force from and after its passage and approval.

Approved, March 13, 1885.

FILING AND RECORDING ARTICLES OF INCORPORATION.

CHAPTER 35.

AN ACT to Amend Sections 389, 390 and 416 of the Civil Code.

Be it enacted by the Legislative Assembly of the Territory of Dakota:

§ 1. SECRETARY TO ISSUE CERTIFICATE.] That section 389 of the Civil Code, be amended to read as follows: 389. Upon the filing of the articles of incorporation with the Secretary of the Territory, he shall issue to the corporation, over the great seal of the Territory, a certificate that the articles containing the required statement of facts have been filed in his office; and thereupon the persons signing the articles, and their associates and successors, shall be a body politic and corporate by the name and for the purposes stated in said articles.

§ 2. RECORDING ARTICLES.] That section 390 of the Civil Code, be amended to read as follows: 390. Upon the filing of any articles of incorporation, as in the last section is prescribed, the Secretary of the Territory shall cause the same to be recorded in a book to be kept in his office for that purpose, to be called "The Book of Corporations," with the date of filing.

§ 3. FILING CERTIFICATE.] That subdivision five of section 416 of the Civil Code, is hereby amended to read as follows: 5. The certificate must be filed in the office of the Secretary of the Territory, there to be recorded in the Book of Corporations, and thereupon the capital stock shall be so increased or diminished.

§ 4. This act shall take effect and be in force from its passage and approval.

Approved, March 2, 1885·

FOREIGN CORPORATIONS.

CHAPTER 36.

AN ACT to Amend Section 569 of the Civil Code of the Territory of Dakota

Be it enacted by the Legislative Assembly of the Territory of Dakota :

§ 1. AGENT TO FILE CERTIFICATE WITH REGISTER OF DEEDS.] That section 569 of the Civil Code of the Territory of Dakota, be and the same is hereby amended by inserting the words, "and register of deeds of the county where said agent resides," immediately after the word " Territory," where said word last occurs in said section and by inserting the words, " or register of deeds " immediately after the word " secretary," where said word last occurs in said section.

§ 2. That this act shall take effect and be in force from and after its passage and approval.

Approved, March 4, 1885.

PROOF OF CORPORATE EXISTENCE.

CHAPTER 37.

AN ACT Relating to Proofs of the Existence of Corporations.

Be it enacted by the Legislative Assembly of the Territory of Dakota :

§ 1. NOT NECESSARY TO PROVE.] In all civil actions brought by or against a corporation, it shall not be necessary to prove on the trial of the cause the existence of such corporation, unless the defendant shall in his answer expressly aver that the plaintiff or defendant is not a corporation.

§ 2. This act shall take effect and be in force from and after its passage and approval.

Approved, February 26, 1885.

REPORTS OF CORPORATIONS.

CHAPTER 38.

AN ACT to Amend Section 515 of the Civil Code.

Be it enacted by the Legislative Assembly of the Territory of Dakota :

§ 1. DIRECTORS LIABLE, WHEN.] That section 515 of the Civil Code, be and the same is hereby amended by striking out the following words where they occur in said section: "And if any such corporation shall fail so to do, the directors shall be jointly and severally liable for all debts of the corporation then existing, and for all that shall be contracted before such report shall be made," and inserting instead thereof, as follows: "Any person who wilfully neglects, fails or refuses to make, sign or publish the report, as provided in this section, shall be guilty of a misdemeanor"

Approved, March 13, 1885.

Costs in Civil Actions.

CHAPTER 39.

AN ACT to Repeal Section Three of Chapter Eleven of the Laws of 1883, entitled "An act Relating to Costs in Civil Actions and to Revive Former Section Three Hundred and Seventy-eight of the Code of Civil Procedure of the Territory of Dakota."

Be it enacted by the Legislative Assembly of the Territory of Dakota :

§ 1. REPEALED.] That section three of chapter eleven of the laws of 1883, entitled "An act relating to costs in civil actions," be and the same is hereby repealed.

§ 2. REVIVED.] That section three hundred and seventy-eight of chapter fifteen of the Code of Civil Procedure, be and the same is hereby revived.

§ 3. That this act shall take effect and be in force from and after its passage and approval.

Approved, March 13, 1885.

County Organization.

CHAPTER 40.

AN ACT to Provide for the Organization of New Counties.

Be it enacted by the Legislative Assembly of the Territory of Dakota :

§ 1. WHEN MAY PETITION.] Whenever the voters of any unorganized county in this Territory shall be equal to one hundred and fifty or upwards, and at least one hundred and fifty thereof shall desire to have said county organized, they may petition the Governor, setting forth that they have the requisite number of legal voters to form a county organization, and request him to organize said county as hereinafter provided.

§ 2. DUTY OF GOVERNOR.] Whenever the voters of any organized county in this Territory shall petition the Governor, as provided in the preceding section, and the said Governor shall be satisfied that such county has one hundred and fifty legal voters, it shall be the duty of the Governor, and he is hereby authorized to call an election in said unorganized county, and fix one or more places in said county as the polling places therein, and shall fix the time for holding said election ; and the Governor shall thereupon issue a notice of election, which notice shall be substantially in the following form, to-wit : Notice is hereby given that on the ....day of........, 18.., at the following place (or places, as the case may be,)............., in the county of........., an election will be held for the following officers of the said county of.........., in the said Territory of Dakota, in the organization of said county, (name the officers to be elected), and also for the temporary location o the county seat of said county, which election will be open at the hour of eight o'clock in the morning, and will continue open until five o'clock in the afternoon of the same day.

Dated this........day of............, 18..

Attest :   ....,
...................,   *Governor.*
Secretary.

§ 3. ELECTION OF OFFICERS.] There shall be elected by the qualified electors of said unorganized county, all of the officers of said county as is or may be provided by law for organized counties, which officers shall hold their respective offices until the next

general election thereafter, and until their successors are elected
and qualified.

§ 4. COUNTY SEAT.] The electors at such election are hereby
empowered to vote for and select a county seat of such county
temporarily by ballot, subject to be changed thereafter as provided
by law; and each voter at such election may designate on his
ballot the place of his choice for county seat, and the place having
the highest number of votes polled shall be the temporary county
seat.

§ 5. ELECTION PRECINCTS—WHO TO PRESCRIBE.] Whenever the
Governor shall have made out and completed said notice of election, he shall cause the same to be delivered to the clerk of the
District Court of the judicial subdivision, to which said unorganized county is attached for judicial purposes, in the county
where the court is held for such judicial subdivision, at least fifty
days prior to the time fixed for said election; and thereupon and
at least forty days prior to the time fixed by the Governor in said
notice for such election, the said clerk of the District Court shall
take to his assistance the chairman of the board of county commissioners and register of deeds, who shall meet at the office of
said clerk of the District Court at the time fixed by him; and the
said officers, or a majority of them, shall thereupon, if the Governor shall fix more than one place for holding the election in
said unorganized county, divide said county into election precincts
in accordance with said notice, regard being had for the convenience of the voters; and the said clerk of the District Court shall
thereupon add at the foot of each certified copy of said notice of
election, a further certificate signed by him, under the seal of the
court, showing the division of the said county into election precincts and the boundaries thereof, as determined by said board;
and the said clerk of District Court of said county, shall cause the
said notice and certificate to be published for at least thirty days
prior to said election, in one newspaper of general circulation in
said judicial subdivision, printed and published in the county
where the court for such subdivision is held, and to deliver to the
sheriff or coroner of the county where such court is held, or other
person designated by him, five certified copies of said notices, and
the certificate at the foot thereof, dividing the county into voting
precincts, if any, which original notice shall be filed in the office
of the clerk of said court as a record therein.

§ 6. JUDGES OF ELECTION.] It shall be the duty of the said
Clerk of District court, Register of Deeds and chairman of the
board of county commissioners, or a majority thereof, at the
same meeting mentioned in the preceding section, to appoint
three capable and discreet persons possessing the qualifications of
electors in said unorganized county to act as judges of election

at each polling place in said county, and thereupon said clerk of the District Court shall make out and deliver to the sheriff, coroner or other person that may be designated by them, after the appointment of said judges, a notice in writing thereof, directed to the judges of election so appointed, and it shall be the duty of the sheriff, coroner or other person so appointed, as provided in this section, within ten days after receiving such notices, to serve the same upon each of the said judges of election.

§ 7. POSTING NOTICES.] The sheriff, coroner or other person to whom such notices of election shall be delivered as aforesaid, shall put up in five of the most public places in each of the voting precincts in said unorganized county, at least twenty days' previous to the time of holding such election, provided for in this act, one of each of the notices of election with the said certificate thereto [and one] shall be posted at the house where said election is authorized to be held.

§ 8. FILLING VACANCIES IN JUDGES OF ELECTION.] If any person appointed to act as judge of election as aforesaid, shall neglect or refuse to be sworn to act in such capacity, or shall not be present, the place of such person shall be filled by the vote of such qualified electors residing within the county or voting precinct as may then be present at the place of election, and the person or persons so elected to fill the vacancy or vacancies, shall be and are hereby vested in that election with the same powers as if appointed judges of election as provided for in this act. Said judges of election shall choose two persons having the qualifications of electors like themselves to act as clerks of such election.

§ 9. ELECTION LAW TO APPLY.] All the provisions of chapter twenty-seven of the Political Code of Dakota, entitled "Elections," and all amendments thereto, not inconsistent with the provisions of this act, shall apply to all elections held under the provisions of this act

§ 10. SUPERVISOR OF ELECTION TO BE APPOINTED.] It shall be the duty of the Governor, at the time of calling said election, or at least thirty days prior to the time fixed for such election, to appoint a supervisor of election for each polling place in said unorganized county, who shall not be a resident of such county, or in any matter interested in the vote therein, but shall possess all the qualifications of an officer of the Territory. Such supervisor shall, before he enters upon the duties of his office, take and subscribe the oath of office required by law; and also that he is not, and will not in any manner be directly or indirectly interested in the location of any county seat in said county, and will not be so interested therein, and is not the owner of any land or interest therein situated in said county, and shall file the same with the Secretary of the Territory.

§ 11. **DUTY OF SUPERVISOR.**] It shall be the duty of the said supervisor of election to furnish at said election at the time and place fixed for such election a ballot box in due form for use at said election. But if the supervisor of election should fail or neglect to so furnish said ballot box at the time and place where such election is held, then any resident and legal voter at such poll shall have authority to furnish a ballot box for use at said election, and the said supervisor shall at the same time and place furnish the proper and necessary poll books for use at said election in the form provided by law, but if said supervisor of election should neglect or refuse to produce and furnish such poll books at said election, then any qualified voter at said election is authorized to produce and furnish such poll books and deliver the same to the judges of election.

§ 12. **POWER AND DUTY OF SUPERVISORS.**] The supervisors of elections, appointed under the provisions of this act, are authorized and required to attend at all times at the places for holding said election for which he is appointed for counting the votes cast at such election, to challenge any vote by any person whose legal qualifications the supervisor may doubt, to be and remain where the ballot boxes are kept, at all times after the polls are opened until every vote cast at such election has been counted, and until the canvass of all votes is completed and the proper and requisite certificates or returns made by the judges and clerks of election, and to personally inspect and scrutinize from time to time, and all times on the day of election, the manner in which the voting is done, and the way and methods in which the poll books and tally sheets therein are kept; and to the end that each candidate voted for at such election, and each place voted for as county seat, shall have the benefit of every vote cast for him or for such place voted for as county seat, the supervisors of election are, and each of them is required to personally scrutinize and assist in the counts and canvass of each ballot in the election precinct for which he was appointed as supervisor, and to make out and deliver to the clerk of said District Court any statement of the truth or accuracy of the poll books, and the truth or fairness of the election and canvass thereof, and whether in the opinion there was illegal voting at said election, and if so the extent of such illegal voting, and the nature and character thereof, if any, in order that the facts as they appear to such supervisors, may become known, which report shall remain among the files of the clerk of the said District Court.

§ 13. **SUPERVISORS TO HAVE CERTAIN PRIVILEGE.**] And to better enable the supervisors of election to discharge their duties, they are authorized and directed on the day of such election to take, occupy and remain in such position from time to time during such election, whether before or behind the ballot boxes, as will in their judgment best enable them to see each person offering to vote, and as will best conduce to their scrutinizing the manner in which the voting is being done; and at the close of the polls for the reception of the votes, they are required to place themselves in such position in relation to the ballot boxes for the purpose of engaging in the work of assisting in the canvass of the ballots as will enable them to fully perform their duties in respect to such canvass provided for, and shall there remain until every duty in respect to such canvass, certificates and returns has been wholly completed.

§ 14. PENALTY FOR ILLEGAL VOTING, ETC.] And if any person shall interfere with the clerks, judges or supervisors of election in the exercise and discharge of their duties or shall interfere, hinder, molest, or threaten to molest any of such officers in the discharge of their duties, or shall cast any illegal vote at such election they shall be deemed guilty of a felony, and shall, upon conviction thereof, be punished as provided in section nineteen of this act.

§ 15. BALLOTS TO BE NUMBERED, ETC.] The ballots at such election shall be folded by the voters and delivered to one of the judges of election, and if the judges and supervisors of election or a majority of them be satisfied the person offering the vote is a legal voter, the clerks of election shall enter the name of the voter and his number under the proper heading in the poll books, and the supervisors of election and also the judges of election shall thereupon endorse on the back of the ticket offered the number corresponding with the number of the voter on the poll book, and shall immediately put the ticket into the ballot box.

§ 16. POLLS TO REMAIN OPEN, BALLOTS HOW PRESERVED.] After the opening of the polls no adjournment shall be had, nor shall any recess be taken until the votes cast at such election shall have been counted and the result publicly announced. All the ballots counted by the judges and supervisors of election, shall, after being read, be strung upon a strong thread or twine, in the order in which they have been read, and after such ballots have been all counted and so strung, the thread shall be tied in a knot, which knot shall be covered by wax, as directed by the supervisors of election, and thereupon it shall carefully be enveloped and sealed up by the judges of election in presence of the supervisors, and immediately placed in the ballot box, together with the said poll books, which ballot boxes shall be carefully locked up or fastened and sealed by the judges of election in the presence of said supervisors before the same shall be delivered to them, or either of them, as provided in this act.

§ 17. RETURN OF POLL BOOKS, ETC.] The judges of election

shall, after the canvass of the votes has been closed, as provided
by law, thereupon enclose and seal one of the poll books, and under cover direct the same to the register of deeds of said county,
tó which said unorganized county is attached for judicial purposes,
and the book thus sealed shall thereupon be delivered to the supervisor of election, and shall that way be conveyed by such supervisor to, and delivered to the said register of deeds, at his office within three days after the closing of the polls; and the other
poll book, enclosed in the ballot box, as aforesaid, together with
the ballots, enclosed and sealed therein, by such judges and supervisors, shall, within the same time, be deposited by said supervisors with the clerk of the district court for such judicial subdivision; and the said poll book in the office of the register of
deeds shall be subject to inspection at any time thereafter, and
said poll book shall be preserved as a public record, and the ballots and the ballot boxes, with the poll book therein, shall be carefully kept closed and sealed until they shall be ordered opened by
the district court of said subdivision, or the Judge thereof.

§ 18. PENALTY OF MISCONDUCT OF, ETC.] If any of the supervisors, judges or clerks of election shall in any manner interfere
with any of the ballots, ballot boxes or poll books, other than as
is provided by this act and the laws of the Territory, or shall wilfully aid or assist in making any false count of the ballots, or wilfully falsify the poll books in any manner, or wilfully
make any false return of the votes, or if any supervisor of
election shall wilfully refuse or neglect to deliver such poll book
and ballot boxes to the officers provided for in this act, within the
time specified in this act, safe, and with the seals unbroken, or if
any supervisor shall in any manner interfere with such poll books,
ballots or ballot boxes, other than to deliver them to the officers
provided for in this act, he shall be deemed guilty of a felony,
and upon conviction thereof, shall be fined in a sum not exceeding five thousand dollars, and be imprisoned in the territorial
prison for not less than one year, or more than five years.

§ 19. CANVASS OF VOTES] The said register of deeds of the
county to which such unorganized county is attached for judicial
purposes shall, within the time prescribed by law for the canvass
of votes, take to his assistance the said probate judge, the said
clerk of the district court, and a majority of the county commissioners of his said county, who shall proceed to open said returns,
and make an abstract of the votes cast at said election in the following manner: The abstract of the votes for county officers
shall be on one sheet, and the abstract of votes for the temporary
location of the county seat shall be on a separate sheet; and it
shall be the duty of said register of deeds, immediately, to make
out a certificate of election to each of the persons having the high-

est number of votes for such county officers, and deliver such certificate to the persons so elected, and immediately after canvassing the returns, and making an abstract of the votes, as provided in this section, the register of deeds shall make a certified copy of each abstract, and forward the same to the Secretary of the Territory, and when the votes are canvassed for county seat, as provided in this section, the place having the highest number of votes shall be the temporary county seat, and such place shall be so declared the county seat by said board, or a majority of them.

§ 20. OFFICERS TO QUALIFY.] The officers elected under the provisions of this act shall proceed to qualify in the manner provided by law for such officers within ·twenty days after the canvassing of such votes as provided for in the preceding section, And the county commissioners after they have so qualified shall immediately convene at the place so selected as the county seat of said unorganized county, as canvassed and declared by said canvassing board, and proceed to the discharge of their duties as said county commissioners in the organization of said county as is now or may be hereafter provided by law; and if any person elected to any office shall fail or refuse to qualify within thirty days after such canvass, his office shall be deemed vacant and shall be filled in the manner provided by law for the filling of vacancies; and if any one or more of the county commissioners shall fail or refuse to qualify as provided by law, then remaining member or members of said board, with the judge of the probate court and register of deeds of said county, even before the said two such officers named have given their bond, shall immediately appoint some suitable person to fill the vacancy in the office of county commissioner.

§ 21. POWER OF COUNTY COMMISSIONERS] The county commissioners elected or appointed under the provisions of this act, shall have power to divide the county into three commissioner districts, which shall be numbered from one to three; and said districts shall not be changed oftener than once in three years, and then only at the regular sessions in January, April or July, and one commissioner shall be elected from each of said districts at the next general election after such organization, one of whom shall be chosen for the term of one year, one for two years, and one for three years, and one annually thereafter as provided by law.

§ 22. COMPENSATION OF SUPERVISORS.] The said supervisors of election shall receive for their services the sum of four dollars per day for the time actually and necessarily employed, and ten cents per mile for necessary travel, to be approved by the Governor and audited, and paid out of the territorial treasury.

§ 23. COMPENSATION OF OTHER OFFICERS.] The officer or person serving the notices on the judges of election, and posting the notices as provided in this act, shall receive for his service the amount authorized by law for like services performed by a sheriff in all organized counties ; and the clerk of the District Court and other county officers required to perform the services required in this act, shall receive two dollars per day for the time actually and necessarily employed, and the printers and publishers shall receive the legal rates for publication of said notices, all of which sum shall be audited and paid by the said unorganized county as soon as the said county shall be organized under the provisions of this act.

§ 24. FAILURE NOT TO INVALIDATE.] Any failure to publish or post the notices provided for in this act shall not invalidate an election held under the provisions of said act ; but if any of the officers shall wilfully fail to perform any of the duties required of him by this act, he shall be deemed guilty of a misdemeanor, and, upon conviction thereof, shall be punished accordingly.

§ 25. WHEN ALL PROCEEDINGS SET ASIDE.] If from any legal cause the whole election held under the provisions of this act for the organization of a county should be set aside by the court or judge thereof, and declared invalid, then the Governor shall have all the authority provided in this act to call a new election, and said county shall be organized as in this act provided.

§ 26. REPEALED.] That sections one, two and three, of chapter twenty-one, of the Political Code, be and the same are hereby repealed.

§ 27. This act shall be in force and effect from and after its passage and approval.

Approved, March 13, 1885.

County Offices.

COMMISSIONERS TO PROVIDE.

CHAPTER 41.

AN ACT to Amend Section Forty-two (42) of Chapter Twenty-one (21) of the Political Code.

Be it enacted by the Legislative Assembly of the Territory of Dakota :

§ 1. That Section Forty-two (42) of Chapter Twenty one (21) of the Political Code be and the same is hereby amended, so as to read as follows:

§ 42. BOARD PROVIDES OFFICERS, JAIL, COURT-ROOM, ETC. In any county where there is no court house or jail erected by the county, or where those erected have not sufficient capacity, it shall be the duty of the Board of County Commissioners to provide for court-room, jail and offices for the following named officers: Sheriff, Treasurer, Register of Deeds, District Attorney, Auditor, Clerk of the District Court, Superintendent of Public Schools and Judge of Probate, to be furnished by such county, in a suitable building or buildings, for the lowest rent to be obtained at the county seat, or to secure and occupy suitable rooms at a free rent within the limits of the county seat or any of the additions thereto until such county builds a court house. They shall also provide the courts appointed to be held therein with attendants, fuel, lights, and stationery, suitable and sufficient for the transaction of their business. If the Commissioners neglect, the court may order the sheriff to do so, and the expense incurred by him in carrying the order into effect, when certified by the court, shall be a county charge.

§ 2. All acts and parts of acts in conflict with the provisions of this act are hereby repealed.

§ 3. This act shall be in force and take effect from and after its passage and approval.

Approved, March 12, 1885.

Damages.

WRONGFUL CONVERSION OF PERSONALTY.

CHAPTER 42.

AN ACT to amend paragraph 1, of Section 1970 of the Civil Code.

Be it enacted by the Legislative Assembly of the Territory of Dakota:

§ 1. MANNER OF DAMAGES.] That paragraph 1 of section 1970 of the Civil Code be amended so as to read as follows: "1, The value of the property at the time of the conversion, with the interest from that time: Or where the action has been prose-

1885—10

cuted with reasonable diligence the highest market value of the property at any time between the conversion and the verdict without interest, at the option of the injured party : And ;"

§ 2. This act shall take effect and be in force from and after its passage and approval.

Approved, March 12, 1885.

Dental Surgery.

CREATING A BOARD OF EXAMINERS.

CHAPTER 43.

AN ACT to Insure the better Education of Practitioners of Dental Surgery, and to Regulate the Practice of Dentistry in the Territory of Dakota.

Be it enacted by the Legislative Assembly of the Territory of Dakota :

§ 1. UNLAWFUL.] That it shall be unlawful for any person to engage in the practice of dentistry in this Territory unless he or she shall have obtained a certificate as herein provided.

§ 2. BOARD OF EXAMINERS. NAME.] A Board of Examiners, to consist of five practising dentists, is hereby created, whose duty it shall be to carry out the purposes and enforce the provisions of this act. The members of said board shall be appointed by the Governor, who shall select them from ten candidates whose names shall be furnished him by the "South Dakota Dental Society" and the "Northwestern Dental Association." Each shall furnish the names of five candidates and the Governor shall select at least two from each five names so furnished, to be members of said board. The term for which the members of said board shall hold their offices shall be five years, except that the members of the board first to be appointed under this act shall hold their offices for the term of one, two, three, four and five years respectively, and until their successors shall be duly appointed. In case of a vacancy occurring in said board, such vacancy shall be filled by the Governor from names presented to him by the "Northwestern Association" and the "South Dakota Dental Society." It shall be the duty of the said dental organizations to present twice the number of names to the Governor of those to be appointed.

§ 3. OFFICERS.] Said board shall choose one of the members President and one the Secretary thereof: And it shall meet at least once in each year, and as much oftener and at such times and places as it may deem necessary. A majority of said board shall at all times constitute a quorum, and the proceedings thereof shall, at all reasonable times, be open to public inspection.

§ 4. PRACTISING DENTISTS TO REGISTER.] Within six months from the time this act takes effect, it shall be the duty of every person, who is at that time engaged in the practice of dentistry in this Territory to cause his or her name and residence, or place of business, to be registered with said board of examiners, who shall keep a book for that purpose. The statement of every such person shall be verified under oath before a Notary Public or Justice of the Peace, in such manner as may be prescribed by the board of examiners. Every person who shall so register with said board, as a practitioner of dentistry, may continue to practice the same as such without incurring any of the liabilities or penalties provided in this act, and shall pay to the board of examiners for such registration a fee of one dollar. It shall be the duty of the board of examiners to forward to the register of deeds of each county in the Territory, a certified list of the names of all persons residing in his county who have registered in accordance with the provisions of this act: And it shall be the duty of all registers of deeds to register such names in a book to be kept for that purpose.

§ 5. EXAMINATION OF PRACTITIONERS.] Any and all persons who shall so desire, may appear before said board at any of its regular meetings and be examined with reference to their knowledge and skill in dental surgery, and if the examination of any such person or persons shall prove satisfactory to said board, the board of examiners shall issue to such persons, as they shall find to possess the requisite qualifications a certificate to that effect, in accordance with the provisions of this act. Said board shall also endorse, as satisfactory, diplomas from any reputable dental college, when satisfied with the character of such institution, upon the holder of such diploma furnishing evidence satisfactory to the board of his or her right to the same: All certificates issued by said board shall be signed by its officers, and such certificates shall be *prima facie* evidence of the right of the holder to practice dentistry in the Territory of Dakota.

§ 6. MISDEMEANOR. PENALTY.] Any person who shall violate any of the provisions of this act shall be deemed guilty of a misdemeanor, and upon conviction may be fined not less than fifty dollars, or more than two hundred dollars, or be confined six months in the county jail. All fines received under this act shall be paid into the common school fund of the county in which such conviction takes place.

§ 7. FEE FOR EXAMINATION.] In order to provide the means for carrying out and maintaining the provisions of this act, the said board of examiners may charge each person applying to or appearing before them for examination for a certificate of qualification, a fee of two dollars, which fee shall in no case be returned : And out of the funds coming into the possession of the board, from the fees so charged, the members of said board may receive, as compensation, the sum of five dollars for each day actually engaged in the duties of their office; and all legitimate and necessary expenses incurred in attending the meetings of said board. Said expenses shall be paid from the fees and penalties received by the board under the provisions of this act, and no part of the salary or other expenses of the board shall ever be paid out of the territorial Treasury. All moneys received in excess of said per diem, allowance and other expenses, above provided for, shall be held by the Secretary of said board as a special fund, for meeting the expenses of said board and carrying out the provisions of this act, he giving such bonds as the board shall from time to time direct, and said board shall make an annual report of its proceedings to the Governor, by the 15th of December of each year, together with an account of all moneys received and disbursed by them pursuant to this act.

§ 8. CERTIFICATE TO BE RECORDED.] Any person who shall receive a certificate of qualification from said board, shall cause his or her certificate to be registered with the register of deeds of any county or counties in which such persons may desire to engage in the practice of dentistry : And the registers of deeds of the several counties in this Territory shall charge for registering such certificates a fee of twenty-five cents for such registration. Any failure, neglect, or refusal on the part of any person holding such certificate to register the same with the register of deeds as above directed for a period of six months, shall work a forfeiture of the certificate; And no certificate when once forfeited shall be restored except upon the payment to the said board of examiners of the sum of twenty-five dollars, as a penalty for such neglect, failure or refusal.

§ 9. PENALTY FOR FALSE PRETENSE.] Any person who shall knowingly and falsely, claim or pretend to have or hold a certificate of license, diploma, or degree, granted by any society, or who shall falsely, and with intent to deceive the public, claim or pretend to be a graduate from any incorporated dental college, not being such graduate, shall be deemed guilty of a misdemeanor, and shall be liable to the same penalty as provided in section VI of this act.

Approved, March 9, 1885.

Depositions.

IN CRIMINAL CASES.

CHAPTER 44.

AN ACT to Provide for Taking Depositions in Criminal Cases.

Be it enacted by the Legislative Assembly of the Territory of Dakota:

CHAPTER I.

§ 1. RIGHT OF DEFENDANT.] When a defendant has been held to answer a charge for a public offense, he may either before or after indictment or information, have witnesses examined conditionally on his behalf as prescribed in this chapter, and not otherwise.

§ 2. IN CASE OF SICK WITNESS.] When a material witness for the defendant is about to leave the Territory, or is so sick or infirm as to afford reasonable grounds for apprehending that he will be unable to attend the trial, the defendant may apply for an order that the witness be examined conditionally.

§ 3. AFFIDAVIT, WHAT TO CONTAIN.] The application must be made upon affidavit, stating:

1. The nature of the offense charged.
2. The state of the proceedings in the action.
3. The name and residence of the witness, and that his testimony is material to the defense of the action.
4. That the witness is about to leave the Territory, or is so sick or infirm as to afford reasonable grounds for apprehending that he will not be able to attend the trial.

§ 4. APPLICATION.] The application may be made to the court or to a judge thereof, and must be made upon five days' notice to the district attorney.

§ 5. ORDER OF COURT.] If the court or judge is satisfied that the examination of the witness is necessary, an order must be made that the witness be examined conditionally at a specified time and place, and that a copy of the order be served on the district attorney within a specified time before that fixed for the examination.

§ 6. ORDER TO DIRECT.] The order must direct that the examination be taken before a magistrate named therein, and on proof being furnished to such magistrate of service upon the district attorney of a copy of the order. If no counsel appear on the part of the people the examination must proceed.

§ 7. WHEN EXAMINATION NOT TO PROCEED.] If the district attorney or other counsel appear on behalf of the people, and it is shown to the satisfaction of the magistrate by affidavit or other proof, or on the examination of the witness that he is not about to leave the Territory, or is not sick or infirm, or that the application was made to avoid the examination of the witness on the trial, the examination cannot take place, otherwise it must proceed.

§ 8. ATTENDANCE ENFORCED.] The attendance of the witness may be enforced by a subpœna issued by the magistrate before whom the examination is to be taken, or from the court where the trial is to be had.

§ 9. TESTIMONY MUST BE WRITTEN—AUTHENTICATION.] The testimony given by the witness must be reduced to writing. The magistrate before whom the examination is had may, in his discretion, order the testimony and proceedings to be taken down in short hand, and for that purpose he may appoint a short-hand reporter. The deposition or testimony of the witness must be authenticated in the following form:

1. It must state the name of the witness, his place of residence and his business or profession

2. It must contain the questions put to the witness and his answer thereto. Each answer being distinctly read to him as it is taken down, and being corrected or added to until it conforms to what he declares is the truth; except in cases where the testimony is taken down in short hand, the answer or answers of the witness need not be read to him.

3. If a question be objected to on either side and overruled, or the witness declines answering it, that fact with the ground on which the question was overruled, or the answer derived, must be stated.

4. The deposition must be signed by the witness, or if he refuses to sign it his reason for refusing must be stated in writing as he gives it; except in cases where the deposition is taken down in short hand it must not be signed by the witness.

5. It must be signed and certified by the magistrate when reduced to writing by him or under his direction, and when taken

down in short hand the manuscript of the reporter, appointed as aforesaid, when written out in long-hand writing, and certified as being a correct statement of such testimony and proceedings in the case, shall be *prima facie* a correct statement of such testimony and proceedings. The reporter shall within five days after the close of such examination transcribe into long hand writing his said short-hand notes, and certify and deliver the same to the magistrate who shall also certify the same and transmit such testimony and proceedings, carefully sealed up, to the clerk of the court in which the action is pending òr may come for trial.

§ 9. DEPOSITION READ IN EVIDENCE.] The deposition or certified copy thereof may be read in evidence by either party on the trial upon its appearing that the witness is unable to attend by reason of his death, insanity, sickness, or infirmity, or of his continued absence from the Territory. Upon reading the depositions in evidence the same objections may be taken to a question or answer contained therein as if the witness had been examined orally in court.

§ 10. WHEN WITNESS IS A PRISONER.] When a material witness for a defendant under a criminal charge, is a prisoner in a territorial prison or in a county jail of a county other than that in which the defendant is to be tried, his deposition may be taken on behalf of the defendant in the manner provided for in the case of a witness who is sick; and the foregoing provisions of this chapter so far as they are applicable, govern in the application for, and in the taking and use of such deposition; such deposition may be taken before any magistrate or notary public of the county in which the jail or prison is situated; or in case the witness is confined in a territorial prison, and the defendant is unable to pay for taking the deposition, before the warden or clerk of the board of trustees of the prisoner, whose duty it shall be to act without compensation. Every officer before whom testimony shall be taken by virtue hereof, shall have authority to administer, and shall administer an oath to the witness, that his testimony shall be the truth, the whole truth and nothing but the truth.

CHAPTER II.

§ 1. WHEN WITNESS NOT IN TERRITORY.] When an issue of fact is joined upon an indictment or information, the defendant may have any material witness, residing out of the Territory, examined in his behalf as prescribed in this chapter, and not otherwise.

§ 2. COMMISSION TO TAKE TESTIMONY.] When a material witness for the defendant resides out of the Territory, the defendant may apply for an order that the witness be examined on a commission, to be issued under the seal of the Court, and the signature of the Clerk, directed to some party designated as commissioner authorizing him to examine the witness upon oath or interrogatories annexed thereto, and to take and certify the deposition of the witness and return it according to the instructions given with the commission.

§ 3. AFFIDAVIT MUST STATE.] Application must be made upon affidavit stating

1, The nature of the offense charged;

2, The state of the proceedings in the action and that an issue of the fact has been joined therein;

3, The name of the witness, and that his testimony is material to the defense of the action;

4, That the witness resides out of the Territory.

§ 4. NOTICE.] The application may be made to the court or judge himself, and must be upon five days notice to the District Attorney.

§ 5. ORDER OF COURT.] If the court or judge, to whom the application is made, is satisfied of the truth of the facts stated and that the examination of the witness is necessary to the attainment of justice, an order must be made that a commission be issued to take his testimony, and the court or judge may insert in the order a direction, that the trial be stayed for a specified time reasonably sufficient for the execution of the commission and return thereof, or the case may be continued.

§ 6. INTERROGATIONS TO BE SERVED.] When the commission is ordered the defendant must serve upon the District attorney, without delay, a copy of the interrogatories to be annexed thereto, within three days notice of the time at which they will be presented to the court or judge. The District attorney may in like manner serve upon the defendant or his counsel cross interrogatories, to be annexed to the commission, with like notice. In the interrogatories, either party may insert any question pertinent to the issue. When the interrogatories and cross interrogatories are presented to the court or judge. according to the notice, the court or judge must modify the questions, so as to conform them to the rules of evidence, and must endorse upon them his alterations, and annex them to the commission.

§ 7. COURT TO DIRECT.] Unless the parties otherwise consent by an endorsement upon the commission the court or judge must endorse thereon the direction and manner in which it must be returned, and may in his *direction* (discretion) direct that it be returned by mail or otherwise, addressed to the Clerk of the Court in which the action is pending, designating his name, and the place where his office is kept.

§ 8. EXECUTING COMMISSION.] The commissioner, unless otherwise specially directed may execute the commission as follows :

1, He must administer an oath to the witness that his answers given to the interrogatories, shall be the truth, the whole truth and nothing but the truth ;

2, He must cause the examination of the witness to be reduced to writing and subscribed by him ;

3, He must write the answers of the witness as nearly as possible in the language in which he gives them, and read to him each answer so taken down, and correct or add to it until it conforms to what he declares is the truth.

4, If the witness declines to answer a question, that fact with the reason assigned by him for declining must be stated.

5, If any papers or documents are produced before him, and proved by the witness, they, or copies of them, must be annexed to the deposition, subscribed by the witness, and certified by the commissioner.

6, The commissioner must subscribe his name to each sheet of the deposition, with the papers and documents proved by the witness, or copies thereof, to the commissioner, and must close it up under seal, and address it as directed by the endorsement thereon.

7, If there be direction on the commission to return it by mail, the commissioner must immediately deposit it in the nearest post office. If any other direction be made by the written consent of the parties, or by the court or judge, or the commissioner as to its return, the commissioner must comply with the directions.

A copy of this section must be annexed to the commission.

§ 9. WHEN COMMISSION DELIVERED TO AN AGENT.] If the commission and return be delivered by the commissioner to an agent, he must deliver the same to the clerk, to whom it is directed, or to the judge of the court in which the action is pending, by whom it may be received and opened upon the agent making affidavit that he received it from the hands of the commissioner, and that it has not been opened or altered since he received it.

§ 10. WHERE AGENT IS INCAPACITATED.] If the agent is dead, or from sickness or other cause, is unable personally to deliver the commission and return, as prescribed in the last section, it may be received by the clerk or judge from any other person, upon his making an affidavit that he received it from the agent; that the agent is dead, or from sickness or other casualty, unable to deliver it, and it has not been opened or altered since the person making the affidavit received it, and that he believes it has not been opened or altered since it came from the hands of the commissioner.

§ 11. COMMISSION TO BE FILED.] The clerk or judge receiving and opening the commission and return must immediately file it, with the affidavit mentioned in the last two sections, in the office of the clerk of the court in which the indictment or information is pending.   If the commission and return is transmitted by mail, the clerk to whom it is addressed must receive it from the the postoffice, and open and file it in his office, where it must remain unless otherwise directed by the court.

§ 12. PUBLIC RECORD.] The commission and return must at all times be open to the inspection of all persons who must be furnished a copy of the same, or any part thereof, on payment of his fees.

§ 13. DEPOSITIONS, ON TRIAL.] Depositions, taken under a commission, may be read in evidence by either party on the trial, upon it being shown that the witness is unable to attend from any cause whatever ; and the same objections may be taken to a question in the interrogatories, or to the answers in the deposition, as if the witness had been examined orally in court.

§ 14. That this act shall be in force and take effect from and after its passage and approval.

Approved, March 13, 1885.

District Attorneys.

CHAPTER 45.

AN ACT to Amend an Act, entitled "An Act to Create the Office of District Attorney for the Several Counties of Dakota Territory," and for other purposes.   Approved March 7, 1883

Be it enacted by the Legislative Assembly of Dakota Territory :

§ 1   SALARY.]   That Section Five of an Act entitled "An act to create the office of District Attorney for the several Counties of Dakota Territory," and for other purposes : Approved, March 7th 1883, be and the same is hereby amended as follows :

The District Attorneys shall severally receive such salaries for their services as the!Board of county commissioners of the proper county shall allow not less than four hundred dollars a year, but the salary of such District Attorneys, shall not be diminished during the term for which they shall be elected or appointed. The Board of county commissioners, however, shall have the power to increase the salary of such District Attorneys, during the term of their office, whenever in their judgment the compensation fixed is inadequate for their services rendered or to be rendered. Said increase to take effect at the time of the passage of the resolution authorizing such increase. All fees and costs received in civil actions in which the county is the successful party, shall be paid into the county treasury for the use and benefit of the county, and it shall not be competent or lawful for the Board of county commissioners to give and pay said fees and costs, or either, or any part thereof to such District Attorney, as a part of his salary, or in addition to his salary.

§ 2. FEES IN CERTAIN CASES] If a judicial sub-division is composed of more than one county, the District Attorney of the county where the court is held for that judicial sub-division, shall have authority to try all cases in which the county or territory is a party, as provided by law, in the District Court, and there shall be charged as a part of the expenses of all criminal prosecutions arising out of said county, the following fees: For each trial in cases of misdemeanor $10, and for each trial in cases of felony $25, and for each judgment upon a plea of guilty, or for costs $10, which fees shall be paid by the counties attached to said counties where the court is held, for judicial purposes; the above fees for all criminal offenses arising in such counties, shall be included in the order of the court or judge as a charge on the said counties together with the other charges against said counties as provided by law.

§ 3. This act shall take effect and be in force from and after its passage and approval.

Approved, March 13, 1885.

Distribution of Laws.

CHAPTER 46.

AN ACT to Amend Section Four of Chapter Three of the Political Code as Amended by Chapter 37 of the Session Laws of 1879.

Be it enacted by the Legislative Assembly of the Territory of Dakota:

§ 1. WHO ENTITLED TO COPIES OF LAWS.] That section four of chapter 3 of the Political Code as amended by chapter 37 of the session laws of 1879, is hereby amended so as to read as follows: § 4. The following named officers of this Territory and of the counties therein and none other, shall be entitled to receive without cost one copy each of the printed volumes of the codes and session laws of Dakota, published or purchased by the Legislative Assembly of this Territory for distribution under the provisions of this act, to wit: The Chief Justice of the Supreme Court of Dakota, each Associate Justice of said Court, each Clerk of the District Court, the United States Attorney for Dakota, the United States Marshal for Dakota, the Governor of the Territory, the Secretary of the Territory, the Auditor, the Treasurer, the Superintendent of Public Instruction, each District Attorney, each Judge of the Probate Court, each Sheriff, each Register of Deeds, each County Clerk or County Auditor, each County Treasurer, each County Justice of the Peace, each Coroner, each County Superintendent of Public Schools, each County Assessor, Chairman of the Board of County Commissioners, each Library Association or Historical Society organized for the benefit of the public in any county or town of this Territory. And to each member of the Legislative Assembly a copy of the laws enacted by the Assembly of which he was a member.

§ 2. All acts in conflict with this act are hereby repealed.

§ 3. This act shall take effect and be in force from and after its passage and approval.

Approved, March 13, 1885.

Drainage.

AMENDING LAND DRAINAGE ACT.

CHAPTER 47.

AN ACT to Amend Chapter Seventy-five (75), of the Laws of 1883, in regard to Drainage.

Be it enacted by the Legislative Assembly of the Territory of Dakota :

§ 1. AMENDMENT.] That section 1, of chapter 75, of the session laws of 1883, be amended by inserting the words, "or special," after the word "regular," where it occurs in the fourth line of said section.

§ 2. AMENDMENT.] That section 2, of chapter 75, be amended by striking out the following words in the 15th line of said section : "if in regular session or ": also by inserting after the word "any," in said line, the words "special or "; also by inserting the word "for" after the word "provided," in line 41 of said section.

§ 3. AMENDING SECTION 4.] That section 4 be amended by striking out the word "construed" in line 7, and inserting the word "constructed" in lieu thereof.

§ 4. AMENDING SECTION 5.] That section 5 be amended by inserting the word "and" after the word "outlet," in line 11.

§ 5. AMENDING SCETION 6.] That section 6 be amended by striking out the work "in" after the word "proportion," where it occurs in the 5th line of said section.

§ 6. VIEWERS, WHEN TO MAKE REPORT.] That section 8 be amended by substituting the following in lieu of said section : " § 8. Viewers, when to make report, &c." Said viewers shall, after having met at the time and place specified in the order issued to them by the county clerk, or township clerk, proceed immediately to perform their said duty, unless for good and sufficient reasons it is necessary to adjourn, and said reasons shall be stated in full in their report, which shall be made out and filed with the county clerk or township clerk, at least two weeks before the next regular meeting of·the said board thereafter; *Provided,* The viewers shall find, upon examination, that the proposed ditch, or drain, or water-course is not of public benefit or utility, they shall so report, and their report need only state such facts.

§ 7. DUTY OF CLERK WHEN REPORT IS FILED.] That section 9

be amended by substituting the following in lieu thereof: "§ 9. Duty of clerk when report is filed. It shall be the duty of the county clerk, or township clerk, when said report is filed, if it be in favor of said work, to give public notice of the pendency of such petition, and the time and place set for the hearing thereof, by publication for three successive weeks, prior to said hearing, in a newspaper, if there be one published in the county; if no newspaper be published in the county, then notices shall be posted in three or more public places in the township or townships where the proposed work is to be done, at least three weeks prior to the day set for said hearing. Said notice shall briefly state where said ditch, drain or water-course commences, through whose land it will pass, and where it will terminate, together with the names of the owners of the lands that will be affected thereby, so far as these can be ascertained with reasonable diligence.

§ 8. WHEN DRAIN TO BE ORDERED] That section 10 be amended by substituting the following in lieu thereof: § 10. "When drain shall be ordered." Said board of commissioners or board of supervisors, at the time set for the hearing of said petition, shall, if no remonstrance be filed, proceed to hear said petition, and consider the report of the viewers. If the report be in favor of the proposed work, and said work will be of public utility, or conducive to public health and convenience, they shall establish the same as specified in the report. But if the viewers report against the proposed work, the board shall dismiss the petition and tax the cost as hereinafter provided. When damages are awarded to any person, persons, or corporations, as provided in this act, the board of commissioners, or board of supervisors, shall order the same to be paid out of the county or township treasury to the person, persons or corporation entitled thereto.

§ 9. AMENDING SECTION 11.] That section 11 be amended by striking out the word "viewers" in the 2d place where it occurs in the 12th line, and inserting the words "the reviewers" in lieu thereof.

§ 10. AMENDING SECTION 12.] That section 12 be amended by inserting the word "if" after the words "except that" in line 6, and inserting the word "the" after the word "find" in line 7, also by striking out the word "reviewers" in line 12 and inserting the word "viewers" in lieu thereof.

§ 11. AMENDING SECTION 13.] That section 13 be amended by striking out the word "free" in line 9 and inserting the word "fee" in lieu thereof.

§ 12. AMENDING SECTION 16.] That section 16 be amended by inserting the word "in" after the word "time" in line 15, also amend section 17 by inserting the words "or township board" after the word "commissioners" in line 18 of said section.

§ 13. AMENDING SECTION 20.] That section 20 be amended by inserting the word "failing" after the word "job" in line 7.

§ 14. AMENDING SECTION 21.] That section 21 be amended by striking out all between the word "land" in line 12 and the word "such" in line 14, also by inserting the word "person" after the words "to the" in line 26.

§ 15. STRIKING OUT SECTION 22.] That section 22 be stricken out.

§ 16. AMENDING SECTION 23.] That section 23 be amended by striking out the word "same" in first line and inserting in lieu thereof the following words: "repairs and cleaning drains and ditches;" also insert after the word "supervisor" the following words: "of roads" in line two.

§ 17. AMENDING SECTION 24.] That section 24 be amended by inserting the word "petition" between the words "the" and "shall" in 4th line and in 5th line. Strike out the word "will" after the word "will" and in line 13 by striking out the word "certain" and inserting the word "certified" in lieu thereof.

§ 18. AMENDING SECTION 26.] That section 26 be amended by striking out the word "but" in 3d line of said section.

§ 19. AMENDING SECTION 27.] That section 27 be amended by striking out the words "in which" where they occur in the 4th line, also strike out the words "shall immediately" where they occur in the 10th line after the word "deeds," also by striking out the word "may" where it occurs in the 23d line, also by striking out the word "to" after the word "to" where it occurs in the 27th line.

§ 20. AMENDING SECTION 28.] That section 28 be amended by inserting the word "or" after the word "county" in line 7, also by striking out the words "or railroad" after the words "or railroad" in line 8, also by inserting the word "private" after the word "as" in the last line of said section.

§ 21. AMENDING SECTION 31.] That section 31 be amended by striking out the word 'in' after the word "employed" in last line of said section.

§ 22. STRIKING OUT SECTION 33.] That section 33 be stricken out.

§ 23. AMENDING SECTION 34.] That section 34 be amended by inserting the word "be" after the word "shall" in line 7.

§ 24. STRIKING OUT SECTON 35.] That section 35 be stricken out.

§ 25. All acts and parts of acts in conflict with this act are hereby repealed.

§ 26. This act shall be in force and take effect from and after its passage and approval.

Approved, March 13, 1885.

CHAPTER 48.

DRAIN VIEWERS CERTIFICATES REDEEMED WITH COUNTY WARRANTS.

AN ACT to Amend Section 33 and 34 of Chapter 75, of the Session Laws of 1883, in regard to Drainage.

Be it enacted by the Legislative Assembly of the Territory of Dakota:

§ 1. POWER OF COMMISSIONERS TO REDEEM VIEWER'S CERTIFI-CATE.] The following shall be added to the end of said section 34 of chapter 75 of the session laws of 1883 : *"Provided,* That the board of county commissioners are hereby authorized to issue a warrant upon the county treasurer payable out of the general funds or from any special fund not overdrawn if they so deem desirable, and accept an assignment of said certificates : which shall be placed in the hands of the county treasurer and collected with, and in the same manner as other taxes levied against said property benefited, and when paid, shall be credited by said treasurer up to such funds as have been debited by the issuance of said warrant.

§ .. That this act shall take effect and be in force from and after its passage and approval.

Approved, March 12, 1885.

Education.

AREA AND ORGANIZATION OF SCHOOL TOWNSHIPS.

CHAPTER 49.

AN ACT to Amend Chapter 44 of the Session Laws of 1883, entitled "Education."

Be it enacted by the Legislative Assembly of the Territory of Dakota:

§ 1. ELECTIONS.] The first election to organize a school township shall be ordered by the Board of county commissioners and the notices shall be made, signed and posted by the proper officers of the county, the same as provided by law for general elections, but no school township shall be organized until the county board are satisfied that it has at least eight thousand dollars of taxable property and not less than twenty children of school age resident within it. All subsequent elections shall be called by the township school board, who shall cause not less than five notices thereof to be posted in five of the most public places in the township not less than ten days before the election, which notices shall be signed by the clerk, or in his absence by the director.

§ 2. AREA.] No township shall hereafter be organized with an area of more than ninety square miles or land sections.

§ 3. BOUNDARIES.] School townships may or may not conform in respect to their boundaries to those of civil townships and may or may not bear the same name.

§ 4. NAME, TAXES, ETC.] School township boards may levy the annual school tax at any time after the assessment is made prior to August 15th in any year.

§ 5. PROHIBITION.] No warrant shall be issued except for an indebtedness incurred prior to its issue.

§ 6. LOCATION OF SCHOOL HOUSES] School houses may be located nearer than one mile to the township boundary when public convenience requires that it be so done.

§ 7. TEACHERS SHALL INSTRUCT, ETC.] In every public school the teacher shall give instruction orally upon the subjects of temperance, physiology and hygiene.

§ 8. SIX MONTHS SCHOOL.] All school corporations and districts in all the counties of the territory shall keep open and maintain public schools for not less than six months each school year where said corporation or district contains twenty or more pupils, and the levy allowed by law upon the assessed valuation is sufficient for that purpose.

§ 9. REPORTS OF SCHOOL CORPORATIONS.] All boards of education, independent school districts, and other school boards, shall make regular annual reports to the county superintendent who shall in time report to the territorial Superintendent. This provision shall apply to all graded and high schools.

§ 10. COMPENSATION.] The boards of education of all school townships and independent school districts may pay their members, for actual services rendered, not more than thirty dollars per annum, and not more than two dollars per day for services duly rendered in connection with their official duties.

§ 11. SCHOOL LAWS.] The territorial Superintendent of Public Instruction shall cause to be printed in pamphlet form a sufficient number of the copies of the laws relating to public schools for distribution among the school boards of the various school corporations and districts of the territory, and there is hereby appropriated out of the territorial treasury a sum sufficient to pay all the necessary cost of printing, binding and distribution of the same, and the accounts therefor shall be certified by the territorial Superintendent, to be true, correct and just, and shall be paid to the proper persons by warrants of the territorial auditor upon the territorial treasurer.

§ 12. SUPERINTENDENT NOT TO BE INTERESTED IN CONTRACT.] No county superintendent shall be interested directly or indirectly in the sale or purchase of any school supplies, or school bonds; but may advise school officers as to their duties regarding the purchase of such supplies or sale of such bonds.

§ 13. OFFICERS TO BELONG TO DIFFERENT SCHOOLS.] Township officers shall belong to different schools, except where there are less than three schools in the township. All those counties having the school district system in force shall be governed by chapter forty of the Political Code of 1877 in every case where the acts of the fifteenth legislative assembly shall be found inconsistent for the government of the same, and the fees of district officers shall in all cases be governed by the district as provided in said chapter forty, regulating the government of school districts, and for the purposes of carrying out the provisions of this section, said chapter forty of the Political Code of 1877 is hereby revived and made of full force and effect so far as it relates to counties excepted from the operations of the school township system.

§ 14. This act shall take effect and be enforced from and after its passage and approval.

Approved, March 13, 1885.

Education.

SCHOOL TOWNSHIP BONDS.

CHAPTER 50.

AN ACT to Amend Chapter Forty-five (45) of the laws of 1883, empowering School Townships to issue their Bonds for Building and Furnishing School Houses.

Be it enacted by the Legislative Assembly of the Territory of Dakota:

§ 1. LIMIT OF AMOUNT TO BE ISSUED.] Chapter forty-five (45) of the laws of 1883 empowering school townships to issue bonds for building and furnishing school houses, is amended as follows:

1. Said bonds shall ¡not be issued to an amount exceeding seven hundred dollars for each single room school house hereafter built: shall draw interest at a rate not to exceed eight per cent. per annum and may be sold at not less than ninety cents on the dollar of their par value including accrued interest, which discount shall cover all cost of preparing, selling and delivering the bonds and receiving the money therefor.

2. Such bonds shall be sold for money only and the money shall be actually paid into the treasury of the school township: and they shall not be exchanged for property of any kind and no contract other than for the sale shall be made in connection therewith.

3. Said bonds shall be made payable at some financial agency in either the city of New York or the city of Boston, and such agency may be inserted in the bonds after their negotiation and sale, but the treasurer of the school township shall enter and keep in his books the number and amount of all bonds sold and the time and place for all payments.

· § 2. MONEY, HOW EXPENDED.] The money raised by the sale of such bonds shall be expended solely for the building and furnishing school houses and shall be paid out only upon warrants duly drawn upon the treasurer by order of the board appearing in the minutes of their proceedings for work already done or material furnished: and the same rule shall apply to all payments of school money for any purpose.

§ 3. CONTRACT FOR BUILDING.] No school house shall be built

by a school township except upon contract in writing let to the lowest possible bidder or bidders after advertisement for proposals upon plans and specifications published not less than three weeks before the letting, in some newspaper printed in the county, and the board may reject any and all bids and advertise for proposals anew. No contract shall be let to any member of the board or to any member of their families or to any brother or sister of any member thereof.

§ 4. WHO NOT TO BE INTERESTED IN CONTRACT.] No member of a school township board and no county superintendent shall be personally or financially interested either directly or indirectly in any contract, purchase or sale of property for the school township or the schools, or in the purchase, sale or adoption of text books for the schools or any other matter bought or sold by the school township, or by its board, or any officer for it or for its schools.

§ 5. This act shall take effect and be in force from and after its passage and approval.

Approved, March 13, 1885.

SCHOOL TONWSHIP BONDS AND WARRANTS.

CHAPTER 51.

AN ACT to Amend Section 9 of Chapter 45 of the Laws of Dakota for 1883.

Be it enacted by the Legislative Assembly of the Territory of Dakota:

§ 1. REDEEMING OLD WARRANTS.] That section 9 of chapter 45 be and the same is hereby amended by inserting the words "and warrants" after the word "bonds" where it occurs in the third line of said section.

§ 2. This act shall take effect and be in force from and after its passage and approval.

Approved, March 13, 1885.

Elections.

VOTER'S QUALIFICATIONS.

CHAPTER 52.

AN ACT to Amend Section 47 of Chapter 27 of the Political Code entitled "Elections."

Be it enacted by the Legislative Assembly of the Territory of Dakota:

§ 1. TIME REQUIRED IN COUNTY, ETC.] That section 47 of chapter 27 of the Political Code entitled "Elections" be amended by striking out from said section the following words: Twenty days in the county and five days in the precinct," and inserting in lieu thereof, as follows: " Sixty days in the county and twenty days in the precinct."

§ 2. This act shall take effect and be in force from and after its passage and approval.

Approved, February 26, 1885.

Elections.

JUDGES, PRECINCTS, ETC.

CHAPTER 53.

AN ACT to Amend Section 3, of Chapter 27 of the Political Code.

Be it enacted by the Legislative Assembly of the Territory of Dakota:

§ 1. JUDGES AND ELECTION PRECINCTS.] That section three of chapter twenty-seven of the political code be, and the same is, hereby amended so as to read as follows: § 3. The several boards of county commissioners shall, respectively, at least thirty days prior to the general election in each, appoint three capable and discreet persons, possessing the qualifications of electors, to act as judges of elections at each precinct for the poll of elections therein, as provided for in this act; and in case of the failure of the said board from any cause to make such appointment, as herein provided, then the county clerk shall make such appointment within thirty days thereafter; and said board shall set off and establish election precincts in so much of the county as is not included in organized civil townships therein, and such precincts shall be set off and established in such manner as that no one precinct shall be within more than one commissioners district, and that there shall be at least one voting precinct in each commissioners district, and the county clerks of the several counties shall make out and deliver to the sheriff, coroner or other person that may be designated by the board of county commissioners of each county, immediately after the appointment of said judges of election, a notice in writing thereof, directed to the judges of election so appointed : and it shall be the duty of such sheriff, coroner, or other person appointed, as provided in this section, within ten days after receiving such notice, to serve the same upon each of the said judges of election, "*Provided,*" That every organized civil township shall constitute an election precinct, and the township supervisors thereof shall be the judges of election for all elections whether general or special held for any purpose whatever in the county.

§ 2. This act shall take effect and be in force from and after its passage and approval.

Approved, March 12, 1885.

CONTESTS AND COUNTY SEATS.

CHAPTER 54.

AN ACT to Provide for Contesting Elections for County Officers, and for the Location of County Seats, and for other purposes.

Be it enacted by the Legislative Assembly of the Territory of Dakota :

§ 1. NOTICE OF CONTEST, SERVING.] Any candidate or person claiming the right to hold an office contested, or any elector of the proper county desiring to contest the validity of an election, or the right of any person declared duly elected to any office in said county, shall give notice thereof in writing to the person whose election he intends to contest within twenty days after the canvass of the votes for such election, which notice shall be served in the same manner as a summons in a civil action. But if the person whose election is contested cannot be found, and shall have ceased to have a residence in said county or territory, then the notice shall be served by leaving said notice at the house where such person last resided in the Territory of Dakota, and if no service as above provided can be made, or if no such residence can be found in the territory, the district court or judge thereof may expressly direct the manner of service, which notice of contest shall be in writing, and shall set forth the facts and grounds upon which the contestant relies in his contest, and may be verified as a pleading in a civil action.

§ 2. ANSWER.] Any person upon whom the notice mentioned in the preceding section may be served, shall, within ten days after the service thereof, answer such notice, admitting or denying the facts alleged therein, and state any other grounds upon which he rests the validity of his election, and shall serve a copy of his answer in the contest, and all allegations set forth in the notice, and not denied in the answer, shall be taken as admitted, and said answer shall be served in the manner provided in the preceding section, except where the contestant appears by attorney, in which case the answer shall be served on the attorney, in the manner provided by the code of civil procedure.

§ 3. WHO MAY BRING CONTEST.] The contest provided for in this act may be brought by a candidate or person claiming said office on his own motion, in his own name as plaintiff, but such contest can not be brought by an elector without the notice is signed by the district attorney of the proper county, or upon his refusal so to sign said notice of contest, the contest may be allowed by the court or judge thereof.

§ 4. TRIAL.] The judge of the district court of the subdivision in which said county is situated, in case no term of said court occurs within twenty days after the said answer is served, may appoint a term of said court (in said court) in said sub-division, but if a term of court occurs before that time in said sub-division then the contest shall be tried at that term, unless otherwise ordered by the court or judge thereof. But the district court or judge upon ten days notice by either party, may try the case at the chambers of the judge at any place fixed by said court or judge of said district; or he may on such application, or his own order, if the pleadings involve a question of fact, order such issues of fact to be tried before a jury, or refer the same as provided in this act, and postpone the trial until such trial can be had in any county in his district, regard being had to the speediest possible trial for the interest of the parties and of the public. The question to be tried, if the issues are ordered to be tried by a jury must be distinctly stated in the order of trial, and the county or sub-division must be designated in the order in which the trial shall be had.

§ 5. TESTIMONY AND PROCEDURE.] All testimony and depositions taken in contests, brought under the provisions of this act, shall be taken in the same manner as civil actions, and depositions may be taken in more than one place at the same time on leave of the court or judge thereof, and all matters relating to the said contest shall be heard and tried by the district court or judge thereof, in the manner that civil actions are tried, except as otherwise provided in this act, and the costs shall be taxed in the same manner as in civil actions, and the court or judge thereof shall have all the power of ordering amendments to notice, and answers and other proceedings as provided in the Code of Civil Procedure, and the court or judge thereof shall have power to enter all orders and final judgment, in such contests, the same as in civil actions.

§ 6. POWER OF ELECTOR.] In any county where there is a vote for the election, or for the removing or changing of the county seat of such county, or changing the county lines of said county, any elector thereof, on leave of the district court or the judge, may contest the validity of such election as to the right of the point declared and selected as the county seat, or as to any county line declared to be established or changed by a vote; such elector shall give notice in writing of such contest to the county commissioners, or a majority of them of the county in which said vote was taken, by serving notice of contest as provided in section one of this act, within thirty days after the result of said vote is canvassed. Said notice shall specify the points on which such election will be contested, and said notice shall be filed with the clerk of the district court where such court is held for the judicial sub-division of which said county forms a part, within ten days after the service of said notice upon the county commissioners as aforesaid, and the said contest shall be tried and determined by the district court or judge thereof, or by a jury as provided for in this act in the contest of county officers; such county commissioners shall appear and defend said contest, and put in an answer to said notice, as is provided for in section two, but if they fail to appear and defend said contest, any elector of said county, at any time before said trial, may on leave of the court or judge appear and defend said contest, and all testimony and depositions shall be taken in the same manner as in civil actions.

§ 7. REFEREE.] All contests brought under the provisions of this act may be referred by the Court, or the Judge thereof, to a referee, as provided in the Code of Civil Procedure, and where the parties do not consent, the Court, or Judge thereof, may direct a reference of such contest.

§ 8. SURETY.] Any person bringing a contest under the provisions of this act, must, before bringing the same, furnish good and sufficient surety for costs, as provided in the Code of Civil Procedure, and the obligation of such surety shall be completed by simply endorsing the notice of contest as security for the costs.

§ 9. APPEALS.] Appeals from any final judgment or decision of the District Court, or Judge thereof, shall be taken in the manner as provided for in the Code of Civil Procedure, except that the undertaking on appeal shall be in the sum fixed by the judge, not less than five hundred dollars, and shall be approved by the judge, or by the clerk of the court of the proper county or subdivision, under the direction of the judge.

§ 10. APPEALS TO SUPREME COURT.] Appeals to the Supreme Court in contests under the provisions of this act, must be taken within sixty days after the entry of final judgment, and the party appealing must immediately procure the transmission of the transcript and papers of appeal to the Clerk of the Supreme Court, and the same may be brought on for hearing and determination before the Supreme Court at any time the said court shall be in session, upon ten days' notice from either party; and the same shall be heard and determined in a summary manner, such notice of hearing may be served during a term, or in a vacation.

§ 11. How CONSTRUED.] This act shall not be construed to affect any of the remedies or rights of action or proceedings provided for in the Code of Civil Procedure.

§ 12. CERTAIN PROVISIONS APPLICABLE.] Except as otherwise provided in this act, the provisions of Part Two of the Code of Civil Procedure are applicable, and constitute the rules of practice in the proceedings mentioned in this act.

§ 13. SAME.] The provisions of Part Two of the Code of Civil Procedure, relative to new trials and appeals, except in so far as they are inconsistent herewith, apply to proceedings mentioned in this act.

§ 14. This act shall take effect and be in force from and [after] its passage and approval.

Approved, March 12, 1885.

1885—13

Exemptions.

CHAPTER 55.

AN ACT to Amend Certain Sections of Part 2, Chapter Thirteen, of the Code of Civil Procedure, subject "Exemptions."

Be it enacted by the Legislative Assembly of the Territory of Dakota:

§ 1. DEBTOR TO MAKE SCHEDULE.] That section three hundred and twenty-six of the code of civil procedure is hereby amended by adding thereto the following: Whenver any debtor against whom an execution, warrant of attachment or other process has been issued, desires to avail himself of the benefit of section 324 of this code, the said debtor, his agent or attorney, shall make a schedule of all his personal property of every kind and character, including money on hand, and debts due and owing to the debtor, and deliver the same to the officer having the execution, warrant of attachment, or other process, which said schedule shall be subscribed and sworn to by the debtor, his agent or attorney, and any property owned by the debtor and not included in said schedule shall not be exempt as aforesaid."

§ 2. APPRAISED.] That section three hundred and twenty-eight of the code of civil procedure be amended by striking out the following words where they occur therein : "The property must be appraised at the usual price of such articles at sheriff's sales," and inserting instead thereof the following : "The property must be appraised at the actual value of the several articles at the place where they are situated."

§ 3. NO EXEMPTION IN CERTAIN CASES.] That section three hundred and thirty-three of the code of civil procedure be hereby amended by adding thereto the following: "6. No exemptions, except the absolute exemptions, shall be allowed any person against an execution or other process issued upon a debt incurred for property obtained under false pretenses."

§ 4. All acts and parts of acts in conflict with the provisions of this act are hereby repealed.

§ 5. This act shall take effect and be in force from and after its passage and approval.

Note by the Secretary of the Territory.

The foregoing act, having been presented (to the Governor for his approval, and not having been returned to the House of Representatives, the

House of the Legislative Assembly in which it originated, within the time prescribed by the Organic Act, has become a law without his approval.

JAMES H. TELLER,
Secretary of the Territory.

Fees.

SHERIFF'S FEES ON FORECLOSURE BY ADVERTISEMENT.

CHAPTER 56.

AN ACT to Provide for Fees in Foreclosures of Mortgages of Real Estate by Advertisement.

Be it enacted by the Legislative Assembly of the Territory of Dakota :

§ 1. FEES TO SHERIFF.] That the sheriff making the sale of real property under the foreclosure of mortgages by advertisement shall receive the same fees and no more that are now or may hereafter be provided by law for the sale of real property under a judgment of foreclosure and sale of real property.

§ 2. This act shall take effect and be in force from and after its passage and approval.

Approved, March 4, 1885.

FOR TRANSPORTING CONVICTS.

CHAPTER 57.

AN ACT Fixing the Fees for Transporting Convicts to the Penitentiary.

Be it enacted by the Legislative Assembly of the Territory of Dakota :

§ 1. NECESSARY EXPENSES AND FEES.] The necessary expenses and legal fees of sheriffs and other officers incurred in conveying convicts to the territorial penitentiary shall be approved by the

Auditor of the Territory and paid out of the territorial treasury. Said Auditor may allow for said expenses and fees the following rates:

Three dollars per day for time of sheriff necessarily spent going to and from the prison by the nearest route.

Two dollars and fifty cents per day for each guard necessary, and such sums as may be necessary for railroad or stage fare and actual traveling expenses.

Not more than one guard shall be allowed for one prisoner, and one additional guard for every two additional prisoners. When conveyance by team is necessary, a team and driver may be employed at a rate of compensation not exceeding five dollars per day—not less than forty miles per day to be estimated as a day's travel. All bills shall be in writing and fully itemized and verified by oath, and accompanied by the receipt of the warden of the state prison for the delivery of such convict or convicts.

§ 2. REPEALED.] That section six hundred and sixty-five and section six hundred and sixty-eight of chapter sixteen of the Code of 1877, and all other acts in conflict with this act are hereby repealed.

Approved, March 13, 1885.

FOR TRANSPORTING INSANE.

CHAPTER 58.

AN ACT Fixing the Fees of Sheriffs and other Officers for Transporting Insane Persons to the Asylums of the Territory, or Convicts to its Penitentiary.

Be it enacted by the Legislative Assembly of the Territory of Dakota:

§ 1. NECESSARY EXPENSES AND FEES.] The necessary expenses and legal fees of sheriffs and other officers incurred in conveying insane persons to the hospitals in this Territory, or convicts to the penitentiary, shall be approved by the Auditor of the Territory and paid out of the territorial treasury. Said Auditor may allow for said expenses and fees the following rates:

Three dollars per day for time of sheriff necessarily spent going to and from the prison, or asylum, by the nearest route.

Two dollars and fifty cents per day for each guard necessary, and such sums as may be necessary for railroad or stage fare and actual traveling expenses.

Not more than one guard shall be allowed for one insane person or convict. All bills shall be in writing and fully itemized and verified by oath and accompanied by the receipt of the superintendent of the insane hospital or warden of the penitentiary for the delivery of such insane person or convict.

§ 2. REPEALED.] That all acts now in force regulating the fees of officers for transporting insane persons, or convicts, are hereby repealed.

Approved, March 13, 1885.

JURORS IN JUSTICES COURT.

CHAPTER 59.

AN ACT to Amend Section Twenty of Chapter Thirty-nine of the Political Code in Relation to Juror Fees in Justice Court.

Be it enacted by the Legislative Assembly of the Territory of Dakota :

§ 1. AMENDMENT.] That section twenty of chapter thirty-nine of the political code is hereby amended by striking out the word "case" in the last line of said section and insert in lieu thereof the words: "day or part of days."

§ 2. This act shall take effect and be in force from and after its passage and approval.

Approved March 2, 1885.

Fish.

CHAPTER 60.

AN ACT to Protect the Passage of Fish in the Dakota, Sioux and Sheyenne Rivers.

Be it enacted by the Legislative Assembly of the Territory of Dakota :

§ 1. PERSONS BUILDING OR OWNING DAMS TO MAKE PASSAGE WAY FOR FISH.] There shall be erected and maintained by the owner or owners of any dam across the Sioux, Dakota and Sheyenne rivers, a fishway, at least one foot in depth at the edge of dam, and of proper width, to allow all fish endeavoring to migrate to the waters of said rivers above the dam, to pass over the same. The said fishway shall be placed at an angle of not more than thirty degrees, and extend entirely to the running water below the dam, and it shall be protected on each side by an apron at least one foot in height, to confine the waters therein. Said fishway shall be constructed under the supervision of the county commissioners of the counties where said dams are located, and be located at such place in said dam, and built in such manner and of such material as they may direct; *Provided*, That the provisions of this act shall not apply to mill dams already in existence on the Sioux river as long as they are in good repair, but whenever such dams need reconstruction the provisions of this act shall be in full force.

§ 2. WHEN COMMISSIONERS OF COUNTY MAY BUILD FISHWAY.] Whenever the owner or occupant of any such dam neglects or refuses to construct such fishway or chute over the same, the commissioners of the county in which such dam is situated shall proceed on notice to them in writing, made by five freeholders of the county, to let the work of erecting such fishway or chute, and providing material therefor, to the lowest responsible bidder, and all expenses attendant upon the erection or maintenance of the same shall be paid by the owner or the occupant of the dam, [and] shall be recovered in the name of the person so building such fishway or chute, upon the acceptance of the same by the county commissioners; and if not paid by said dam owners or occupants, the same shall become a lien on said property, and shall be collected as is provided in enforcing mechanics' liens.

§ 3. All acts or parts of acts in conflict with this act are hereby repealed.

[§ 4.] This act shall take effect and be in force from and after its passage and approval.

Approved, March 12, 1885.

Fuel.

GOVERNING THE TRANSPORTATION.

CHAPTER 61.

AN ACT to Regulate the Receiving and Transportation of fuel on Railroads in this Territory.

Be it enacted by the Legislative Assembly of the Territory of Dakota:

§ 1. RAILWAY COMPANY REQUIRED TO TRANSPORT FUEL.] Any railroad company doing business in this Territory, when desired by any person wishing to ship coal or other fuel over its road, shall receive and transport such coal or other fuel in bulk, within a reasonable time, and permit the same to be loaded either on its track near the depot or at any warehouse or side-track without any distinction, discrimination or favor between one shipper and another, and without discrimination or distinction as to the manner in which such coal or other fuel is offered for transportation, or as to the person, warehouse or place, where or to which it may be consigned. Every railroad company shall permit connections to be made and maintained in a reasonable manner with its track to and from any coal mine adjacent to or near any station or side track on its line, *Provided, however,* That such railroad company shall not be required to pay the cost of making or maintaining said connections or of the siding or switch track necessary to make the same: and, *Provided, further,* That a majority of the railroad commissioners shall direct such railroad to make such connections and siding.

§ 2. NO DISCRIMINATION.] No railroad corporation shall charge, demand or receive from any person, company or corporation, for the transportation of coal or other fuel, a greater sum than it shall at the same time charge, demand or receive from any other person, company or corporation for a like service from the same place and all concessions of rates, rebates, drawbacks and contracts for special rates, shall be open to and allowed to all persons, companies and corporations, and they shall charge no more for transporting from any point on its line than a fair and just proportion of the price it charges for the same kind of freight transported from any other point within the Territory.

§ 3. CERTAIN LAW TO APPLY.] All the provisions of an act entitled "an act to provide for the establishment of a board of railroad commissioners, defining their duties and to regulate the receiving and transportation of freight on railroads in this Territory" shall apply to the receiving and shipments of coal and other fuel so far as the same is applicable: and it shall be the duty of the railroad commissioners to enforce the provisions of this act.

§ 4. This act shall take effect and be in force from and after its passage and approval.

Approved, March 12, 1885.

Grand Juries.

CHAPTER 62.

AN ACT to Amend Section Six of Chapter Nineteen of the Political Code and to Amend Section One Hundred and Sixty-three of the Code of Criminal Procedure.

Be it enacted by the Legislative Assembly of the Territory of Dakota:

§ 1. HOW SUMMONED. NUMBER.] That section six of chapter nineteen of the Political Code of the Territory of Dakota is hereby amended to read as follows: § 6. "A grand jury shall be summoned in the same manner provided for summoning petit jurors; *Provided,* that in all cases the grand jury shall consist of not less than sixteen nor more than twenty-three jurors.

§ 2. DEFINED.] That section one hundred and sixty-three of the Code of Criminal Procedure be and the same is hereby amended to read as follows: § 163. "A grand jury as (is) a body of men consisting of not less than sixteen nor more than twenty-three jurors impanneled and sworn to inquire into and true presentment make of all public offenses against the territory committee or triable within the county or sub-division for which the court is holden.

§ 3. This act shall take effect and be in force from and after its passage and approval.

Approved, March 12, 1885.

Health.

ESTABLISHMENT OF TERRITORIAL AND COUNTY BOARDS.

CHAPTER 63.

AN ACT Establishing Territorial and County Boards of Health, and Providing for the Protection of the Health of Persons and Animals.

Be it enacted by the Legislative Assembly of the Territory of Dakota:

§ 1. TERRITORIAL BOARD, OF WHOM COMPOSED.] That there is hereby established a territorial Board of Health of the Territory of Dakota, composed of a president, vice president and superintendent of public health. The Attorney General of said Territory shall be *ex-officio* president of said board. The Governor shall appoint some suitable person, resident of this Territory, vice president, and he shall also appoint by and with the advice and consent of the council said superintendent of public health, who shall be learned in medicine, a graduate of some medical college recognized by the American Medical Association and a resident of this Territory, and the several persons thus appointed shall hold their offices for two years and until their successors are elected and qualified.

§ 2. DUTIES OF OFFICERS.] The president of said board shall preside at the meetings thereof, and the vice president shall perform the duties of president in his absence. The superintendent of public health shall be *ex-officio* secretary of said board. He shall keep a record of all proceedings of the territorial board of health, and of his own acts as such superintendent, and he shall perform such other duties as are prescribed by this act, or may be prescribed by the territorial board of health. The records kept by said superintendent shall be by him at all times kept open to the inspection of the public.

§ 3. MEETINGS.] The several persons composing said territorial board of health shall meet at the capital of said Territory on the ——— day of April, 1885, and they shall thereafter meet as often as once in every six months at such place in said Territory as they may from time to time appoint.

§ 4. POWERS AND DUTIES.] Said territorial board of health shall have power, and it shall be their duty:

1. To fix the time and place of the meeting of said board, subject only to the provisions of section three of this act.

1885—14

2. To make rules and regulations for the government of said board, its officers and its meetings.

3. To make and enforce any and all needful rules and regulations for the prevention and cure, and to prevent the spread of, any contagious, infectious or malarial diseases among persons and domestic animals.

4. To establish quarantine, and isolate any person affected with contagious or infectious disease.

5. To isolate, kill or remove any animal affected with contagious or infectious disease.

6. To remove or cause to be removed any dead, decaying or putrid body, or any decayed, putrid or other substance that may endanger the health of persons or domestic animals.

7. To condemn and cause to be destroyed any impure or diseased article of food that may be offered for sale.

8. To superintend the several boards of health in cities, villages and towns, and the county boards of health of the several counties.

9. To empower and direct the superintendent of public health to do or cause to be done any or all the things mentioned in subdivisions four, five, six, seven and eight of this act.

§ 5 SALARY, ETC.. OF SUPERINTENDENT.] The superintendent of public health shall be paid a yearly salary of five hundred dollars, in equal installments, at the end of every three months. He shall also be paid five cents per mile for every mile actually and necessarily traveled in the performance of his official duties, and such other sum or sums as he may necessarily pay or become liable to pay for the official books, records and papers kept by him, and for the printing of his reports, and such circulars and blanks as may be required for the proper conduct of the business of his office not to exceed in the aggregate the sum of three hundred dollars. The accounts of the superintendent for his mileage and said other expenses of his office shall be audited by said territorial board of health, and the same together with his salary shall be paid out of the territorial treasury

§ 6. CERTAIN EXPENSES ALLOWED.] The president and vice president of the said territorial board of health shall receive no compensation for the performance of their official duties, but they shall be paid five cents for every mile actually and necessarily traveled, and such other necessary expenses as they may pay or incur in attending the meetings of said board or in the performance of their duties as such officers.

§ 7. COUNTY BOARD] At the first meeting of said territorial board of health they shall appoint two persons from each county, residents thereof, who, with the district attorney of the county from which they are appointed, shall constitute a county board of health for such county. The district attorney shall be the president of such county board of health. One of the persons so appointed from each county shall be learned in medicine, and shall hold a license to practice medicine from the superintendent of public health, who shall be superintendent of health in the county for which he is appointed. The other person so appointed by said board from such county shall be vice president of the county board of health.

§ 8. DUTIES OF OFFICERS.] The president of each county board of health shall preside at the meetings thereof, and in his absence the vice-president shall perform the duties of president. The county superintendent of health shall be *ex-officio* secretary of the board of health of his county, The said county superintendent of health shall keep a record of all the proceedings of such board, and of his official acts, and he shall, at the end of every month, make a full report in writing to the superintendent of public health of the proceedings of the county board of health and of his official acts, and shall, whenever danger to the health of persons or domestic animals is threatened, or whenever any contagious or infectious disease occurs in his county, either among persons or domestic animals, immediately report the same to the superintendent of public health.

§ 9. MEETINGS.] The several county boards of health shall meet at the county seat in their respective counties, at such time within thirty days after the appointment of the county superintendent of health as he may designate. Notice of the time and and place of such meeting shall be by him given to the other members of said county board, at least five days prior to such meeting, and thereafter said county board of health shall meet at the county seat as often as once in every three months.

§ 10. POWERS AND DUTIES.] The several county boards of health shall have power within their respective counties, subject to the supervisory control of the territorial board of health, and the superintendent of public health, to do and perform all the things mentioned in subdivisions three, four, five, six, seven and eight, of section four of this act; all expenses actually and necessarily paid or incurred by the county boards of health in carrying out the provisions of this act shall be audited by said board, and certified to the county commissioners of the county where such expenses are incurred, and shall be paid the same as other county expenses are paid. •

§ 11. POWERS OF SUPERINTENDENT.] The county superintendent of health shall have charge of and superintend, subject to the approval of the board of which he is a member, and the supervisory control of the territorial board of health and superintendent of public health, all the matters and things mentioned in subdivisions four, five, six and seven of section four of this act, within his county, and in case of immediate danger to the health of persons or of domestic animals, he may act as in his judgment he may deem best without consultation with the other members of the county board of health, for the prevention of such danger, and he shall immediately report such action to the president of the county board of health, and to the superintendent of public health.

§ 12. COMPENSATION.] The president of the county board of health shall receive no other compensation than that which is provided for; shall receive five cents for every mile actually and necessarily traveled in the performance of his duties as a member of said board. The county superintendent of health shall receive five dollars per day for every day in which he may be actually and necessarily engaged, and five cents per mile for every mile actually and necessarily traveled in the performance of his duties, and he shall also receive such other sum or sums as he may necessarily pay or become liable to pay in carrying out and performing the various duties imposed upon him under the provisions of this act, or by the county board of health, all of which accounts for services, mileage and other expenses shall be audited by the county board of health, and certified to the county commissioners of the county, and paid as other county expenses are paid.

§ 13. REPORTS.] The superintendent of public health shall, on the first day of December, 1886, and bi-ennially thereafter, make a full report to the Governor, and to the Legislative Assembly of the Territory of Dakota, which report shall show all that has been done by the territorial board of health, and by such superintendent of public health during the two years preceding the making of such report, the number of cases treated by said superintendent of public health, and in each of the counties by the county superintendents of health, the character and extent during such time of all the contagious or infectious diseases that have been reported to said superintendent of public health; and he shall also report a full statement of all expenditures by said territorial board of health, and in each of the organized counties in this territory by the county boards of health, and he shall also report such recommendations as he may deem advisable for the better protection of the public health, and the prevention and cure of contagious or infectious diseases of persons and of domestic animals.

§ 14. WHO MAY PRACTICE MEDICINE.] No person shall be permitted to practice medicine in any of its departments in this Territory unless he be a graduate of a medical college, or unless upon examination before a board composed of the superintendent of public health and two other physicians to be selected by the territorial board of health, such person shall be found proficient in the practice of medicine and surgery and shall also be found upon proo' to have been actually engaged in the practice of medicine for a term of not less than ten years, and no person shall practice medicine unless he be of good moral character, and is not an habitual drunkard. Any person possessing the qualifications mentioned in this section, shall upon presentation of his diploma, or of proof thereof by affidavit if the same is lost or destroyed, and upon the affidavit of two reputable citizens from the county where he resides that such applicant possesses the qualifications of a physician as prescribed herein, to the superintendent of public health, together with a fee of two dollars, receive from such superintendent of public health a license, certifying the applicant to be a practising physician, and having the qualifications for such prescribed by this section, which license shall be recorded in the office of the register of deeds in the county where such practising physician resides. Any person who practices medicine or attempts to practice medicine without complying with the provisions of this section, shall be deemed guilty of a misdemeanor, and any person shall be regarded as practising medicine within the meaning of this section who shall profess publicly to be a physician and to prescribe for the sick, or who appends to his name the letters "M. D.," but nothing in this section shall be construed to prohibit students from prescribing, under the supervision of preceptors, or to prohibit gratuitous services in case of emergency, nor shall this section apply to commissioned surgeons in the United States army and navy. Any person violating any of the provisions of this act, or who shall prevent or attempt to prevent the several officers of the public health, or persons employed by them, from performing any of the duties prescribed in this act to be performed by any such officer or any practising physician, who shall fail to report to the county superintendent of health the existence of any contagious or infectious disease, and any person who shall willfully conceal any case of contagious or infectious disease either among persons or animals, shall be deemed guilty of a misdemeanor. The district court shall upon the complaint of any member of the territorial board of health or the county board of health, where he resides, have power to cancel any license that may be issued to any person to practice medicine where such license was fraudulently obtained or where the person to whom such license was issued has been guilty of violating any of the provisions of this act.

§ 15. VACANCIES.] In case any vacancy shall occur in the office of vice-president or superintendent of public health, such vacancy shall be filled by appointment by the Governor, and the person so appointed to fill such vacancy shall hold for the unexpired term of office in which such vacancy occurs.   In case any vacancy occurs in the office of vice president or superintendent of health in any of the county boards of health, the superintendent of public health shall appoint some suitable person to fill such vacancy, and the person so appointed shall hold such office until the next meeting of the territorial board of health, and until a successor to such officer has been appointed by said territorial board of health

§ 16.   Nothing contained in this act shall in any manner affect any board of health heretofore established, or that may be hereafter established in any city, village or incorporated town, *Provided, however*, That all such boards of health shall be under the superintending control of the territorial board of health.

Approved, March 12, 1885.

UNWHOLESOME FOOD.

CHAPTER 64.

AN ACT to Secure the Public Health and Safety against Unwholesome Provisions.

Be it enacted by the Legislative Assembly of the Territory of Dakota:

§ 1.   PENALTY FOR SELLING.]   Whoever sells diseased, corrupted or unwholesome provisions for food or drink, knowing it to be such, without informing the buyer, or fraudulently adulterates for the purpose of sale, any substance intended for food or drink, so as to render them injurious to health, shall be punished by imprisonment for not more than five years or by a fine not exceeding one thousand dollars: and whoever kills or causes to be killed, for the purpose of sale any calf less than four weeks old, or knowingly sells or has in his possession with intent to sell for food the meat of any calf killed when less than four weeks old, shall be punished by imprisonment in the jail or house of correction, not exceeding thirty days, or by fine not exceeding fifty dollars, or both: and all such meat exposed for sale, or kept with intent to sell, may be seized and destroyed by any board of health, or health officer, or any sheriff, deputy sheriff, constable or police officer.

§ 2.   MAGISTRATE TO ISSUE SEARCH WARRANT.]   When com-

plaint is made on oath to any court or justice of the peace authorized to issue warrants in criminal cases, that meat or calves killed
when less than four weeks old is kept or concealed with intent to
sell the same for purposes of food, such magistrate, when satisfied
that there is reasonable cause for such belief, may issue a warrant
in search therefor.

§ 3. OLEOMARGERINE.] Whoever, by himself or by his
agent, sells, exposes for sale or has in his possession
with intent to sell, any article, substance, or compound,
made in imitation of cheese or butter, or as a substance
for cheese or butter, and not made exclusively and wholly
of milk or cream, or containing any fats, oils or grease not
produced from milk or cream, shall have the words "imitation
cheese" or "adulterated butter," or if such substitute is the compound known as oleomargerine then the word "oleomargerine,"
stamped, labeled, or marked, in printed letters of plain roman type
not less than one inch in length, so that said words cannot be
easily defaced upon the side of every cheese cloth, or band around
the same, and upon the top and side of ever tub, firkin, box or
package, containing any of said article, substance or compound.
And in case of retail sales of any of said articles, substance or
compounds not in the original packages, the seller shall attach to
each package so sold and delivered therewith to the purchaser, a label or wrapper bearing in a conspicuous place upon the
out side of said package the words "imitation cheese," "adulterated butter," or "oleomargerine," as herein provided, in printed
letters of plain roman type not less than half an inch in length.

§ 4. PENALTY FOR ERASING MARKS, ETC.] Whoever sells, exposes for sale, or has in his possession with intent to sell, any article, substance or compound made in imitation or semblance of
cheese or butter, or as a substitute for cheese or butter, except as
provided in the preceding section, and whoever defaces, erases,
cancels or removes any mark, stamp, brand, label or wrapper provided for by the preceding section, or changes the contents of any
box, tub, article or package, marked, stamped or labeled as aforesaid, with intention to deceive as to the contents thereof, for the
first offense forfeits one hundred, and for the second and every
subsequent offense, two hundred dollars, to be recovered by indictment, with costs.

§ 5. DUTY OF HEALTH AND OTHER OFFICERS.] Every health
officer, sheriff, deputy sheriff, or constable, shall institute complaint for the violation of the two preceding sections whenever he
has reasonable cause for suspicion, and on the information of any
person who shall lay before him satisfactory evidence of the same.
Said officer shall take specimens of suspected butter or cheese, and
cause the same to be analyzed or otherwise satisfactorily tested.

The expense of such analysis or test, not exceeding twenty dollars in any one case, may be included in the costs of prosecution, and taxed and allowed to the officer paying the same.

§ 6. DEFINITIONS.] For the purposes of the three preceding sections, the terms "butter" and "cheese" mean the products usually known by those names, and which are manufactured exclusively from milk or cream, or both, with salt and rennet, and with or without coloring matter.

§ 7. That this act shall take effect and be in force from and after its passage and approval.

Approved, March 10, 1885.

Homestead.

THE CONVEYANCE THEREOF.

CHAPTER 65·

AN ACT Supplementary to and Explanatory of Chapter 38 of the Political Code.

Be it enacted by the Legislative Assembly of the Territory of Dakota :

§ 1. NOT TO INCLUDE.] That chapter 38 of the Political Code, relating to homesteads and the conveyance thereof, shall not be deemed or construed to include any gold or silver mine, or gold or silver mill, or any mill, smelter, or machinery intended or used for the reduction or milling of gold or silver ores.

§ 2. AREA ON MINERAL LANDS.] Section 8 of said chapter is hereby amended by adding thereto the following : "If the homestead is claimed upon any land, the title or right of possession to which was acquired or claimed under the laws of the United States relating to mineral lands, then the area of the homestead shall not exceed one acre whether within or without a town plat."

§ 3. This act shall take effect and be in force from and after its passage and approval.

Approved, March 12, 1885.

Immigration.

CHAPTER 66.

AN ACT Creating the office of Commissioner of Immigration and for the Appointment of a Commissioner of Immigration for the Territory of Dakota.

Be it enacted by the Legislative Assembly of the Territory of Dakota:

§ 1. COMMISSIONER OF IMMIGRATION.] The office of Commissioner of Immigration is hereby created and established.

§ 2. DUTIES—APPOINTMENT.] The duties of the said office shall be performed by a commissioner of Immigration, who shall be appointed by the Governor by and with the advice and consent of the council, for the term of two years from the date of his appointment, and shall serve during the said term of two years and until his successor is appointed and shall have qualified. The commissioner must be a resident of Dakota and shall possess the requisite qualifications required by law for holding office in the Territory.

§ 3. OATH AND BOND.] The person so appointed shall, upon his confirmation, proceed to qualify by subscribing the proper oath of office and depositing with the Secretary of the Territory his official bond in the sum of five thousand dollars, with such surety as the Secretary shall approve, conditioned for a faithful discharge of the duties of his office.

§ 4. FURTHER DUTIES] It shall be the duty of the commissioner to look after and devise means to advance the immigration interests of Dakota, and to encourage and promote the permanent settlement and improvement of all sections of the Territory. He shall have charge of the preparation in manuscript, the publication, and the distribution by mail and otherwise of any and all documents and articles of reading matter, designed to convey correct and full information on all matters pertaining to the growth and development of the agricultural, manufacturing, commercial and mining interests of the Territory of Dakota. He shall attend to all correspondence relating to immigration, and shall do all in his power by letter; by the use of published printed matter, and through personal efforts, to secure the most liberal and extensive advertisement of the resources and opportunities of Dakota. It shall be his aim to induce the investment of capital in agriculture, in mining, and in different industrial and mercantile pursuits, and to facilitate the coming to Dakota of persons and families seeking permanent location for new homes. It shall be the duty of the commissioner to procure the most favorable rates of fare obtainable from railroad and other transportation companies, for persons coming to Dakota, and where such persons have formed a colony or party of considerable numbers, he shall be required to visit them, if necessary, and do all in his power to direct and assist them in making the necessary arrangements for transportation and in reaching Dakota.

§ 5. TO HAVE CHARGE OF EXHIBIT.] The commissioner shall have charge of any exhibit of the products and resources of Dakota which may be made at any fair or exhibition held at any point in the United States, and shall have authority to co-operate with any railroad company or companies doing business in the Territory, and with any other parties interested, with the view of securing such exhibit at any fair or exposition held as aforesaid.

§ 6. TERRITORIAL STATISTICIAN.] The commissioner shall and is hereby declared to be *ex-officio* territorial statistician. It shall be his duty to obtain from county assessors and other officers of the organized counties of the Territory, and to collate and prepare in tabulated form for reference, statistics showing county, township, and other municipal indebtedness of all kinds : the assessed valuation of real and personal property, the acreage in wheat, corn, and other kinds of grain : the number of cattle, horses, hogs, and other live stock, and the population, vital statistics, and all other information pertaining to and showing the condition, growth, and development of the Territory by counties.

§ 7. REPORT.] The commissioner shall make a report on the first day of each month, or at any time, upon the request of the Governor, showing the work done by his office, and shall make a biennial report to the Governor, at the regular session of the Legislative Assembly, showing the operations and affairs of his office in detail.

§ 8. GOVERNOR MAY REMOVE.] The commissioner may at any time during his term of office be removed from office by the Governor, on presentation of satisfactory evidence of his incompetency or failure to perform the duties of his office properly, and the Governor shall have power to fill the vacancy during the interim, for the balance of the unexpired term.

§ 9. SALARY.] The commissioner shall have an annual salary of two thousand dollars ($2,000).

§ 10. APPROPRIATION, OFFICE EXPENSE.] The sum of nine

hundred (900) dollars per annum shall be allowed the commissioner for clerk hire and other office expenses. For traveling expenses incurred while in the performance of the duties of his office embraced within the provisions of this act, the commissioner shall be allowed the sum of five hundred (500) dollars for each year of his term of office.

§ 11. APPROPRIATION—ADVERTISING.] To defray the expenses of the office of the commissioner incurred in the publication and distribution of advertising and reading matter, and documents of all kinds, and in any and every other manner contracted under the authority of this act for the purpose of carrying out its provisions, there shall be and is hereby appropriated out of any funds belonging to the Territory not otherwise appropriated, the sum of four thousand (4,000) dollars, or so much thereof as may be necessary for the two years ending on the thirty-first day of December, 1886.

§ 12. This act shall take effect and be in force from and after its passage and approval.

Approved, March 11, 1885.

Imprisonment.

CHAPTER 67.

AN ACT to Amend Section 759 of the Penal Code, relating to Terms of Imprisonment.

Be it enacted by the Legislative Assembly of the Territory of Dakota:

§ 1. TERM OF SENTENCE.] That the last sentence of section 759 of the Penal Code in the words following, to-wit: "But no person can in any case be sentenced to imprisonment in the territorial prison for any term less than one year" is hereby repealed, and said sentence is stricken out of said section.

§ 2. This act shall take effect and be in force from and after its passage and approval.

Approved, March 12, 1885.

Insane.

NORTH DAKOTA HOSPITAL.

CHAPTER 68.

AN ACT Establishing the North Dakota Hospital for the Insane and Providing for the Government of the Dakota Hospitals for the Insane.

Be it enacted by the Legislative Assembly of the Territory of Dakota:

§ 1. WHERE LOCATED.] That the North Dakota Hospital for the Insane, until otherwise provided by law, is established as now located on parts of sections six (6) and seven (7), in township one hundred and thirty-nine (139), north of range sixty-three west of the fifth principal meridian, in the county of Stutsman, near the city of Jamestown.

§ 2. APPOINTMENT OF TRUSTEES.] The board of trustees of each Hospital for the Insane shall consist of five members, and the Governor, by and with the consent of the council, shall at this session of the Legislative Assembly of the Territory of Dakota, appoint five persons as trustees respectively for the North Dakota Hospital for the Insane, and five persons as trustees for the Dakota Hospital for the Insane; three persons of each board shall be residents respectively of the counties in which the Hospital for the Insane are situated as trustees of such Hospital, each of whom shall hold their offices respectively for the term of two years and until their successors are appointed and qualified, except to fill vacancies, which shall only extend to the end of the next session of the Legislature. In case of any vacancy occasioned by the removal from the Territory by such trustee, or death, resignation, or non-acceptance of the office, the Governor shall immediately fill such vacancy; and unless the person so appointed shall accept the office within twenty days, the Governor shall immediately thereafter appoint some other person; and the Governor at each session of the Legislature hereafter shall appoint the trustees for each of said hospitals for the term of two years, as in this section provided, and each of said members of the said board shall before entering upon the duties of his office take and subscribe the oath of office provided by law.

§ 3. OBJECT OF HOSPITAL.] The object of the said Hospitals for the Insane shall be to receive and care for all insane or distracted persons residing within its jurisdiction, as limited and prescribed in this act, who may be committed to their care in accordance with law, and to furnish all needed medical treatment, seclusion, rest, restraint, attendance, amusement, occupation and support which may tend to restore their health and recover them from insanity or to alleviate their sufferings : *Provided,* That the trustees shall have power to discharge patients and to refuse additional applications for admission to the Hospital under their care, whenever in their judgment the interests of the insane demand such discharge or refusal ; and that in the admission and attention of patients, curables and . recent cases shall have the preference over cases of long standing, and that violent, dangerous or otherwise troublesome cases shall have preference over those of an opposite description.

§ 4. TRUSTEES MAY TAKE LANDS, ETC —PROVISO.] The board of trustees of each Hospital may take in the name of the Territory and hold in trust for the hospitals, any lands conveyed or derived, and any money or personal property given or bequested, to be applied for any purpose connected with either institution ; *Provided,* They shall not have power to bind the Territory by any contract, beyond the amount of the appropriation which may at the time have been made for the purpose expressed in the contract, nor to sell or convey any part of the real estate belonging to said hospitals without the consent of the Legislature, except that they may release any mortgage or convey any real estate which may be held by them as security for any money or upon any trust, the terms of which authorize such conveyance. No trustee or officer of either Hospital shall be either directly or indirectly interested in any contract for the purchase of building material, supplies or other articles for the use of the institution They shall provide and keep a seal upon which shall be inscribed the name of the Hospital, with such other words and devices as they may deem appropriate.

§ 5. PER DIEM.] The trustees shall be paid at the rate of three dollars per day for the time necessarily incurred in the discharge of their official duties, and five cents per mile going and returning necessarily traveled in the discharge of said duties. Upon the presentation of the proper vouchers, containing an itemized statement of the sum due each trustee for services rendered, and for mileage, duly signed by the president of the board of trustees and countersigned by the secretary of said board, the territorial Auditor shall draw his warrant upon the territorial Treasurer therefor to be paid out of the territorial treasury.

§ 6. OFFICERS OF BOARD.] The trustees of each board shall elect a president and secretary from their own number, whose term of office shall be for one year, or until said board shall elect their successors. They shall make a record of their proceedings at all meetings in a book kept for that purpose, and at their annual meeting next preceding the regular session of the Legislature, they shall each make a report to the Governor of the condition and wants of their respective hospitals, which shall be accompanied by a full and accurate report of the superintendent which shall show the annual cost per capita of the inmates and the per cent. of discharges and recoveries, and a detailed account of all monies received and paid out by the steward, and shall have not less than five hundred copies of said report printed.

§ 7. FISCAL YEAR—MEETINGS.] The fiscal year of the Hospital shall close on the 30th day of November each year, and the annual meeting of the board of trustees respectively shall be held on the first Wednesday of December thereafter at the Hospital. Special meetings for the appointment or removal of resident officers, or for the transaction of general business may be held upon the written request of the president or any three members of the board. Three members of the board shall constitute a quorum for the transaction of business.

§ 8. GENERAL POWERS AND DUTIES.] The board of trustees shall have general control and management of their Hospital; shall make all by-laws, rules and regulations necessary for the government of the same, not inconsistent with the laws of the Territory; they shall appoint a superintendent, who shall be a physician of acknowledged skill and ability, a graduate of a reputable, regular medical college, and of good moral character; one or more assistant physicians, who shall be of like skill and ability, and a graduate of a medical college, as aforesaid, when the superintendent shall deem such appointment necessary; a steward and matron, all of whom shall be styled the resident officers of the Hospital, and shall reside therein, and shall be governed by the laws and by-laws established for the same. The salaries of the resident officers of the Hospital for the Insane shall be, per annum, as follows: Superintendent, two thousand dollars; steward, one thousand two hundred dollars; assistant physicians, one thousand dollars; matron, five hundred dollars. These salaries shall be audited and paid monthly out of the territorial treasury, upon the presentation of the proper voucher therefor, duly verified, which voucher shall be approved by the president of the board of trustees, and countersigned by the secretary.

§ 9. MONTHLY VISITS.] One or more of the trustees shall visit his Hospital monthly, and the president of the board, with the superintendent, shall make monthly examinations of the accounts of the steward, and certify their approval on the same page with his monthly balance.

§ 10. BOND AND OATH OF SUPERINTENDENT.] The superintendent of the Hospital shall, before entering upon the duties of his office, give a bond to the Territory of Dakota in the penal sum of twenty-five hundred dollars, conditioned that he will faithfully and impartially discharge the duties of his office, according to law and the by-laws of said Hospital, to be approved by said board, and take and subscribe an oath faithfully and diligently to discharge the duties required of him by law and the by-laws of the board of trustees, which bond and oath shall be filed with the Treasurer of the Territory; he shall be the chief executive officer of the Hospital, and have entire control of the medical, moral and dietetic treatment of the patients; he shall employ all employes and assistants necessarily connected with the institution, below the grade designated as officers in section seven in this act, and may discharge any employe at will, and suspend any resident officers of the Hospital, except steward, being responsible to the board for the proper exercise of that duty in regard to officers.

§ 11. DUTIES OF STEWARD.] The steward shall keep the accounts, pay those employed in and about the Hospital, and have a personal superintendence of the farm, garden and grounds, and perform such other duties as may be assigned him under the by-laws of the hospital, under the direction of the board of trustees; he shall purchase all supplies for the Hospital, wherever the best grade of articles, in suitable quantities, can be bought at the lowest price, and, so far as practicable, in large rather than in small quantities; and shall, if in his judgment it can be done to advantage, advertise [for proposals for staple supplies, such as meat, flour, sugar, coffee, tea, fuel and other staple articles, and make contracts for the furnishing of the same, in bulk or in quantity, as may be needed for use.

§ 12. SAME, ACCOUNTS.] The steward shall keep an accurate account of all receipts and expenditures in detail which shall be open to the inspection of the superintendent and board of trustees and these accounts shall be carefully balanced on or before the 15th day of each month and closed biennially on the 30th day of November next preceding each regular session of the legislature. There shall be provided and submitted for the inspection of the superintendent and board of trustees, on or before the 15th day of each month, an original and duplicate balance sheet, which balance sheet shall show the balance of appropriations in the territorial treasury, to be applied to the maintenance of the patients, or to the general use of the Hospital or from any source whatever. These balance sheets shall also show a detailed statement of all receipts and disbursements during the month, and to what appropriation each belongs together with the name of each payee and the price paid. There shall be submitted with the balance sheet the original bills of purchase; vouchers for the same and receipts of all other disbursements of whatever kind, which bills of purchase, vouchers and receipts shall have endorsed on the back of each the signatures attached thereto with the month and year of payment. After the original duplicate balance sheets have been endorsed as correct by the superintendent and presidents of the board of trustees the steward shall within five days thereafter file the original balance sheet in the office of the superintendent, and the duplicates·thereof with the original bills of purchase, vouchers and receipts pertaining thereto he shall file in the office of the territorial Auditor, and upon the presentation of the monthly balance sheet, properly signed and endorsed as correct by the president of the board of trustees, together with the original bills of purchase, vouchers and receipts pertaining thereto, the territorial Auditor shall draw his warrants upon the territorial Treasurer for the respective amounts therein stated, from the appropriations to which they are properly chargeable.

§ 13. New buildings.] Whenever any additional building is to be erected, or extensions, or alterations, or repairs are to be made in connection with either Hospitals the board of trustees shall have authority to procure all necessary plans, drawings and specifications for such buildings, alterations or repairs, to advertise for proposals for the erection and completion thereof and to accept such bid as may seem to them most advantageous, the contractor in every case to give adequate security for the faithful performance of his contract, to appoint and discharge a building superintendent who shall superintend the work, and perform such other duties in that respect as they may require, and to fix his compensation, and to examine and certify to the correctness of his estimates and accounts for work under the contract and of the superintendent and the employes.

§ 14. Appropriations not to be diverted.] No portion of any special appropriation for the erection of any building or for the doing of any work or for any purpose other than ordinary expenses shall be drawn from the territorial Treasury in advance of the work done or the material furnished and then only upon proper estimates thereof, approved by the trustees, and no portion of any appropriation for any purpose, shall be drawn from the treasury before it shall be required for the purpose for which it is made, and no appropriation which is or may be made for one purpose shall be drawn or used for any other purpose, and if at any time hereafter the sum appropriated by the Legislative Assembly for any specific purpose shall be found insufficient to complete and accomplish the purpose for which said appropriation is made, then no part of the said sum so appropriated shall be expended or drawn from the territorial Treasury, nor shall any liability on the part of the Territory be created on account of said appropriation.

§ 15. PATIENTS.] All residents of the Territory of Dakota, who are or may become inmates of either Hospital, shall receive their board, tuition and treatment free of charge during their stay. The residents of other states or territories may be admitted to said Hospitals; upon the payment of the first cost of said board, tuition and treatment as provided by the by-laws adopted by the board of trustees; *Provided*, That no resident of another state or territory shall be received or retained to the exclusion of any resident of any part of the Territory of Dakota: And, *Provided further*, That should any inmate be unwilling to accept gratuitous board, treatment or tuition, then the superintendent of the Hospital is hereby authorized to receive pay therefor, and is required to account for the same in an itemized, monthly statement to the trustees, as donations to be duly credited to the persons from whom they were received, and if the superintendent shall receive any money for the purpose of furnishing extra attention and comforts to any inmates of the Hospital he shall account for the same, and for the expenditures, in like manner to the trustees.

§ 16. REMOVAL OF PATIENTS.] As soon as the North Dakota Hospital for the Insane shall be ready for the reception of patients, the boards of commissioners of Insanity, constituted under chapter 23 of the laws of 1879, in each organized county lying north of the 46th parallel of latitude, and in each county of which the greater portion shall be north of said parallel, shall transact all business arising under said chapter 23 with the trustees and officers of the said North Dakota Hospital for the Insane. The boards of commissioners of all organized counties south of the above described territory, shall transact all business with the said Dakota Hospital for the Insane at Yankton, and the territory of Dakota is hereby divided into two districts as above described for the purposes of this act, and shall be known as the District of South Dakota, [and] the District of North Dakota, and the patients from the district of south Dakota shall be taken to and cared for at the said Dakota Hospital for the Insane, and the patients from the district of north Dakota shall be taken to and cared for at the said North Dakota Hospital for the Insane, and all patients belonging to said northern district under treatment at the Dakota Hospital for the Insane, at the time said north Dakota Hospital shall be ready for patients as aforesaid, shall be transferred to said north Dakota Hospital at the expense of the last named institution.

§ 17. REPEALED.] Chapter eighty-three of the laws of 1881 and all acts and parts of acts in conflict with the provisions of this act are hereby repealed.

§ 18. This act shall be in force and effect from and after its passage and approval.

Approved, March 2, 1885.

1885—16

Insurance.

GENERAL PROVISIONS.

CHAPTER 69.

AN ACT to Revise and Amend Article 11 of Chapter 3, Title 2 of Part 3 of Division Second of the Civil Code, entitled "Insurance Corporations."

Be it enacted by the Legislative Assembly of Dakota :

§ 1. MAY FORM COMPANIES.] That any number of persons, not less than seven, may associate, form and incorporate a company for the following purposes, to-wit : To make insurance upon dwelling houses, stores and all kinds of buildings, and upon household furniture and other property, against loss or damage by fire, lightning, cyclone, tornado or hail, and the risks of inland navigation and transportation. Any and all insurance companies incorporated under the provisions of this act shall, in a declaration and charter provided to be filed, have expressed an intention to make an insurance, or which shall have power to make insurance against loss or damage by the risks of inland navigation or transportation, shall have power to make insurance upon vessels, boats, cargoes, goods, merchandise, freights and other property, against loss and damage by all or any of the risks of lake, river, canal and inland navigation and transportation.

§ 2. RE INSURANCE.] Any companies organized under this act shall have power to effect re-insurance of any risks taken by them respectively.

§ 3. DECLARATION TO BE FILED.] Such persons shall file in the office of the territorial auditor a declaration, signed by all the incorporators, expressing their intention to form a company for the purpose of transacting the business of insurance, as expressed in the first section of this act, which declaration shall also comprise a copy of the charter proposed to be adopted by them, and shall publish a notice of such intention, once in each week, for at least four weeks, in a public newspaper published in the county in which such insurance company is proposed to be located.

§ 4. CHARTER—WHAT TO CONTAIN.] The charter comprised in such declaration shall set forth the name of the company, the place where the principal office for the transaction of its business shall be located, and the mode and manner in which the corporate powers granted by this act are to be exercised, the mode and manner of electing directors, a majority of whom shall be citizens of this territory, and filling of vacancies—and each director of the company shall be the owner, in his own right, of at least five hundred (500) dollars worth of the stock of such company--and the period for the commencement and termination of its fiscal year and the amount of capital to be employed in the transaction of its business ; and the territorial auditor shall have the right to reject any name or title of any company applied for, when he shall deem the name too similar to any one already printed or likely to mislead the public in any respect.

§ 5. COMPANY MAY NOT ENGAGE IN TRADE.] No company formed under this act shall, directly or indirectly, deal or trade in buying or selling any goods, wares, merchandise or other commodities whatever, except such articles as may have been insured by such company and are claimed to be damaged by fire, lightning, cyclone, tornado, hail or water.

§ 6. CAPITAL STOCK.] No company shall be incorporated under this act with a capital less than one hundred thousand (100,000) dollars, actually paid in cash, and shall at all times, be provided with cash on hand equal, at least, to twenty per centum of its capital. No joint-stock fire, cyclone, tornado, hail, inland or marine insurance company, of any other state, territory, or nation, shall do business in this Territory, unless it has at least one hundred thousand (100,000) dollars capital, actually paid in cash.

§ 7. LIMIT OF RISK.] No fire insurance company organized under this act, or transacting business in this Territory, shall expose itself to any loss by any one fire or inland navigation risk or hazard, to an amount exceeding ten per centum of its paid up capital; and it shall be lawful for any company doing business in the Territory to insure houses, buildings, and all other kinds of property against loss or damage by fire, lightning, cyclone or tornado, and to make all kinds of insurance on goods, merchandise or other property in the course of transportation, whether on land or water, or any vessel or boat, wherever the same may be. To insure growing crops against damage or loss by hail, to insure horses, cattle and other live stock, against loss or damage by accident, theft, or any other unknown or contingent event whatever, which may be subject to legal insurance, and to cause itself to be insured against any loss or risk it may have occurred in the course of its business, and upon any interest which it may have in property, and generally to do and perform all other matters and things proper to promote these objects, and no company organized under this act for transacting business in this Territory, shall expose itself to loss on any one risk or hazard, to an amount exceeding ten per centum of its paid up capital, unless the excess shall be re-insured in some other good reliable company.

§ 8.   STOCK BOOKS.]   It shall be lawful for the individuals associated for the purpose of organizing any company under this act, after having published the notice and filed the declaration and charter as required by the third section of this act, and also on filing in the office of the territorial auditor, proof of such publication, by the affidavit of the publisher of said newspaper, his foreman or clerk, to open books for subscription to the capital stock of the company so intended to be organized, and to keep the same open until the full amount specified in the charter is subscribed.

§ 9.   INVESTING CAPITAL.]   It shall be lawful for any insurance company organized under this act, or any such company incorporated under any law of this Territory, to invest its capital and the fund accumulated in the course of its business, or any part thereof, in bonds and mortgages on improved unincumbered real estate within the Territory of Dakota, worth double the sum loaned thereon (exclusive of buildings, unless such buildings are insured and the policy transferred to said company), and also in the bonds of the Territory, or stocks, or treasury notes of the United States, and also the bank stock of national banks, and also in the stock and bonds of any county or incorporated city in the Territory, authorized to be issued by the legislature; to loan the same, or any part thereof on the security of such stocks, or bonds, or treasury notes, or upon bonds or mortgages as aforesaid, and to change and reinvest the same as occasion may, from time to time, require; but the surplus money over and above the capital stock of such insurance company, incorporated under any law of this Territory, may be invested in or loaned upon the pledge of public stocks or bonds of the United States, or any of the states, or stocks, bonds, or other evidence of indebtedness of any solvent, dividend-paying institution, incorporated under the laws of this Territory, or United States, except their own stock; *Provided, always,* That the market value of such stocks, bonds or other evidence of indebtedness, shall be at all times, during the continuance of such loan, at least ten per centum more than the amount loaned thereon.

§ 10   PURCHASE REAL ESTATE.]   No company organized by or under this act shall purchase, hold or convey real estate, except for the purpose and in the manner herein set forth, to-wit: .

1.   Such as shall be requisite for its convenient accommodation in the transaction of its business; or,

2.   Such as shall have been mortgaged to it in good faith as security for loans previously contracted, or for money due; or,

3.   Such as shall have been conveyed to it in satisfaction of

debts previously contracted in their legitimate business, or for
money loaned ; or,

4. Such as have been purchased at sales upon judgment, decrees or mortgage foreclosures obtained or made for such debts.
And it shall not be lawful for any such company to purchase, hold
or convey real estate in any other case or for any other purpose.

§ 11. AUDITOR TO ISSUE CHARTER.] The charter or proof of
publication herein required to be filed by every such company,
shall be examined by the district attorney of the county in which
the principal office of the company is located, and if found con-
formable to this act, and not inconsistent with the laws of the Territory, shall be certified by him to the territorial auditor, who
shall thereupon cause an examination to be made, either by himself or three disinterested persons specially appointed by him for
that purpose, who shall certify under oath that the capital herein
required of the company named in the charter, according to the
nature of the business proposed to be transacted by such company,
has been paid in, and is possessed by it in money, or in such stocks
and bonds and mortgages as are required by the ninth section of
this act. Such certificates shall be filed in the office of the
said Auditor, who shall thereupon deliver to such company a certified copy of the charter and of such certificates, which, on being filed in the office of the register of deeds of the county where
the company is to be located, shall be their authority to commence business and issue policies; and such certified copy of the
charter and of said certificates may be used for or against such
company with the effect as the originals, and shall be conclusive
evidence of the fact of the organization of such company.

§ 12. BY-LAWS.] The incorporators or directors, as the case
may be, or any company organized under this act, shall have the
power to make such by-laws, not inconsistent with the laws of this
Territory, as may be deemed necessary for the government of its
officers and conduct of its affairs, and the same, when necessary,
to alter and amend. And they and their successors may have a
common seal, and change and alter the same at their pleasure.

§ 13. DIVIDENDS.] It shall not be lawful for the directors,
trustees or managers of any insurance company organized under
this act, or incorporated under any law of this Territory, to make
any dividends, except from the surplus profits arising from their
business ; and in estimating such profits there shall be reserved
therefrom a sum equal to forty per cent. of the amount received
as premiums on all unexpired risks and policies, which amount,
so reserved, is hereby declared to be unearned premiums; and
there shall be also reserved all sums due the corporation on bonds,
mortgages, stocks and book account of which no part of the principal or interest thereon has been paid during the year preceding

such estimate of the profits, and upon which suit for foreclosure or collection has not been commenced, or which, after judgment has been obtained thereon, shall have remained more than two years unsatisfied, and on which interest shall not have been paid·

§ 14. MAY EXTEND CHARTER.] Any existing insurance company heretofore incorporated under the laws of this Territory, or any company organized under this act, having a capital of at least one hundred thousand (100,000) dollars, may, without increasing its capital at any time within two years previous to the termination of its charter, after giving notice at least once a week for four weeks successively, in a newspaper published in the county where such company is located, of such intention, with declaration under its corporate seal, signed by the president and two-thirds of the directors of their desire for such extension—provided such directors have been so instructed by a majority vote of the stock—may extend the term of its original charter in accordance with the provisions of this act, by altering or amending the same so as to agree therewith, and filing a copy of such amended charter, with the declaration aforesaid, in the office of the territorial Auditor, whereupon the same proceedings shall be had as are required in the eleventh section of this act.

§ 15. MAY INCREASE CAPITAL STOCK.] Any existing insurance company or any company formed under this law, may at any time increase the amount of its capital stock, after giving notice once a week for four consecutive weeks in any newspaper published in the county where such company is located, of such intention, with the written consent of three-fourths in amount of its stock, unless otherwise provided in its charter or by-laws, by altering or amending its charter or by-laws in this respect, upon filing a copy of its charter or by-laws so amended, together with the declaration under its corporate seal, signed by its president and directors of their desire to do so, with such consent of three-fourths in amount of its stock to such increase, in the office of the territorial Auditor, and upon the same proceedings had as are required by the eleventh section of this act.

§ 16. ANNUAL STATEMENT.] Every insurance company doing business in this Territory must transmit to the territorial Auditor a statement of its condition and business for the year ending on the preceding thirty-first day of December, which shall be rendered on the first day of January in each year, or within one month thereafter, except that foreign insurance companies shall transmit their statement of business other than that taken in the United States prior to the following first day of May; such statement must be published at least three times in a newspaper of general circulation, printed and published in each judicial district of this Territory in which said insurance company shall have an agency, and a duplicate thereof, upon which shall be indorsed the names of the attorneys on whom process of law can be served as required by this act, shall be filed in the office of the register or deeds of the county wherein the agency may be established, but the provisions of this section as to the appointment of attorneys shall not apply to companies organized within this Territory. Statements for publication shall be made out on blanks furnished by the territorial Auditor, and the territorial Auditor's certificate of authority for the company to do business in this Territory shall be published in connection with the said statement of each company doing business in this Territory. Proof of publication, to-wit: the printer's affidavit of the fact, shall be filed with the territorial Auditor in all cases; *Provided*, The territorial Auditor shall select three newspapers of general circulation, published in each of the judicial districts, from which said company shall select one in which said statement shall be published.

§ 17. WHAT TO CONTAIN.] The annual statements required by the last action must be in form, and state particulars, as follows:

1. The name of the company and where located.
2. The name and residence of the attorney for this Territory.
3. The amount of capital stock actually paid in cash.
4. The property or assets of the company, specifying:

(*a*) The value, as nearly as may be, of the real estate owned by the company.

(*b*) The amount of cash on hand, in office.

(*c*) The amount of cash on deposit in banks.

(*d*) The amount of cash in hands of agents and in course of transmission.

(*e*) The amount of loans secured by bonds and mortgages, being first lien on real estate worth double the amount of the sum loaned thereon.

(*f*) The amount of stocks and bonds owned by the company, specifying the amount, number of shares, and market value of each kind of stock, on the day of making the statement.

(*g*) The amount of stocks held by them, as collateral security for loans, with the amount loaned on each kind of stock, par value and market value thereof on the day the statement is made.

(*h*) The amount of all other sums due the company.

5. The liabilities of such company, specifying:

(*a*) The amount of losses unpaid.

(*b*) The amount of claims for losses, resisted by the company.

(*c*) The whole amount of unearned premiums on outstanding risks.

(*d*) The amount of dividends declared and due and remaining unpaid.

(e) The amount of dividends, if any, declared and not yet due.

(f) The amount of money borrowed and remaining unpaid, and the securities, if any, given for the payment thereof.

(g) The amount of all other existing claims.

6. The income of the company during the preceding year, specifying:

(a) The whole amount of cash premiums received, stating separately the amount of premiums received on policies written in the Territory of Dakota.

(b) The whole amount of interest money received, stating separately the amount of interest received on loans in the Territory of Dakota.

(c) The whole amount of income received from all sources.

7. Expenditures during the preceding year, specifying:

(a) The whole amount of losses paid during the preceding year, stating how much of the same accrued prior, and how much subsequent, to the date of the preceding statement; also stating separately the amount of losses paid upon risks taken in this Territory, and how much accrued prior, and how much subsequent, to the preceding statement.

(b) The amount of dividends paid during the preceding year.

(c) The whole amount of fees and commissions paid to officers and agents during the preceding year.

(d) The amount of taxes paid during the preceding year, stating separately the amount paid in this Territory.

(e) The amount of fees paid the auditor of this Territory, not including taxes.

(f) The whole amount paid for salaries of officers and agents during the preceding year.

(g) The whole amount of all other expenditures.

8. Specifying:

(a) The gross amount of risks taken during the preceding year, stating the amount in this Territory separately.

(b) The whole amount of risks outstanding.

(c) The whole amount of losses incurred during the year, including those claims not yet due, stating separately those incurred in this Territory.

(d) The number of agents in this Territory.

§ 18. SPECIAL STATEMENTS.] The territorial Auditor may require at any time statements from any company doing business in this Territory, or any of their officers and agents, on such points as he may deem necessary to elicit a full exhibit of its business and standing.

§ 19. VERIFICATION OF STATEMENTS.] The statements required under this act must be verified by the signature and oath of the president or vice president, with those of the secretary or actuary, or by the manager or general agent of a foreign company doing business in this Territory ; and it shall be the duty of the territorial Auditor to cause the information contained in the statements required by this act to be arranged in a tabular form and printed annually, and transmitted to the territorial legislature with his biennial report ; also for distribution to the companies doing business in the Territory.

§ 20. COMPANY PROHIBITED FROM DOING BUSINESS, WHEN.] No company having neglected to file the statements required from it within the time and manner prescribed, shall do any new business after a notification by the Auditor, while such neglect continues.

§ 21. FORFEIT FOR NEGLECT] Any company willfully neglecting to make and transmit any statement required by this act shall forfeit one hundred (100) dollars for each week's delay.

§ 22. AUDITOR MAY PREVENT PUBLICATION.] The territorial Auditor has authority to prevent the publication of any part or all of the statement of any company made under this act until its annual report is made.

§ 23. REPRESENTATIVE OF COMPANY RETIRING FROM BUSINESS.] In case any insurance company not incorporated in this Territory shall cease to transact business in this Territory according to the laws thereof, the attorney last designated shall be deemed to continue the attorney for such corporation, for the purpose of serving papers or process for the commencement of any action or proceedings for any violation or any liability accruing on their policies while transacting business in this Territory, and service of such papers in the action or proceedings aforesaid, upon any such attorney, shall be deemed valid and personal service upon such corporation.

§ 24. SHALL FILE STATEMENT AND COPY OF CHARTER.] And every company or association shall also file a certified copy of its charter, together with a statement, under oath of the president (or vice president) and secretary, stating the name of the company and where located, the amount of its capital, with a detailed statement of its assets, showing the amount of cash on hand, in bank, or in the hands of agents ; the amount of real estate, and how much the same is incumbered by mortgage ; the number of shares of stock of every kind owned by the company ; the par and market value of the same ; amount loaned on bond and mortgage ; the amount loaned on other security, stating the kind and the amount loaned on each, and the estimated value of the whole amount of such securities and other assets or property of the company ; also stating the indebtedness of the company ; the amount of losses adjusted and unpaid; the amount incurred and in process of adjustment; the amount resisted by the company as illegal and fraudulent, and all other claims existing against the company; also a report of the last annual report, if any, made under the laws of the state or county, and under which such company was incorporated. And no agent shall be allowed to transact business for any such company whose capital is impaired to the extent of twenty per cent thereof while such deficiency continues.

§ 25. AGENT TO PROCURE CERTIFICATE.] It shall not be lawful for any agent or agents to act for any company or companies referred to in this act. directly or indirectly, in taking risks or transacting the business o' fire, cyclone, tornado, hail and inland navigation insurance in this Territory, without procuring from the territorial Auditor a certificate of authority, stating that such company has complied with all the requisites of this act which applies to such company. The statements and evidences of investment required by this act shall be renewed from year to year, in such manner and form as required by this act, and the Auditor on being satisfied with the capital, securities and investments remaining secured as hereinbefore provided, shall furnish a renewal of the certificate as aforesaid.

§ 26. PENALTY.] Any violation of any of the provisions of this act shall subject the party violating the same to a penalty of five hundred (500) dollars for each violation, and to the additional sum of one hundred (100) dollars for each month during which any such agent shall neglect to file such affidavits and statement as herein required.

§ 27. PROVISIONS SHALL APPLY TO ALL COMPANIES.] The provisions of this act shall apply to all foreign companies, partnerships, associations and individuals, whether incorporated or not. All insurance companies, associations or partnerships incorporated or organized under the laws of any other state or territory of the United States or any foreign government, transacting the business of fire, cyclone, tornado, hail or marine insurance, or any other kind ' insurance, in this Territory, shall make annual statements of their condition and affairs to the Auditor, in the same manner and the same form as similar companies organized under the law of this Territory.

§ 28. REVOCATION OF AUTHORITY.] If the Auditor has, or shall have at any time after examination, reason to believe that any annual statement or other report required or authorized by this act, made or to be made out by any officer or officers, agent or agents of any corporation, association or partnership, incorporated by or organized under the laws of any state or territory of the United States or any foreign government, is false, it shall be the duty of said Auditor to immediately revoke the certificate of authority granted on behalf of such corporation or association and mail a copy of such revocatioh to such company, and the agent or agents of such corporation, association or partnership, after such notice, shall discontinue the issuing of any new policies or of the renewal of any policy previously issued; and such revocation shall not be set aside nor any new certificate of authority be given until satisfactory evidence shall have been furnished to said Auditor that such corporation or association is in substance and in fact in the condition set forth in such statement or report, and that all requirements of said act have been fully complied with.

§ 29. AUDITOR TO MAKE EXAMINATION.] It shall be the duty of the territorial Auditor, whenever he shall deem it expedient to do so, in person or by one or more persons appointed by him for that purpose, not officers or agents of, or in any manner interested in, any insurance company doing business in this Territory, except as policy holders, to examine into the affairs of any company incorporated under this act in this Territory, or companies of other states or territories or any foreign companies doing business by its agents in this Territory; it shall be the duty of the officers or agents of any such company, doing business in this Territory to cause their books to be opened for the inspection of the Auditor or persons so appointed, and to otherwise facilitate such examination so far as it may be in their power to do, and pay all reasonable expenses incurred therein, in no case to exceed ten dollars per diem. And for that purpose the said Auditor, or person or persons so appointed by him, shall have the power to examine, under oath, the officers and agents of any such company, relative to the business of said company. And whenever the said Auditor shall deem it for the best interests of the public so to do he shall publish the result of such investigation in two newspapers in this Territory.

§ 30. DUTY OF AUDITOR IN CERTAIN CASES.] And whenever it shall appear to said Auditor, from such examination, that the assets of any such company incorporated in this Territory are insufficient to justify the continuance in business of any such company, he may direct the officers thereof to require the stockholders to pay in the amount of such deficiency within such a period as he may designate in such requisition, or he shall communicate the fact to the District Attorney, whose duty it shall be to apply to the district court of the county in which the principal office of the company shall be located, for an order requiring them to show cause why the business of such company shall not be closed; and the court shall thereupon proceed to hear the allegations and proof of the respective parties; and in case it shall appear to the satisfaction of said court that the assets and effects of said company are not sufficient, as aforesaid, and that the interests of the public so require it, the said court shall decree the dissolution of said company and a distribution of its effects. The said district court shall have the power to refer all applications for distribution to a referee, who shall inquire into and report upon the facts stated therein. Any company receiving the aforesaid requisition from such Auditor, shall forthwith call upon the stockholders for such amount as shall make the capital equal to the amount fixed by the charter of said company. And in case any stockholder of such company shall refuse or neglect to pay the amount so called for, after notice personally given, or by advertisement in such time and manner as the Auditor shall approve, it shall be lawful for said Auditor to require the return of said original certificate of stock held by said stockholder, and in lieu thereof to issue new certificates for such number of shares as said stockholder may be entitled to, in the proportion that the ascertained value of the funds of said company may be found to bear to the original capital of said company ; the value of such shares for which the new certificates shall be issued, to be ascertained under the direction of said Auditor, and the company paying for the fractional parts of shares ; and it shall be lawful for the directors of such company to create new stock, dispose of the same and issue new certificates of stock to the amount sufficient to make up the original capital of the company.

§ 31. WHEN DIRECTORS LIABLE.] And it is hereby declared that in the event of any additional losses incurring upon new risks, taken after expiration of the period limited by said Auditor, in the aforesaid requisition for the filling up of the deficiency in the capital of said company, and before said deficiency shall have been made up, the directors shall be individually liable to the extent thereof.

§ 32. WHEN TRANSFER WILL NOT RELEASE.] No transfer of the stock of any company organized under this act, made during the pendency of any such investigation, will release the party making the transfer from his liability for the losses which may have occurred previous to the transfer.

§ 33. AUDITOR TO REVOKE.] And whenever it shall appear to said Auditor, from the report of the person or persons appointed by him, that the affairs of any company not incorporated by the laws of this Territory are in unsound condition, he shall revoke the certificates granted in behalf of said company, and shall cause a notification thereof to be published in any newspaper of general circulation published at the capital, and mail a copy thereof to each agent of the company. The agent or agents of such company shall, after such notice, be required to discontinue the issuing of new policies and the renewal of any policies previously issued.

§ 34. PENALTIES, HOW RECOVERED.] Every penalty provided for by this act, shall be sued for and recovered in the name of the Territory by the district attorney in whose jurisdiction the company or agent or agents so violating shall be doing business, and one-half of all such penalties shall be paid, when recovered, into the treasury of said county, and the other half to the informer; and in case of the non-payment of such penalties, the party so offending shall be liable to imprisonment for a period not exceeding six months, in the discretion of any court having cognizance thereof.

§ 35. DURATION OF CHARTERS.] All companies incorporated or extended under this act, may provide in their charter for not more than thirty years' duration, but the legislature may at any time alter or amend this act, and provide for the closing up of the business and affairs of any company formed under it. Nothing herein contained shall be so construed as to prevent the subsequent extension of the charter of companies organized or extended under this act.

§ 36. REDUCING CAPITAL STOCK.] Whenever it shall appear to the territorial Auditor, from examination made by him, in the manner prescribed by law, that the capital stock of any company organized under this act, is impaired to an amount exceeding twenty per cent. of such capital, and he shall be of the opinion that the interests of the public will not be prejudiced by permitting such company to continue business with the reduced capital, it shall be lawful for such company, with the permission of the said Auditor, to reduce its capital stock, and the par value of the shares thereof, to such amount as the Auditor may, under his hand and seal, certify to be proper, and as shall, in his opinion, be justified by the assets and property of such company; *Provided*, That no part of such assets and property shall be distributed to the stockholders; *Provided further*, That the capital stock of any such company shall not be reduced to an amount less than the sum now required by law for the organization of a new company under the general insurance laws, for the transaction of business at the place where such a company is located, and of the kind which said company is authorized to transact. No reduction of the capital of any such company shall be made except upon a resolution of the board of directors, approved by at least two-thirds of the directors, certified under its corporate seal, signed by the president and at least two-thirds of the directors and proved or acknowledged in the manner required by law for the proof or acknowledgment of conveyances, which certificate shall be filed in the office of said Auditor before any action shall be had by him thereon. The territorial Auditor, in case he shall permit any such company to reduce its capital in the manner provided in this act, shall execute the certificate required by this act in duplicate, and deliver one of said certificates to the officers of said company, who shall forthwith file the same with the clerk of said county in which said company is located, and the other to be filed in the office of said Auditor Such company upon filing the certificate with the county clerk as required by this act, shall with such reduced capital, possess the same rights and be subject to the same liabilities as it possessed and was subject to at the time of the reduction of its capital, and the charter of such company shall be deemed to be amended in all respects to the amount of capital, and per value of the shares, so as to conform to the reduction. It shall be lawful for the said company to require the return of the original certificate of stock held by each stockholder, in lieu thereof to issue new certificates for such number of shares as each stockholder may be entitled to; in the proportion that the reduced capital may be found to bear to the original capital of the company. It shall be lawful for any such company after its capital shall be so reduced as aforesaid, to increase its capital stock in the manner prescribed by this act.

§ 37. STATEMENT OF RECEIVERS.] It shall be the duty of all receivers of insurance companies, on or before the 1st day of March of each year, and at any other time, when required by the territorial auditor, to make and to file, annually, their statements of their assets and liabilities, and of their income and expenditures, in the same manner and form, and under the same penalties, as the officers of such companies are now required by law to make annual and other statements to the Auditor.

§ 38. PUBLICATION OF STATEMENT.] And the said Auditor shall also require its annual statement, required to be filed by this act, to be published, in conformity with the provisions of section 16 of this act.

§ 39. FEES.] There shall be paid by every company, association, person or persons, or agent, doing business in this Territory, to whom this act shall apply, the following fees :

Upon filing declaration, or certified copy of charter, $25.

Upon filing the annual statement, $10.

For each certificate of authority, and certified copy thereof, $2.

For every copy of any paper filed in the department, the sum of twenty cents per folio ; and for fixing official seal to such copy and certifying the same, the sum of $1.

For official examinations of companies under this act, the actual expense incurred, not to exceed $10 per diem.

And companies organized under the laws of this Territory, shall pay the following fees :

For filing and examination of the first application of any company, and the issuing of the certificates of license thereon, $10.

For filing each annual statement, and the issuing renewal of license required by law, $3.

For each certificate of authority to its agents, fifty cents. *Provided*: That the net amount of all fees over and above the cost of performing the clerical labor connected therewith shall not exceed under this act, the sum of two thousand dollars, and that any amount above that sum shall be paid over to the territorial Treasurer for the general fund of the Territory.

§ 40. TAX.] Every insurance company doing business in this Territory, except in joint-stock and mutual companies organized under the laws of this territory, shall, at the time of making the annual statement, as required by law, pay into the [territorial] *state* treasury, as taxes, two and a-half per cent. of the gross amount of premiums received in this Territory during the preceding year, taking duplicate receipts thereof, one of which shall be filed with the Auditor; and upon the filing of said receipts—not until then—the said Auditor shall issue the annual certificate as provided by law; and the said sum of two and a-half per cent. shall be in full of all taxes, state [territorial] and local

§ 41. WHEN COMPANY MAY COMMENCE BUSINESS.] No company formed under this act for the purpose of doing the business of insurance on the mutual plan, shall commence business within this Territory, nor establish agencies for the transaction of business within this Territory, until agreements have been entered into for insurance with at least one hundred applicants, the premiums of which shall amount to not less than fifty thousand dollars, of which ten thousand dollars at least, shall have been paid in cash, and notes of solvent parties, founded on actual and *bona fide* applications for insurance, shall have been received for the remainder, and no one of the notes received as aforesaid, shall amount to more than two hundred dollars, and no two shall be given for the same risk, or be made by the same person or firm, except where the whole amount of such notes shall not be more than two hundred dollars, nor shall any such note be represented as capital stock, unless a policy be issued upon the same within thirty days after the organization of the company, upon a risk which shall not be for a shorter period than twelve months. Each of said notes shall be payable, in part or in whole, at any time when the directors shall deem the same requisite for payment of any loss and such incidental expenses as may be necessary for the transaction of said business. And no note shall be and appear as a help to said capital stock, unless the same shall be accompanied by a certificate of the register of deeds or clerk of the district court of the county where the person making such note shall reside, that the person making the note is, in his opinion, pecuniarily good and responsible for the same; and no such note shall be surrendered during the life-time of the policy for which it was given.

§ 42. AGENTS' RESPONSIBILITY.]   Agents appointed by any company doing business in this Territory, to solicit for applications for insurance, collect the premiums on the same, and transact other duties of agents in such cases, shall be held personally responsible to such company for any money received by them for such company; and in case any such agent shall embezzle or fraudulently convert to his own use, or shall take or secrete the same with the intent to embezzle and convert to his own use, without the consent of such company, any money belonging to such company, which shall come into his possession, or shall be under his care by virtue of his agency, he shall be deemed by so doing to have committed the crime of larceny, and on conviction shall be subject to the fine and penalties provided by the statutes in such cases.

§ 43. RECIPROCAL OBLIGATIONS.]   When by the laws of any state or territory, any taxes, fines, penalties, licenses, fees, deposits of moneys or securities, or capital requirements, or other obligations, or prohibitions are imposed or would be imposed on insurance companies of this Territory, doing or that might seek to do, business in such state or territory, or upon their agents therein; so long as such laws continue in force, the same obligations and prohibitions, of whatever kind, shall be imposed upon all insurance companies of such state or territory doing business within this Territory or upon their agents here.

§ 44. ANNUAL STATEMENTS.]   All insurance companies heretofore organized in the Territory of Dakota, and now doing business in this Territory, shall be required to make the annual statement provided for and required by companies formed or organized under this act.   But this shall not be construed to interfere with, or in any manner abridge, the rights and privileges of any company already in existence, or doing business under any law now or heretofore existing in the Territory.

§ 45. CHANGING PRINCIPAL OFFICE.]   It shall be lawful for any insurance company to change the location of its principal office to any place within the Territory of Dakota, by a majority vote of the stock of said company, and said company shall also publish a notice of such change of location for three consecutive months immediately thereafter, in some newspaper of general circulation published in said Territory, a copy of which notice must be filed with the Auditor of the Territory.

§ 46. REPEALED—PROVISO.]   All of chapter 69 of the Civil Code, with the amendments thereto regulating insurance companies and the business of insurance is hereby repealed; *Provided,* That nothing contained in this act shall prevent the complete organization of any insurance company under the laws heretofore in force, where the declaration of intention to form and the charter of such insurance company, was filed in the office of the Auditor of said Territory at the time of the passage of this act.

§ 47. NOT TO APPLY.] This act shall not apply to the organization, duties or powers of county mutual insurance companies.

§ 48. This act shall take effect and be in force from and after its passage and approval.

Approved, March 13, 1885.

COUNTY MUTUAL INSURANCE COMPANIES.

CHAPTER 70.

AN ACT Authorizing the Formation of County Mutual Insurance Companies.

Be it enacted by the Legislative Assembly of the Territory of Dakota :

§ 1. WHO MAY UNITE TO FORM COMPANY.] It shall be lawful for any number of persons, not less than twenty-five (25) residing in any county in this Territory, who collectively shall own property of not less than twenty-five thousand dollars ($25,000.00) in value, which they desire to have insured, to form themselves into a company for mutual insurance against loss or damage by fire, lightning, hail and tornado, which corporation shall possess the usual powers and be subject to the usual duties of corporations, and the corporated name thereof shall embrace the name of the county in which the business office of the said company shall be located.

§ 2. DIRECTORS.] Every company so formed shall choose of their number not less than five, nor more than nine (9) directors to manage the affairs of such company, who shall hold their office for one year, or until others are elected, and such directors shall choose one of their members president, vice president, secretary and treasurer. Said treasurer shall give such bond as may be required by the board of directors of said company.

§ 3. ARTICLES TO BE FILED.] The directors of such company shall file their articles of association, together with a copy of their

1885—18

by-laws and the names of the officers of such company, in the office of the county clerk of the county in which such company is located, and shall keep a record of their proceedings in a book kept for that purpose, together with the names of all persons insured, and the amount each person is insured, which record shall be kept open for the inspection of all the members of such company at the office of the secretary.

§ 4. MAY ISSUE POLICIES.] The directors of such company may issue policies, signed by the president and secretary, agreeing in the name of the company to pay all loss or damage by fire or lightning, for a term not exceeding five (5) years, by the holder of such policies and not exceeding the sum named in such policy.

§ 5. OBLIGATION OF INSURED.] Every person so insured shall give his undertaking, bearing even date with the policy so issued to him, binding himself, his heirs and assigns to pay his *pro rata* share to the company of all losses or damages by fire, lightning, hail and tornado, which may be sustained by any member thereof, and every such undertaking shall within five days after the execution thereof be filed with the secretary in the office of said company, and shall remain on file in such office except when required to be produced in court as evidence. He shall also at the time of effecting such insurance pay such percentage in cash and such reasonable sum for a policy as may be required by the rules and by-laws of the company.

§ 6. IN CASE OF LOSS.] Every member of such company who may sustain loss or damage by fire or lightning, shall immediately notify the president of such company, or in case of his absence the secretary thereof, who shall forthwith convene the directors of such company, whose duty it shall be to appoint a committee of not less than three (3) nor more than five (5) members of such company to ascertain the amount of such loss, and in case of the inability of the parties to agree upon the amount of such damages, the claimant may appeal to the probate judge of the county in which the company is situated, whose duty it shall be to appoint three disinterested persons as a committee of reference, who shall have full authority to examine witnesses and to determine all matters in dispute, who shall make their award to the president in writing, or in his absence, to the secretary of such company, which award thereon shall be paid. The said committee of reference shall each be allowed the sum of two dollars per day for each day's service so rendered, and the sum of five cents for every mile necessarily traveled in the discharge of such duties, which shall be paid by the claimant unless the award of such committee shall exceed the sum offered by the company in liquidation of such loss or damage, in which case said expenses shall be paid by the company.

§ 7. MAY CLASSIFY PROPERTY.] The companies under the provisions of this act, may classify the property insured at the time of issuing the policies thereon under different rates, corresponding as nearly as may be to the greater or less risk from fire, and loss which may attach to each several buildings. personal property insured, or damage by hail or tornado. Whenever the amount of any loss shall be ascertained, the president shall convene the directors of said company, who shall make an assessment upon all property insured, taken in connection with the rate of premium, under which it may have been classified.

§ 8. COLLECTING ASSESSMENTS.] It shall be the duty of the secretary whenever such assessment shall have been completed to immediately notify every person composing such company by letter sent to his usual post office address, of the amount of such loss, the sum due from him as his share thereof, and of the time when and to whom such payment is to be made, but such time shall not be less than thirty nor more than sixty days from the date of such notice, and the person designated to have such money by the directors, may demand not to exceed two per cent. in addition to the amount due on each assessment as aforesaid for his fees in securing and paying over the same.

§ 9. SUITS.] Suits at law may be brought against any member of such company who shall refuse or neglect to pay any assessment made upon them by the provisions of this act, and the directors of any company so formed, who shall wilfully neglect or refuse to perform the duties imposed upon them by the foregoing sections of this act, shall be liable in their individual capacity to the persons sustaining such loss.

§ 10. PROHIBITORY.] No company formed under the provisions of this act shall insure any property outside the limits of the county in which said company is located, nor shall they insuure any property other than detached dwellings and their contents and farm buildings, and their contents, and live stock when on the premises or running at large, and hay or grain in the bin or stack, and growing grain against damage by hail or tornado, nor shall they insure any property within the limits of any incorporated city in the Territory.

§ 11. ELECTION OF DIRECTORS.] The directors of each company so formed shall be chosen by ballot at the annual meeting thereof, which shall be held on the first Tuesday in January of each year, and every person shall have one vote for each two hundred dollars which he may be insured, but no person shall be allowed to vote by proxy at such election.

§ 12. STATEMENT.] It shall be the duty of the Secretary of every company as aforesaid, to prepare a statement, showing the condition of such company on the day preceding the annual meeting, which statement shall contain the amount insured, the number of policies issued, and to whom, and the amount insured by each policy and all other matters pertaining to the interests of such company, which statement shall be filed in the office of the county clerk of the county in which such company is located, on or before the 15th day of January in each year, and which statement shall also be read to the members at their annual meeting.

§ 13. WITHDRAWALS.] Any member of such company may withdraw therefrom at any time by giving notice in writing to the president, or in his absence to the secretary thereof, and paying his share of all claims then existing against said company, and the directors or a majority thereof shall have power to annul any policy by giving notice in writing to the holder thereof.

§ 14. NON-RESIDENTS.] Non-residents of any county in this Territory, owning property therein may become members of any company founded under this act, and shall be entitled to all rights and privileges appertaining thereto except that it shall not be lawful for such non-residents to become a director in said company.

§ 15. BY-LAWS.] The company so formed may adopt such by-laws for its regulation as are not inconsistent with the provisions of this act and may therein prescribe the compensation of its officers.

§ 16. No company formed under this act shall continue for a longer term than thirty years.

§ 17. All acts or parts of acts inconsistent with the provisions of this act are hereby repealed.

§ 18. This act shall take effect and be in force from and after its passage and approval.

Approved, March 13, 1885.

Judicial Districts.

CERTAIN TERMS CONSIDERED GENERAL.

CHAPTER 71.

AN ACT to Amend Section 9 of an act Entitled an Act to Amend Chapter Thirteen of the Political Code Relating to the Subdivision of Judicial Districts.

Be it enacted by the Legislative Assembly of the Territory of Dakota:

§ 1. ADDITIONAL TERMS CONSIDERED GENERAL.] That section nine, of chapter twenty -seven, of the laws of 1879, be and is hereby amended by striking out in said section the word "Additional" wherever it occurs therein.

§ 2. This act shall take effect and be in force from and after its passage and approval.

Approved, March 13, 1885.

SECOND DISTRICT—SUBDIVISION OF MINER COUNTY.

CHAPTER 72.

AN ACT Creating a Judicial Subdivision of the Second Judicial District, and Fixing Time of Holding Court Therein.

Be it enacted by the Legislative Assembly of the Territory of Dakota:

§ 1. MINER COUNTY A SUBDIVISION.] That the county of Miner shall constitute a judicial subdivision of the second judicial district.

§ 2. TERM OF COURT.] And one term of the District Court is hereby appointed to be held therein at Howard, the county seat of Miner county, on the first Tuesday of May of each year, and such other special terms of the District Court may be held in said county in each year at said county seat, as the Judge of said district may appoint.

§ 3. This act shall take effect on and after its passage and approval.

Approved, March 13, 1885.

THIRD DISTRICT—SUBDIVISION OF RANSOM AND SARGENT COUNTIES.

CHAPTER 73.

AN ACT Constituting Ransom and Sargent Counties one Judicial Subdivision in the Third Judicial District, to fix the Terms of Court Therein and for other purposes.

Be it enacted by the Legislative Assembly of the Territory of Dakota:

§ 1. SUBDIVISION OF RANSOM AND SARGEANT COUNTIES.] That the counties of Ransom and Sargent in the Territory of Dakota, shall constitute one Judicial Subdivision in the Third Judicial District; and the District Court therein shall be held at the county seat of said Ransom county on the second Thursday of March in each year.

§ 2. ACTIONS MAY BE CHANGED.] All actions or proceedings, civil or criminal, now pending in the subdivision formerly composed of the counties of Richland, Ransom and Sargent, which properly belong in said counties of Ransom and Sargent under the provisions of the code of civil procedure and code of criminal procedure, the venue thereof may be changed by order of the court or judge thereof upon the demand of either party, which demand shall be served upon the opposite party or his attorney if either can conveniently be found in the Territory, but if neither can conveniently be found in the Territory, then such change of venue may be made as therein provided upon filing such demand with the clerk of the district court of said Richland county.

§ 3. PROCESS RETURNABLE.] All process, writs, bonds, notices, appeals, continuances, recognizances and proceedings in actions arising or properly belonging in said Ransom and Sargent counties issued and made returnable to the terms of the district court in said Richland county as fixed by law prior to the passage of this act, shall be taken and considered as made, taken and returnable to the terms of said district court for Ransom and Sargent counties as fixed by this act.

§ 4. All acts and parts of acts in conflict with the provisions of this act are hereby repealed.

§ 5. This act.shall take effect and be in force from and after its passage and approval.

Approved, February 20, 1885.

THIRD DISTRICT—SUBDIVISION OF NELSON COUNTY.

CHAPTER 74.

AN ACT Creating the County of Nelson, Dakota Territory, as a Legal Subdivision of the Third Judicial District, and Providing for a Term of Court Therein.

Be it enacted by the Legislative Assembly of the Territory of Dakota :

§ 1. NELSON COUNTY A SUBDIVISION.] That the county of Nelson, in the Territory of Dakota, be and the same is hereby created a legal subdivision of the third judicial district of Dakota.

§ 2. TERM OF COURT.] There shall be held on the third Monday of August in each year at Lakota, the county seat of said county, a term of court for the trial of all causes within the jurisdiction thereof.

§ 3. This act shall take effect and be in force from and after its passage and approval.

Approved, March 12, 1885.

THIRD DISTRICT—SUBDIVISION OF RICHLAND COUNTY.

CHAPTER 75.

AN ACT Creating and Defining a Subdivision of the Third Judicial District.

Be it enacted by the Legislative Assembly of the Territory of Dakota :

[§ 1.] RICHLAND COUNTY A SUBDIVISION.] That the county of Richland shall constitute one subdivision of the third judicial district, and the District Court shall be held therein at the county seat of said Richland county, on the fourth Tuesday of March and the first Tuesday of October of each year.

[§ 2] This act shall take effect and be in force from and after the 1st day of June, 1885.

Approved, March 13, 1885.

THIRD DISTRICT—SUBDIVISION OF SARGENT COUNTY.

CHAPTER 76.

AN ACT Authorizing the Judge to Create a New Subdivision in the Third Judicial District, and for other Purposes.

Be it enacted by the Legislative Assembly of the Territory of Dakota:

§ 1. JUDGE MAY MAKE SUBDIVISION OF SARGENT COUNTY.] That upon a petition signed by a majority of the board of county commissioners of Sargent county, the Judge of the District Court within and for said third judicial district, shall, by an order to that effect, create the county of Sargent a judicial subdivision; and upon the making of such order, the said county of Sargent shall be and become a judicial subdivision, and such Judge may hold court at the county seat of said county at such time as he may elect.

§ 2. JUDGE MAY ORDER TRANSFER.] Whenever said county shall have been created a subdivision under the provisions of this act, the Judge shall order all actions or proceedings that may at that time be pending in the counties of Richland or Ransom, properly belonging to said Sargent county, to be transferred, together with all papers and files relating to such actions or proceedings, to the clerk of the District Court of said Sargent county.

§ 3. All acts or parts of acts in conflict with this act are hereby repealed.

§ 4. This act shall take effect and be in force from and after the fifteenth (15) day of April, 1885.

Approved, March 13, 1885.

THIRD DISTRICT—SUBDIVISION OF RAMSEY COUNTY.

CHAPTER 77.

AN ACT to Create a New Subdivision of the (3) Third Judicial District.

Be it enacted by the Legislative Assembly of the Territory of Dakota:

§ 1. RAMSEY AND TOWNER COUNTIES A SUBDIVISION.] That the counties of Ramsey and Towner are hereby created and constituted a subdivision of the (3) third judicial district.

§ 2. The judge of the (3) third judicial district shall annually appoint and hold terms of the district court for said subdivision at Devils Lake, the county seat of said Ramsey county; and the county of Towner is attached to Ramsey county for judicial purposes.

§ 3. This act shall take effect and be in force from and after its passage and approval.

Approved, March 13, 1885.

FOURTH DISTRICT—BOUNDARIES OF.

CHAPTER 78.

AN ACT Defining the Boundaries of the Fourth Judicial District, and Fixing the Time for Holding Court Therein.

Be it enacted by the Legislative Assembly of the Territory of Dakota:

§ 1. COUNTIES INCLUDED IN FOURTH DISTRICT—TERMS OF COURT.] That the counties of Union, Clay, Lincoln, Turner, Minnehaha, McCook, Moody and Lake shall constitute the fourth judicial district, and each of said counties shall constitute a judicial subdivision, and the terms of the District Court shall be held therein as follows, to-wit:

Clay county, the first Tuesday in February and the first Tuesday in September.

1885—19

Union county, the third Tuesday in February and the third Tuesday in September.

Lincoln county, the fourth Tuesday in February and the fourth Tuesday in September.

Turner county, the second Tuesday in March and the third Tuesday in October.

Minnehaha county, the second Tuesday in April and the second Tuesday in November.

McCook county, the fourth Tuesday in May.

Lake county, the first Tuesday in June.

Moody county, the third Tuesday in June and the first Tuesday in January.

§ 2. All acts and parts of acts in conflict with the provisions of this act are hereby repealed.

§ 3. This act shall take effect and be in force from and after its passage and approval.

Approved, March 2, 1885.

FIFTH DISTRICT—BOUNDARIES OF.

CHAPTER 79.

AN ACT Defining the Boundaries of the Fifth Judicial District, and Fixing the Time for Holding Court therein.

Be it enacted by the Legislative Assembly of the Territory of Dakota:

§ 1. COUNTIES INCLUDED IN—TERMS, WHEN HELD.] That the counties of Roberts, Day, Brown, McPherson, Edmunds, Campbell, Walworth, Potter, Faulk, Sully, Hughes, Hyde, Hand, Spink, Beadle, Clark, Codington, Grant, Deuel, Hamlin, Kingsbury, Brookings, shall constitute the fifth judicial district, and each of said counties shall constitute a judicial subdivision, excepting the counties of Edmunds, McPherson, Campbell and Walworth, which counties shall constitute one judicial subdivision; and in case of the organization of the county of Marshall the said county shall be attached to the county of Day for judicial purposes, and the terms of the District Court shall be held therein as follows, to-wit:

Brookings, the second Tuesday in June and the second Tuesday in December.

Kingsbury, the third Tuesday in June and the third Tuesday in December.

Codington, the first Tuesday in June and the first Tuesday in December.

Deuel, the fourth Monday in May

Hamlin, the fourth Tuesday in November.

Hughes, the second Tuesday in April and the second Tuesday in September.

Hand, the fourth Tuesday in April and the third Tuesday in October.

Beadle, first Tuesday in May and the first Tuesday in October.

Spink, the second Tuesday in July and the second Tuesday in January.

Brown, the third Tuesday in July and the third Tuesday in January.

Grant, the third Tuesday in March and the third Tuesday in November.

Edmunds, McPherson, Walworth and Campbell shall constitute one judicial subdivision of the fifth judicial district, and a term of court shall be held in Edmunds county on [the] second Tuesday in September.

Hyde—A term of court shall be held in Hyde county, commencing on the 3d Tuesday in September.

Sully—A term of court shall be held in the county of Sully, commencing on the 4th Tuesday in October.

The counties of Marshall and Day shall constitute one judicial subdivision, and a term of court shall be held in the county of Day commencing on the 2d Tuesday of August.

Potter county—A term of court shall be held in Potter county the 3d Tuesday of February.

Faulk—At such time in the year, 1885, as the Judge of said district may designate, and thereafter there shall be two terms of court annually held in said county on the first Tuesday of September and fourth Tuesday of January.

Clark—Terms of court shall be held on the first Tuesday of February and third Tuesday in August.

For other counties of said district, not otherwise provided for, at least one term shall be held each year, and two if deemed necessary by the Judge, at such times as he shall designate.

§ 2. All acts and parts of acts in conflict with provisions of this act are hereby repealed

Approved, March 13, 1885.

SIXTH DISTRICT—FIXING TERMS OF COURT THEREIN.

CHAPTER 80.

AN ACT to fix the Terms of the District Court within and for the Sixth Judicial District of the Territory of Dakota, exercising the Power and Jurisdiction of the District and Circuit Courts of the United States.

Be it enacted by the Legislative Assembly of the Territory of Dakota :

§ 1. TERMS OF COURT—WHEN AND WHERE HELD.] That the terms of the district court in and for the Sixth Judicial District of the Territory of Dakota, having and exercising in all cases arising under the constitution and laws of the United States, the same jurisdiction as is vested in the circuit and district courts of the United States, shall be held at Bismarck, in the county of Burleigh and Territory of Dakota, on the first Tuesday in March and the first Tuesday of September in each year, and the judge of said court shall have power to appoint and hold such other special terms of said district court as he may deem necessary for the due administration of justice.

§ 2. This act shall take effect from and after its passage and approval.

Approved, March 12, 1885.

SIXTH DISTRICT—BOUNDARIES AND SUBDIVISIONS.

CHAPTER 81.

AN ACT to define the Sixth Judicial District of the Territory of Dakota and To Subdivide the same, and to fix the terms of Court therein, and for other purposes, in pursuance of the act of Congress dividing said Territory in six Judicial Districts.

Be it enacted by the Legislative Assembly of the Territory of Dakota :

§ 1. COUNTIES INCLUDED IN.] That the sixth judicial district of the Territory of Dakota shall consist of the following counties in said Territory, namely: Bowman, Villard, Billings, Dunn,

McKenzie, Allred, Buford, Flannery, Wallace, Mountraille, Williams, Stark, Hettinger, Boreman, Morton, Mercer, McLean, Ward, Stevens, Renville, Wynn, Bottineau, McHenry, Sheridan, Burleigh, Emmons, McIntosh, Logan, Kidder, Wells, DeSmet, Rolette, Benson, Foster, Eddy, Stutsman, LaMoure, Dickey, Griggs, Steele and Barnes.

§ 2. SUBDIVISION FIRST.] That the said sixth judicial district be, and the same is hereby divided into subdivisions, as follows: The first subdivision shall consist of the counties of Burleigh, Emmons, McLean, Stevens, Boreman, and Sheridan, Mountraille, Flannery, Buford. The district court in and for this subdivision shall be held at the city of Bismarck, in the county of Burleigh, on the first Tuesday in March and the first Tuesday in September in each year.

§ 3. SECOND.] The second subdivision shall consist of the counties of Morton, Stark, Hettinger, Boreman, Bowman, Villard, Billings, Dunn, McKenzie, Allred, Wallace, Williams and Mercer. The district court in and for this subdivision shall be held at the city of Mandan in the county of Morton on second Tuesday of August of each year.

§ 4. THIRD.] The third subdivision shall consist of the counties of Kidder, Logan and McIntosh. The district court in and for this subdivision shall be held at the city of Steele in the county of Kidder, at such time as the judge may direct in each year.

§ 5. FOURTH.] The fourth subdivision shall consist of the counties of Stutsman, Foster, Wells and La Moure. The district court in and for this subdivision shall be held at the city of Jamestown in the county of Stutsman on the second Tuesday in November of each year and one term commencing second Tuesday in April, 1885, shall be held.

§ 6. FIFTH.] The fifth subdivision shall consist of the counties of Barnes, Griggs, Steele. The district court in and for this subdivision shall be held at the city of Valley City in the county of Barnes on the second Tuesday in July of each year.

§ 7. SIXTH.] The sixth subdivision shall consist of the counties of Benson, Rolette, Bottineau, McHenry, Ward, DeSmet, Eddy, Wynn. The district court in for this subdivision shall be held at the town of Minnewaukan in the county of Benson on the second Tuesday in January of each year.

§ 8. SEVENTH.] The seventh subdivision shall consist of the county of Dickey. The district court in and for this subdivision shall be held at Ellendale at such time in each year as the judge of said court may direct.

§ 9. PENDING ACTIONS.] All actions and proceedings, both civil and criminal, now pending in any subdivision of said sixth judicial district, heretofore created by act of the Legislature of this Territory, shall be respectively tried, heard and determined in the district court held in the subdivision hereby created, in which the county, wherein the cause of action arose, or the offense was committed, or the venue is laid, is situate or forms a part.

§ 10.   All acts or parts of acts conflicting with this act, or any of its provisions, are hereby repealed.

§ 11.   This act shall take effect from and after its passage.

Approved, March 13, 1885.

SIXTH DISTRCT—DICKEY AND McINTOSH COUNTY

CHAPTER 82.

AN ACT to Create a New Sub-division of the Sixth Judicial District.

Be it enacted by the Legislative Assembly of the Territory of Dakota:

§ 1.   SUB-DIVISION.]   The counties of Dickey and McIntosh are hereby created and constituted a sub-division of the sixth judicial district.

§ 2.   JUDGE SHALL APPOINT TERM.]   The judge of the sixth judicial district shall annually appoint and hold court for said subdivision at the county seat of said Dickey county, and the county of McIntosh is hereby attached to Dickey county for judicial purposes.

§ 3.   This act shall take effect and be in force from and after its passage and approval.

Approved, March 4, 1885.

ACTIONS TRANSFERRED FROM THE THIRD TO SIXTH DISTRICT.

CHAPTER 83.

AN ACT Concerning Actions and Proceedings Brought in the Third Judicial District of Dakota Territory, in the Counties or Sub-divisions now included in the Sixth Judicial District of said Territory, and the Jurisdiction thereof since the Creation of the said Sixth Judicial District.

WHEREAS, The judge of the district court of the sixth judicial district of the Territory of Dakota, as created by act of congress, has held that the said court has no jurisdiction "To hear, try or determine any action or proceeding" pending in the sub-divisions in said district prior to the creation of said district; Therefore,

Be it enacted by the Legislative Assembly of the Territory of Dakota:

§ 1. ACTIONS TO CONTINUE, ETC.] That all actions, motions, orders and proceedings, pending at the time of the passage of said act of congress are hereby declared to continue in said 6th judicial district in every sub-division therein, with full force and effect, the same as though said judge had not so held; *Provided, however,* That this act shall not be construed as a legislative construction that such decision is correct, but this act is passed to avoid the effect of such decision on pending cases and proceedings and to avoid litigation and unnecessary appeals.

Approved, March 13, 1885.

Juries.

CHAPTER 84.

AN ACT Providing for Struck Juries.

Be it enacted by the Legislative Assembly of the Territory of Dakota:

§ 1. MANNER OF SELECTING JURY.] That whenever a struck jury is deemed necessary, by either party, for the trial of the issue in any action or proceeding in the district court, or brought there by appeal or otherwise, such party may file with the clerk of the court a demand in writing for such jury, whereupon such clerk shall forthwith deliver a certified copy of such demand to the sheriff of the county, who shall give to both parties four days notice of the time of the striking of the same. At the time designated said sheriff shall attend at his office, and in the presence of the parties, or their attorneys, or such of them as attend for that purpose, shall select from the number of persons qualified to serve as jurors within the county, forty such persons as he shall think most indifferent between the parties, and best qualified to try such issue, and then the party requiring such jury, his agent or attorney shall first strike off one of the names, and the opposite party, his agent or attorney, another, and so on alternately, until each have struck out twelve. If either party shall not attend in person, or by attorney, the sheriff shall strike for the party not attending. When each party has stricken out twelve names as above aforesaid, the sheriff shall make a fair copy of the names of the remaining sixteen persons, and certify the same under his hand, to be the list of jurors struck for the trial of such case or proceeding, and shall deliver the same to the clerk, who shall thereupon issue and deliver to the sheriff or other officer, a *venire facias*, with the names in said list contained, annexed thereto, and such sheriff or other officer shall summon the persons named according to the demand of such writ, and upon the trial of the cause, the jury so struck shall be called as they stand upon the panel, and the first twelve of them who shall appear and are not challenged for cause or set aside by the court, shall be the jury, and shall be sworn to try the issue joined in said cause or proceeding, *Provided*, That if a sufficient number does not appear for the trial of said cause, the court shall cause talesmen to be called as in other cases.

§ 2. WHEN SHERIFF NOT TO ACT.] That if the said sheriff is interested in the cause or proceedings or related to either of the parties, or does not stand indifferent between them the judge of the said court may name some judicious and disinterested person to select and strike the jury, and to do and perform all things required to be done by said sheriff relating to the striking out of the same, but in no case shall it be necessary to strike such jury more than six days previous to the term of the court at which the action or proceeding is to be tried, and three days service of the venire shall be held sufficient.

§ 3. FEES—HOW PAID.] That the party requiring such struck jury shall pay the fees for striking the same, and the legal fees for mileage and attendance for each juror so attending, and shall not have any allowance therefor in the taxation of costs.

§ 4. JURY TO BE ALLOWED BY COURT.] That no struck jury

shall be had under the provisions of this act unless the same has been allowed by the court or judge thereof on due notice, *Provided,* That this act shall not be construed to apply to trials and juries in criminal cases.

§ 5. This act shall take effect and be in force immediately on and after its passage and approval.

Approved, March 13, 1885.

Justices of the Peace.

CHANGE OF VENUE.

CHAPTER 85.

AN ACT to Amend "An act the Establish a Code of Proceedings in Courts of Justice of the Peace, and to Limit the Jurisdiction of the Same.

Be it enacted by the Legislative Assembly of the Territory of Dakota:

§ 1. THIS SECTION TO APPLY.] Section one hundred and twelve of the Justice's Code of the Territory of Dakota, be and the same is hereby amended by adding at the end of said section the following proviso: *Provided,* That this section shall apply to all examinations and proceedings under chapter three of title two of the Code of Criminal Procedure, relating to the jurisdiction and duties of justices of the peace in cases of security to keep the peace; and also to examinations held under, or pursuant to, chapter seven of title four of said Code, in all cases where the person complained of is not brought before a Judge of the Supreme Court or of the District Court.

§ 2. This act shall take effect and be in force from and after its passage.

Approved, March 12, 1885.

1885—20

TIME OF TRIALS AND POSTPONEMENTS.

CHAPTER 86.

AN ACT to Amend Section Forty-seven of the Justices' Code of the Territory
of Dakota.

Be it enacted by the Legislative Assembly of the Territory of Dakota:

§ 1. DEPOSITIONS.] That section forty-seven of the Justice's
Code of the Territory of Dakota, be and the same is hereby
amended by adding at the end of said section the following:
" And if the trial be postponed the depositions of witnesses residing
out of the county or territory may be taken either upon commission issued by the justice, or upon notice to take depositions in the
same manner as is provided by the Code of Civil Procedure ; and
such depositions shall, when completed, be directed to the justice,
and be published by the justice in the same manner as depositions
are published by the clerk of the District Court."

Approved, February 27, 1885.

Justices Practice.

CHAPTER 87.

AN ACT Authorizing County Boards to Purchase the "Dakota Justice Court
Practice, Civil and Criminal," for Justices of the Peace.

Be it enacted by the Legislative Assembly of the Territory of Dakota:

§ 1. COUNTY BOARD MAY PURCHASE] That the county board
of each county in the Territory of Dakota, is hereby authorized to
purchase for each justice of the peace in their respective counties,
at a price not exceeding five dollars per volume, one copy of the
" Dakota Justice Court Practice, Civil and Criminal," prepared,
copy-righted and published by Americus B. Melville.

§ 2. HOW TO PURCHASE.] Whenever any county board shall

purchase and receive one or more of said books, the chairman of said board, together with the county clerk, shall sign a warrant of the county in an amount equal to the price agreed to be paid for said books, and shall deliver the same on demand to the publishe..

§ 3   This act shall take effect from and after its passage and approval.

Note by the Secretary of the Territory.

The foregoing act, having been presented to the Governor for his approval, and not having been returned to the House of Representatives, the House of the Legislative Assembly in which it originated, within the time prescribed by the Organic Act, has become a law without his approval.

JAMES H. TELLER,
Secretary of the Territory.

Legal Holidays.

CHAPTER 88.

AN ACT to Amend Section Twenty one Hundred and Fifteen of the Civil Code of the Territory of Dakota.

Be it enacted by the Legislative Assembly of the Territory of Dakota :

§ 1.   DECORATION DAY.]   That section twenty-one hundred and fifteen of the Civil Code, be and the same is hereby amended by inserting after the word " December," in the third line of said section, the following words :   " The thirtieth day of May."

§ 2.   This act shall take effect and be in force from and after its passage and approval.

Approved, March 12, 1885.

Legislative Assembly.

APPROPRIATION FOR WATER IN CAPITOL BUILDING.

CHAPTER 89.

JOINT RESOLUTION Providing for the Purchase of Water for Capitol Building.

Be it enacted by the Legislative Assembly of the Territory of Dakota:

[§ 1.] APPROPRIATION.] That there is hereby appropriated out of any funds in the territorial treasury not otherwise appropriated a sufficient sum to pay for water for the use at the capitol building at Bismarck, and the Secretary of the Territory is hereby authorized to contract for and provide water for such purposes.

Approved, February 11, 1885.

APPROPRIATION FOR WINDOW SHADES.

CHAPTER 90.

AN ACT to provide Shades for Windows in the "House."

Be it enacted by the Legislative Assembly of the Territory of Dakota:

§ 1. APPROPRIATION.] That C. H. Phelps is hereby directed to purchase and place in position nineteen (19) shades for windows in the "House" not already provided therewith.

§ 2. That there is hereby appropriated out of any funds in the territorial treasury not otherwise appropriated forty-seven and 50-100 dollars to be used in payment of shades so furnished.

Approved, March 2, 1885.

APPROPRIATION FOR PAGES OF THE COUNCIL.

CHAPTER 91.

AN ACN making Appropriation to pay Geo. Hughes and Charles Healy for Services as Pages of the Council.

Be it enacted by the Legislative Assembly of the Territory of Dakota.

§ 1. PER DIEM.] That Geo. Hughes and Charles Healy be and are hereby allowed the sum of two dollars per day for each and every day actually employed as pages of the council.

§ 2. APPROPRIATION.] That the sum of two hundred and forty dollars, or so much thereof as may be necessary, is hereby appropriated out of any moneys in the territorial treasury, not otherwise appropriated, for the payment of the service herein mentioned.

§ ˙. This act shall take effect and be in force from and after its passage and approval.

Approved, March 9, 1885.

APPROPRIATION FOR PURCHASE OF FUEL.

CHAPTER 92.

AN ACT Authorizing the Secretary of the Territory to Purchase Fuel for the Capitol Building during the Present Session of the Legislature.

Be it enacted by the Legislative Assembly of the Territory of Dakota:

[§ 1.] SECRETARY AUTHORIZED TO PURCHASE.] That the secretary of the Territory is hereby authorized and instructed to provide the necessary fuel for heating the capitol building during the present session of the legislature; and a sufficient amount is hereby appropriated out of any funds in the territorial treasury not otherwise appropriated for the payment thereof, *Providing*, That the amount furnished by the general government for that purpose as provided by law shall be found insufficient.

Approved, March 7, 1885.

APPROPRIATION FOR PURCHASE OF FUEL.

CHAPTER 93.

JOINT RESOLUTION.

Resolved by the Council and House of Representatives :

APPROPRIATION.] That the secretary of the Territory be, and is hereby instructed to contract and pay for one hundred tons of coal for the use of the capitol building, and that sufficient money is hereby appropriated out of the general fund to pay for the same, to be paid out by an order from the territorial Auditor.

Approved, January 29, 1885.

APPROPRIATION TO PAY FOR FUEL.

CHAPTER 94.

AN ACT Appropriating Money to Pay for Fuel used in Heating the Capitol Building.

Be it enacted by the Legislative Assembly of the Territory of Dakota :

§ 1. SUM ALLOWED.] That there is hereby allowed to William M. Pye, Sr., the sum of ($931.36) nine hundred and thirty-one and 36-100 dollars, as payment for fuel furnished by him and used in heating the capitol building of the Territory of Dakota.

§ 2. APPROPRIATION.] The sum of ($931.36) is hereby appropriated out of the general fund of the Territory of Dakota for the purpose of paying the same.

§ 3. This act shall have effect and be in force from and after its passage and approval.

Approved, March 13, 1885.

APPROPRIATION DONATED TO O. N. FARLEY.

CHAPTER 95.

AN ACT to Appropriate the sum of Two Hundred and Sixty Dollars as a Donation to O. N. Farley.

Be it enacted by the Legislative Assembly of the Territory of Dakota :

§ 1. APPROPRIATION.] That there shall be appropriated from the funds now in the hands of the treasurer of the Territory, the sum of two hundred and sixty dollars to be paid to O. N. Farley, as a donation from the Territory of Dakota, and the territorial Auditor shall be and hereby is instructed to draw his warrant for said amount.

§ 2. This act shall take effect and be in force from and after its passage and approval.

Approved, March 13, 1885.

APPROPRIATION FOR PAGES OF THE HOUSE.

CHAPTER 96.

AN ACT Making Appropriations to pay Fred H. Lounsberry, Frank Armstrong and Henry Murphy for Services as Pages of the House.

Be it enacted by the Legislative Assembly of the Territory of Dakota :

§ 1. APPROPRIATION.] That Fred Lounsberry, Frank Armstrong and Henry Murphy be and are hereby allowed the sum of two (2) dollars per day for each and every day actually employed as pages of the house.

§ 2. ACCOUNT TO BE CERTIFIED.] That the sum of two hundred and forty (240) dollars, or so much thereof as may be necessary, is hereby appropriated out of any moneys in the territorial treasury, not otherwise appropriated, for the payment of the sum herein mentioned.

§ 3.   That said sum shall be audited and paid out of the territorial treasury upon an account certified by the Speaker of the House.

§ 4.   This act shall take effect and be in force from and after its passage and approval.

Approved, March 13, 1885.

APPROPRIATION FOR PRINTING JOURNALS.

CHAPTER 97.

JOINT RESOLUTION to provide for the Payment of Printing and Binding Council and House Journals for the Sixteenth Legislative Assembly.

Be it resolved by the House of Representatives, the Council Concurring:

§ 1.   APPROPRIATIONS.]   There is hereby appropriated out of the treasury of the Territory a sum sufficient to pay for the printing and binding of the journals of the Sixteenth Legislative Assembly in accordance with resolutions passed by the Council and House of Representatives.

§ 2.   DUTY OF CLERKS.]   It is hereby made the duty of the chief clerks of the respective houses to prepare for the printer any appendix, record of bills or index necessary to complete the bound edition, and it is further made the duty of said clerks to place at the disposal of the territorial Librarian fifty copies of the journal of each house, the balance of the bound edition to be distributed among the various territorial officers and the members of the legislature.

§ 3.   BILLS TO BE CERTIFIED.]   All bills for the printing and binding required by this resolution shall be certified to by the respective chief clerk of each house and the secretary of the Territory, whereupon it is the duty of the Auditor to draw a warrant on the general fund in payment of such bills out of any money not otherwise appropriated.

§ 4.   This resolution shall [take] effect and be in force from and after its passage and approval.

Approved, March 13, 1885.

APPROPRIATION FOR POSTMASTER AND CLERK.

CHAPTER 98.

AN ACT Appropriating funds for paying the Postmaster and Clerk of Committee on Counties of the Council.

Be it enacted by the Legislative Assembly of the Territory of Dakota :

§ 1. APPROPRIATED.] There is hereby appropriated from the funds in the territorial treasury the sum of one hundred and sixteen dollars or so much thereof as is necessary to pay for the services of J. A. Fry, the postmaster of the council.

§ 2. AMOUNT TO BE CERTIFIED.] The amount due such officer shall be audited and paid out of the territorial treasury upon an account certified by the president of the council.

§ 3. That there is hereby appropriated out of any funds in the territorial treasury not otherwise appropriated the sum of one hundred [and] fifty two dollars to pay for the services of F. W. Rogers as clerk of the committee on counties and as assistant enrolling clerk of the council.

§ 4. This act shall take effect and be in force from and after its passage and approval.

Approved, March 13, 1885.

APPROPRIATION FOR ALL EMPLOYES AT CAPITOL.

CHAPTER 99.

AN ACT to Appropriate funds for the Payment of all Persons Employed in and about the Capitol Building by Authority of the Legislative Assembly.

Be it enacted by the Legislative Assembly of the Territory of Dakota :

§ 1. ACCOUNTS TO BE CERTIFIED] That the accounts of all persons employed by the authority of the Legislative Assembly

1885—21

in and about the capitol building when approved by the president of the Council and the speaker of the House of Representatives, shall be a sufficient authority for the territorial Auditor to draw his warrant on the territorial treasury for the several sums named in such accounts for services rendered.

§ 2. APPROPRIATION.] That there is hereby appropriated out of the territorial treasury a sum sufficient to pay for services of persons so employed.

§ 3. This act shall take effect and be in force from and after its passage and approval.

Approved, February 12, 1885.

APPROPRIATION FOR ASSISTANT CLERKS AND ASSISTANT SERGEANT AT-ARMS.

CHAPTER 100.

AN ACT Appropriating funds for Paving the Assistant Clerks and Assistant Sergeant at-arms of the Council and House.

Be it enacted by the Legislative Assembly of the Territory of Dakota:

§ 1. APPROPRIATION.] That there is hereby appropriated from the funds in the territorial treasury the sum of twelve hundred dollars, or so much thereof as is necessary, to pay for the services of the assistant clerks in the House of Representatives and for the assistant sergeant-at-arms of the respective bodies.

§ 2. AMOUNT CERTIFIED.] The respective amounts due each officer shall be audited and paid out of the territorial treasury upon an account certified by the respective presiding officers of the two houses of said assembly.

§ 3. This act shall take effect and be in force from and after its passage and approval.

Approved, February 4, 1885.

APPROPRIATION FOR PRINTING FOR LEGISLATIVE ASSEMBLY.

CHAPTER 101.

JOINT RESOLUTION Providing for certain Public Printing, and Making Appropriation for the same.

Resolved by the Council and House of Representatives :

SECRETARY AUTHORIZED TO PROCURE PRINTING.] That the Secretary of the Territory is hereby authorized to procure from the public printer the printing, at a rate not exceeding that established by the government for similar work, of not more than one hundred copies each of all bills, resolutions and memorials ordered printed by the House of Representatives or the council of this session, and for which payment has not been otherwise provided for. Upon presentation to the territorial Auditor of a properly verified account for printing done under the provisions of this resolution, such account having been approved in writing by the secretary of the Territory, the Auditor shall draw his warrant on the territorial treasurer or the amount of said bill or bills; and there is hereby appropriated from the territorial treasury such sum as may be necessary to pay for said printing.

Approved, January 31, 1885.

APPROPRIATION FOR PAY OF STENOGRAPHERS.

CHAPTER 102.

JOINT RESOLUTION Authorizing the President of the Council and Speaker of the House to Appoint Stenographers for their Respective Bodies.

Be it resolved by the Council and House of Representatives of the Territory of Dakota:

AUTHORITY TO EMPLOY APPROPRIATION.] The president of the Council and speaker of the House of Representatives of the Territory of Dakota are authorized and it is hereby made their duty to appoint a competent and skilled stenographer for their respective houses. Such stenographers shall be under the direction and control of the president and speaker respectively for the service of the various committees of the respective houses. Each of said stenographers shall receive six dollars per day for the time actually employed by them in the performance of their duties, which services shall be audited and paid out of the territorial treasury on the certificate of the president of the Council and speaker of the House of Representatives that said services were actually performed and that the bill for such services was [is] correct and just.

Approved, February 11, 1885.

APPROPRIATION FOR ASSISTANT ENROLLING CLERKS.

CHAPTER 103.

JOINT RESOLUTION Authorizing the President of the Council and Speaker of the House to Appoint an Assistant Engrossing Clerk, and Assistant Clerk of the Council and House of Representatives.

Be it resolved by the Council and House of Representatives of the Territory of Dakota:

AUTHORITY TO APPOINT—APPROPRIATION.] That the president of the Council and speaker of the House of Representatives are authorized to appoint when necessary an assistant enrolling and engrossing clerk, and an additional assistant clerk of the Council and House of Representatives respectively. Each of said clerks shall receive for their services the sum of five dollars per day for the time actually and necessarily employed in the discharge of their duties, to be audited and paid out of the territorial treasury on the certificate to and allowance of, their account of services by the said president and speaker respectively.

Approved, February 11, 1885.

APPROPRIATION FOR EMPLOYMENT OF ENROLLING CLERKS.

CHAPTER 104.

JOINT RESOLUTION.

Resolved by the Council, the House of Representatives concurring:

AUTHORITY TO EMPLOY, ETC.] That the president of the Council and the speaker of the House are hereby authorized to employ such additional engrossing and enrolling clerks for both branches of the Legislature as are in their judgment deemed necessary for a proper fulfillment of the duties required of the committees of each House; and there is hereby appropriate ! out of any funds in the treasury a sum of money sufficient to cover the expenses of such additional service.

Approved, March 13, 1885.

APPROPRIATION FOR CLERKS AND OTHER SUBORDINATE OFFICERS.

CHAPTER 105.

AN ACT Compensating the Clerks and other Subordinate Officers of the Council and House of Representatives for extra Services.

Be it enacted by the Legislative Assembly of the Territory of Dakota :

§ 1. EXTRA COMPENSATION.] That the chief clerks, assistant chief clerks and enrolling and engrossing clerks of the Council and House of Representatives and the sergeant-at-arms, assistant sergeant-at-arms and other subordinate officers, excepting pages, be paid the sum of $25 each for extra services rendered during the sixteenth session of the Legislative Assembly.

§ 2. WARRANT AUTHORIZED.] Upon the certificate of the president of the Council and speaker of the House of Representatives, duly attested by the chief clerks of their respective Houses, the territorial Auditor shall draw his warrant for the sum so named on the territorial Treasurer, whereupon the territorial Treasurer shall pay the same out of any moneys in the territorial treasury not otherwise appropriated.

§ 3. APPROPRIATION.] There is hereby appropriated the sum of six hundred dollars, or so much thereof as may be necessary to carry out the provisions of this act, out of any money in the territorial treasury not otherwise appropriated.

§ 4. This act shall take effect and be in force from and after its passage and approval; *Provided*, That this act shall apply only to such officers as had taken the oath of office prior to March 5th.

Approved, March 13, 1885.

APPROPRIATION FOR ENROLLING CLERKS.

CHAPTER 106.

AN ACT Providing for Compensation for V V. Barnes and Chas. Richardson for Labor on Committees of Engrossment and Enrollment in House and Council respectively.

Be it enacted by the Legislative Assembly of the Territory of Dakota:

§ 1. APPROPRIATION] There is hereby appropriated out of any money in territorial treasury not otherwise appropriated, fifty dollars each to V. V Barnes and Charles Richardson as compensation for labor performed on committee of engrossment and enrollment of their respective Houses.

Approved, March 13, 1885.

APPROPRIATION FOR EXTRA SERVICES OF CLERKS.

CHAPTER 107.

APPROPRIATION] WHEREAS, Under a joint resolution passed by the Council and House of Representatives on the 13th day of

March, 1885, known as House bill 426, there was appropriated $600 (six hundred dollars) for extra services by the clerks and other subordinate officers of the session ; and

WHEREAS, There is a deficiency of $200 (two hundred dollars) existing for the purpose named in said bill, *therefore be it*

Resolved, By the Council, the House concurring, that there is hereby appropriated $200 (two hundred dollars) or as much thereof as is necessary to carry out the provisions of said act.

Approved, March 13, 1885.

APPROPRIATION FOR CLERK FOR COMMITTEE.

CHAPTER 108.

AN ACT Providing a Clerk for the Committee on Appropriations.

Be it enacted by the Legislative Assembly of the Territory of Dakota :

§ 1. AUTHORITY TO EMPLOY.] That the committee on appropriations of the house be authorized to employ a clerk for said committee during the remainder of the sixteenth session of the Legislative Assembly of Dakota Territory, to receive the same pay and be paid in the same manner as the clerk of the judiciary committee, whose duty in addition to that of clerk of said appropriation committee and when not so employed, shall be to assist other committees as clerk, under and by direction of the speaker of the house.

§ 2. APPROPRIATION.] There is hereby appropriated from the territorial treasury such an amount as may be necessary to pay said clerk according to provisions of said act.

Approved, February 13, 1885.

APPOINTMENT OF ASSISTANT SERGEANT-AT-ARMS.

CHAPTER 109.

AN ACT to amend an Act Entitled an Act to employ an Assistant Sergeant at-Arms for the Council and House of Representatives and to provide their Compensation.

Be it enacted by the Legislative Assembly of the Territory of Dakota :

That section one, chapter 78, of the laws of 1883 be amended so as to read as follows:

§ 1. PRESIDING OFFICERS TO APPOINT.] There shall be appointed by the president of the council and the speaker of the House one watchman and one assistant sergeant at-arms and the president of the council shall appoint a postmaster to discharge the duties pertaining to that office for both council and house, the duties of which postmaster shall be prescribed by the president of the council. The assistant sergeant at-arms shall discharge the several duties of the sergeant at-arms in case of his absence, or inability to serve, and shall, alternately with the watchman. serve as night watchman of the halls of the Council and House of Representatives.

§ .2 This act shall take effect from and after its approval.

Approved, February 10, 1885.

EXTENDING THE EXTRA TIME FOR CHIEF CLERKS.

CHAPTER 110.

AN ACT to amend Chapter 49 of the Session laws of 1883 Entitled "AN ACT to amend Section 13 of Chapter 20 of the Political Code" relating to extra per diem to Chief Clerk.

Be it enacted by the Legislative Assembly of the Territory of Dakota :

§ 1. SIXTY DAYS ALLOWED.] That section one (1) of said act is hereby amended by striking out the word "forty" (40) where it occurs in said section and inserting in lieu thereof the word "sixty" (60).

§ 2. All acts and parts of acts in conflict with this act are hereby repealed.

§ 3. This act shall take effect and be in force from and after its passage and approval.

Approved, March 13, 1885.

License Funds.

CHAPTER 111.

AN ACT to amend Section 53 of Chapter 44 of the laws of 1883, and to provide what Fund, money paid to the County Treasurer for Licenses to sell Intoxicating liquors, shall be applied.

Be it enacted by the Legislative Assembly of the Territory of Dakota :

§ 1. LICENSE FUNDS WITHDRAWN FROM PUBLIC SCHOOLS.] That section 53 of chapter 44, of the laws of 1883, be, and the same is hereby amended by striking out the words: "And all money paid into the county treasury for license to sell intoxicating liquors."

§ 2. PAID TO GENERAL COUNTY FUND.] All fines, forfeitures and pecuniary penalties prescribed as a punishment for crime and collected under the general laws of the Territory : and all money paid into the county treasury for license to sell intoxicating liquors in the various counties, shall be placed in and become a part of the general county fund.

§ 3. This act shall take effect and be in force from and after July 15, 1885.

Approved, February 26, 1885.

1885—22

Live Stock Lien.

CHAPTER 112.

AN ACT to amend Section One (1) of Chapter Eighty-five (85) of the Session laws of 1883 entitled "Live Stock."

Be it enacted by the Legislative Assembly of the Territory of Dakota:

§ 1. FINE FOR FILING LIEN EXTENDED.] That section one (1) of chapter eighty-five (85) be and the same is hereby amended by striking out the word, "ten" where it occurs in said section and inserting in lieu thereof the word "ninety."

§ 2. This act shall take effect and be in force from and after its passage and approval.

Approved, March 3, 1885.

Militia.

CHAPTER 113.

AN ACT to Amend Chapter 30 of the Political Code, Revised 1877, of the Territory of Dakota, and making an Annual Appropriation to Provide for the Maintenance of the Militia.

Be it enacted by the Legislative Assembly of the Territory of Dakota:

§ 1. UNIFORMS.] That chapter 30 of the Political Code be amended as follows: That every company or battery of the Dakota National Guard shall provide suitable uniforms, subject to the inspection and approval of the officer who may muster such company into service. For the purpose of aiding in procuring uniforms, and keeping them in repair, there shall be paid annually to each officer and soldier, who shall be uniformed and duly mustered, and is in attendance at the annual encampment or the annual inspection of such company, a sum equal to five dollars.

§ 2. ARMORY.] Every company and battery shall provide at their own expense a suitable room or building for an armory, with proper racks, frames and other needful provision for the safe keeping of the arms, accoutrements, and stores issued by the Territory, and shall therein keep the same when not in lawful use. The Governor of the Territory is hereby authorized and empowered to receive and execute bonds in the name of the Territory for such arms and accoutrements as may be deemed necessary to fully carry out the provisions of this act.

§ 3. WHEN ENTITLED TO FUNDS.] Each company or battery which shall be organized and mustered, and shall possess minimum number of members, and are uniformed and equipped with the necessary arms and accoutrements for its members, that has a suitable armory and has its arms, accoutrements and stores in good condition, which shall have been annually mustered and inspected by the company commander, and made return thereof to the adjutant general, shall, upon the certificate thereof from the adjutant general, approved by the Governor, be annually paid out of the territorial treasury three hundred dollars, on the receipts of the commander, which shall be in full compensation on the part of the Territory for all pay when not called into active service, and for rent of armory. Whenever any of the companies shall lapse into ill condition, become lax in discipline, negligent in instruction, drill or other duties, or the members lose interest in their organization, the Governor may retire such company from the service, and shall admit in place thereof some other company of later organization, which shall have complied with the requirements of the law; *Provided, however,* That compensation shall not be allowed to more than one company in any county. The Governor, however, may divide the compensation between two companies, where the same have already been organized.

§ 4. EXEMPT FROM JURY DUTY.] Every member of the Dakota National Guard shall be exempt from jury duty, and from the payment of poll tax, and every member who shall be honorably discharged after four years' service, or by reason of disability received while in service, shall be forever so exempt, and also exempt from military duty in time of peace; the proper discharge certificate shall be conclusive evidence of the right of such exemption.

§ 5. ORGANIZATION.] The Governor may form the volunteer companies into battalions and regiments, and appoint officers therefor; not less than two nor more than five companies shall constitute a battalion, and two battalions shall be deemed a regiment; the officers of such regiment shall be a colonel, lieutenant colonel and one major.

§ 6. GENERAL TRAINING.] The Governor shall, with or without permanently organizing battalions or regiments, order rendezvous and encampments of the several companies for instruction in drill and duties, not to exceed four nor less than two days in any one year, and shall fix the point at which such companies shall rendezvous, and the Governor shall designate the officer to command at each camp. The Governor shall allow toward the expense of subsistence of the troops during such rendezvous, one dollar and fifty cents per day for each officer and enlisted man actually attending in uniform for the time he is absent from home to attend such rendezvous. Such allowance shall be paid out of the territorial treasury to the companies on such vouchers and proofs as the Governor may require and on his approval. Transportation, subsistence and suitable camp and garrison equipage shall be provided at the expense of the Territory.

§ 7. MUSTER ROLLS. ETC.—ADJUTANT GENERAL'S SALARY.] The adjutant general and quarter-master general shall prepare, subject to the Governor's approval, blanks and forms for muster rolls, ordnance and property returns, reports, receipts and other papers necessary to carry out the provisions of this act, with proper accompanying instructions from time to time. The adjutant general shall preserve and cause to be recopied, when necessary, such muster rolls or other records of his office as require to be transcribed for presentation; that the adjutant general shall receive the sum of ($1000) one thousand dollars per annum as salary, and there is hereby appropriated the sum of five hundred dollars for the purpose of necessary records, keeping the same, traveling expenses, rents, caring for and storing arms, freights and other necessary expenses belonging to the adjutant general's office.

§ 8. INSPECTION.] The entire territorial militia and all armories, ordnance stores, camp and garrison equipage, belonging to the Territory, shall be inspected at least once each year, under such rules and regulations as may be provided by the inspector general with the approval of the commander-in-chief.

§ 9. CLERKS.] Such clerical assistance shall be employed in the adjutant general's office as shall, in the opinion of the Governor, be actually necessary, and any person so employed shall receive for the time actually and necessarily on duty such compensation as the Governor may prescribe. There shall be allowed annually for postage, stationary and office incidentals to each regimental headquarters, twenty-five dollars, and each company headquarters the sum of ten dollars.

§ 10. CALLING OUT MILITIA.] When the sheriff or other officer authorized to execute process finds, or has reason to apprehend that resistance will be made to the executive thereof, he may command as many male inhabitants of his county as he may think proper; and upon application of the sheriff and by order of the

Governor, any military companies in the county, armed and equipped, shall assist him in overcoming the resistance, and if necessary, in seizing, arresting and confining the resistors and their aiders and abettors, to be punished by law.

§ 11. MILITIA, HOW PAID.] All officers and soldiers while on duty or assembled therefor, pursuant to the order of any sheriff of any county in cases of riot, tumult, breach of the peace, or whenever called upon by the civil authorities to aid in the enforcement of the laws, shall receive the same compensation as provided for in section 12 of this act. and shall be a portion of the county charges of said county from the Territory, to be levied and raised as other county charges are levied and raised.

§ 12. PAY OF OFFICERS AND MEN] The military forces of the Territory, when in the actual service of the Territory in time of insurrection, invasion, or immediate danger thereof, shall, during their time of service, be paid by an appropriation especially made therefor, the following sums each for every day actually on duty :

To each general, field and staff officer,.......... $4 00
To every other commissioned officer,........... 2 50
To every non-commissioned staff officer,........ 2 00
To every other enlisted man,................. 1 50

§ 13. RULES FOR GOVERNING.] The Governor shall from time to time make, publish and distribute in a neat pamphlet form, rules, regulations and orders for the government of the Dakota National Guard, not inconsistent with law.

§ 14 APPROPRIATION.] For the purpose of carrying out the provisions of chapter 30 of the Political Code of the Territory of Dakota as herein amended, there is hereby made an appropriation of fifteen thousand dollars per annum, or so much thereof as may be necessary, out of any money in the territorial treasury, and all warrants against said appropriation shall be drawn by the territorial Auditor upon the territorial Treasurer, upon the certificate of the adjutant general approved by the Governor. All laws in conflict with the foregoing provisions being hereby so amended as to conform thereto.

§ 15. This act being deemed of immediate importance shall take effect from and after its passage and approval.

Approved, March 12, 1885.

COMMISSIONS—WHEN TO EXPIRE.

CHAPTER 114

AN ACT to Amend Chapter (30) Thirty, Section Fourteen of the Political Code. Revised 1877.

Be it enacted by the Legislative Assembly of the Territory of Dakota :

§ 1. COMMISSIONS EXPIRE.] That section fourteen of said chapter thirty be amended by striking out the words "except the quarter master general, adjutant general and paymaster general."

§ 2. This act shall take effect immediately after its passage and approval.

Approved, March 13, 1885.

New Trials.

CHAPTER 115.

AN ACT to Amend Sections Four Hundred and Twenty-three and Four Hundred and Twenty-four of the Code of Criminal Procedure of the Territory of Dakota.

Be it enacted by the Legislative Assembly of the Territory of Dakota :

§ 1. WHEN COURT MAY POSTPONE.] That section four hundred and twenty-three of the Code of Criminal Procedure of the Territory of Dakota, be and the same is hereby amended by adding thereto as paragraph seven : "When new evidence is discovered material to the defendant, and which he could not with reasonable diligence have discovered and produced at the trial when a motion for a new trial is made upon the ground of newly discovered evidence, the defendant must produce at the hearing, in support thereof, the affidavits of the witnesses by whom such evidence is expected to be given, and if time is required by the defendant to produce such affidavits, the court may postpone the hearing of the motion for such length of time as, under all the circumstances of the case, may seem reasonable."

§ 2. APPLICATION—WHEN TO BE MADE.] That section four hundred and twenty-four of the Code of Criminal Procedure of the Territory of Dakota be and the same is hereby amended to read as follows:

§ 424. The application for a new trial must be made before judgment, but the court or judge thereof may upon good cause shown, allow such application to be made at any time within thirty days after the entry of such judgment. And motions for a new trial on the ground of newly discovered evidence, may be made after judgment at the term in which the cause is tried, or during vacation before the court or judge thereof, at any time before the next succeeding term or at such term.

Approved, February 27, 1885.

Normal School.

MADISON.

CHAPTER 116.

AN ACT to Repeal Section 4, Chapter 99 of the Session Laws of 1881 and for other purposes.

Be it enacted by the Legislative Assembly of the Territory of Dakota :

§ 1. REPEALED.] That section 4 of chapter 99 of the session laws of 1881 be and the same is hereby abrogated and repealed.

§ 2. HOW GOVERNED.] That the board of education for the Normal school for the Territory of Dakota located and established at Madison, Lake county, Dakota Territory, shall consist of five (5) members who shall be appointed by the Governor, and by and with the consent of the legislative council. Two of said members of the board shall hold their office for the term of two (2) years and three for the term of four (4) years. The territorial Treasurer by virtue of his office shall be treasurer of said board, and the board shall annually elect from their number a president and secretary. It shall be the duty of the secretary to keep an exact detailed account of the doings of said board, and he shall submit such reports to the legislature as are required by this act, and no member of said board of education shall, during his continuance in office as a member of said board, act as an agent of any publishers of school books and school library books, either directly or indirectly, and the Governor of the Territory is hereby authorized and required upon satisfactory evidence being produced to him that any member of said board is employed as such agent or interested as aforesaid, to remove such member of said board from office, and to appoint another in his place to fill such vacancy.

§ 3. All acts and parts of acts in conflict with this act are hereby repealed

§ 4. This act shall take effect and be in force from and after its passage and approval.

Approved, March 9, 1885.

Notice of Pendency of Action.

CHAPTER 117.

AN ACT to Amend Section One Hundred and One of the Code of Civil Procedure.

Be it enacted by the Legislative Assembly of the Territory of Dakota:

§ 1. EFFECT OF LIS PENDENS.] That section one hundred and one of the Code of Civil Procedure be and the same is hereby amended so as to read as follows:

§ 101.] In an action affecting the title to real property, the plaintiff at the time of filing the complaint, or at any time afterwards, or whenever a warrant of attachment of property shall be issued, or at any time afterwards, the plaintiff or defendant, when he sets up an affirmative cause of action in his answer, and demands substantive relief at the time of filing his answer, or at any time afterwards, if the same be intended to affect real property, may file for record with the Register of Deeds of each county in which the real property is situated, a notice of the pendency of the action, containing the names of the parties, the object of the action, and the description of the real property in that county affected thereby; from the time of filing only shall the pendency of the action, be constructive notice to a purchaser or incumbrancer of the property affected thereby; and every person whose conveyance or incumbrance is subsequently executed or subsequently recorded, shall be deemed a subsequent purchaser or incumbrancer, and shall be bound by all proceedings taken after the filing of such notice to the same extent as if he were a party to the action. For the purpose of this section an action shall be deemed to be pending from the time of filing such notice, *Provided, however,* That such notice shall be of no avail unless it shall be followed by the first publication of the summons, or by the personal service thereof, on a defendant within sixty days after such filing. And the court in which the said action was commenced, may at any time on application of any person aggrieved and on good cause shown, and on such notice as shall be directed or approved by the court order the notice authorized by this section to be canceled of record in whole or in part by the Register of Deeds of any county in whose office the same may have been filed or recorded, and such cancellation shall be made by an endorsement to that effect on the margin of the record, which shall refer to the order, and for which the Register of Deeds shall be entitled to a fee of twenty-five cents.

§ 2. This act shall take effect and be in force from and after its passage and approval.

Approved, March 13, 1885.

NOTICE OF PENDENCY OF ACTION.

CHAPTER 118.

AN ACT to Amend Section One Hundred and One (101), of Chapter Nine (9), of the Code of Civil Procedure.

Be it enacted by the Legislative Assembly of the Territory of Dakota:

§ 1. FILE FOR RECORD.] That section one hundred and one (101), of the Code of Civil Procedure of the Territory of Dakota be, and the same is, hereby amended by inserting after the words " may file," where they occur in said section, the following words : " for record."

§ 2. This act to take effect and be in force from and after its passage and approval.

Approved, February 19, 1885.

1885—23

Notice of Motion.

CHAPTER 119.

AN ACT to Amend Section Five Hundred and Eleven of the Code of Civil Procedure.

Be it enacted by the Legislative Assembly of the Territory of Dakota:

§ 1. SERVING NOTICE.] That section five hundred and eleven of the code of civil procedure of the Territory of Dakota is hereby amended so as to read as follows:

§ 511. When notice of motion is necessary it must be served eight days before the time appointed for the hearing, but the court or judge may, by order to show cause, prescribe a shorter time.

Approved, March 9, 1885.

Official Bonds.

CHAPTER 120.

AN ACT providing for the Recording of the Official Bonds of Civil Officers

Be it enacted by the Legislative Assembly of the Territory of Dakota:

§ 1. BONDS TO BE RECORDED AT LENGTH.] The bonds of all county, township and precinct officers, immediately after the approval of the same, shall be recorded at length in the office of the register of deeds of the county to which such bonds are given, in a book to be provided and kept for that purpose. When the said bonds are so recorded they shall be forthwith filed respectively as provided in section 5, of chapter V of the political code.

§ 2. BONDS NOW ON FILE TO BE RECORDED.] Upon the taking effect of this act the bonds of all such officers as are now in office, shall be taken from the files by the persons having the custody of the same, recorded at length by the register of deeds as provided in section 1, of this act, and thereupon returned forthwith to the files from which they were taken respectively.

§ 3. FEE FOR RECORDING.] That the register of deeds shall be entitled to charge and receive a fee of fifty (50) cents for recording each official bond recorded by him pursuant to this act to be paid by the principal in said bond.

§ 4. This act shall take effect and be in force from and after its passage and approval.

Approved, February 26, 1885.

Opium.

CHAPTER 121.

AN ACT in regard to the Selling and Smoking of Opium.

Be it enacted by the Legislative Assembly of the Territory of Dakota.

§ 1. UNLAWFUL TO SELL OPIUM WITHOUT PERMIT.] It shall be unlawful for any person by himself, by agent or otherwise, to either directly or indirectly sell or give away opium or any other commodity of which opium is an ingredient, unless the person so selling or giving away the said article has a written permit or license from the authorities of the city or town in which such person carries on business or from the board of county commissioners of the county wherein said person resides, in case he does not carry on business in any city or town, and unless the person to whom opium or other articles are sold or given away shall obtain and present to the person selling the same a prescription for the said articles in writing, signed by a reputable practising physician.

§ 2. UNLAWFUL TO SMOKE OPIUM.] It shall be unlawful for any person to smoke opium or any commodity whatever of which opium is an ingredient.

§ 3 UNLAWFUL TO ALLOW PREMISES TO BE USED FOR OPIUM SMOKING.] It shall be unlawful for any person owning or having in charge or possession any room, building, cellar, or other place or premises, to permit opium or any commodity of which opium .

is an ingredient to be smoked in, upon or about such place or premises.

§ 4. Penalty.] Any person violating the provisions of section one, two or three of this act shall be guilty of a misdemeanor and upon conviction thereof shall be punished by a fine not exceeding one hundred dollars or by imprisonment in the county jail not exceeding thirty days, or both such fine and imprisonment.

§ 5. Places used for opium smoking a nuisance.] Any room, building, cellar or other place or premises used or permitted to be used for smoking of opium or any commodity of which opium is an ingredient, shall be considered and is hereby declared a public nuisance: and the district court or the judge thereof may at any time, upon satisfactory proof that the smoking or use of opium is permitted or carried on in any such premises, order and cause any such premises to be abated as a public nuisance.

§ 6. Jurisdiction.] Justices of the peace shall have concurrent jurisdiction with the district court to hear, try and determine any case arising under this act within their county. It is hereby made the especial duty of all ministerial officers to enter complaint in each case of the violation of this act, and they are hereby required to ascertain by inquiry and examination as to any such violations.

§ 3. This act shall take effect and be in force from and after its passage and approval.

Approved, March 13, 1885.

Passage Tickets.

CHAPTER 122.

AN ACT Relative to Dealing in Passage Tickets.

Be it enacted by the Legislative Assembly of the Territory of Dakota:

§ 1. Right to deal in passage tickets.] Any person having an established place of business in any village, town, or city within this Territory, shall have the right to buy, sell and exchange passage tickets or other evidences of a right of passage from one place to another upon any railroad line or steamboat line and their connections that said tickets may have been regularly issued over and for.

§ 2. THAT PURCHASERS MAY SELL.] Any person purchasing a ticket from the authorized office of any line for the transportation ol passengers, shall have the right to sell his ticket or tickets to any person doing business under this act; *Provided*, That nothing in this act shall be construed to prevent any incorporated village, town or city to regulate this business by any law deemed necessary for the protection of the public.

§ 3. ACTS IN CONFI ICT REPEALED.] All acts or parts of acts conflicting with the provisions of this act be and the same are hereby repealed.

§ 4. This act shall take effect and be in force from and after its passage and approval.

Approved, March 13, 1885.

Penitentiary.

SIOUX FALLS—GOVERNMENT OF.

CHAPTER 123.

AN ACT to Repeal Section Two and Amend Section Twelve of Chapter One Hundred and Four of the Session Laws ol 1881.

Be it enacted by the Legislative Assembly of the Territory of Dakota:

§ 1. REPEALED.] That section two of chapter one hundred and four of the session laws of 1881, entitled "An act to locate and provide for the building and government of a territorial penitentiary," is hereby repealed.

§ 2. DIRECTORS APPOINTED—VACANCIES.] That the penitentiary at Sioux Falls, Dakota, shall be under the direction and government of five directors who shall be appointed by the Governor of the Territory, with the advice and consent of the Council. Said directors to hold their office for the term of two years or until their successors are appointed and qualified, and in case a vacancy shall occur in the position of director, such vacancy shall be filled by the other members of the board who shall vote by ballot in filling such vacancy, which person so elected shall hold his office until the end of the next Legislative Assembly thereafter or until his successor is elected and qualified.

§ 3. OFFICERS, OF WHOM TO CONSIST.] That section twelve of chapter one hundred and four of the laws of 1881 is hereby amended so as to read as follows: The officers of the prison shall consist of five directors, one warden, one deputy warden, one gate keeper, one turnkey and such guards, overseers and laborers as may be necessary ; *Provided, however,* That the present directors shall continue to serve until their successors under this act are appointed and qualify

Approved, February 20, 1885.

CARE OF UNITED STATES PRISONERS.

CHAPTER 124.

AN ACT to Authorize the Directors of the Penitentiary at Sioux Falls to Make a Contract with the United States for the Care of United States Prisoners, and to Rent the United States Wing to said Penitentiary.

Be it enacted by the Legislative Assembly of the Territory of Dakota :

§ 1. DIRECTORS MAY MAKE CONTRACT.] The directors oi the penitentiary at Sioux Falls are hereby authorized to rent the United States wing of the penitentiary at Sioux Falls, upon such terms and conditions as they may deem for the best interests of the Territory. Said directors are also authorized to contract with the United States for the support and care of United States prisoners at said penitentiary.

§ 2. This act shall take effect and be in force from and after its passage and approval.

Approved, March 13, 1885.

Proof of Service.

CHAPTER 125.

AN ACT to Amend Section 107 of the Code of Civil Procedure.

Be it enacted by the Legislative Assembly of the Territory of Dakota :

§ 1. CERTIFICATE OF PERSON SERVING.] That section 107 of the Code of Civil Procedure, be and the same is hereby amended by inserting the words " or other officer," after the word " sheriff " in subdivision 1 of said section.

Approved, March 13, 1885.

Railroad Commission.

CHAPTER 126.

AN ACT to Provide for the Establishment of a Board of Railroad Commissioners, defining their duties, and to Regulate the Receiving and Transportation of Freight on Railroads in this Territory.

Be it enacted by the Legislative Assembly of the Territory of Dakota :

§ 1. APPOINTMENT OF COMMISSIONERS.] The Governor, with the advice and consent of the council, shall bi-ennially appoint three competent persons, who shall constitute a board of railroad commissioners, and who shall hold their office for the term of two years from the first of April next after such appointment. The Governor shall, by appointment, fill any vacancy caused by death, removal or resignation ; said commissioners shall hold their offices until their successors are duly appointed and qualified. No person owning stock, bonds or other property in any railroad company, or who is in the employment of, or who is in any manner pecuniarily interested in any railroad corporation, public ware house or elevator, shall be eligible to the office of railroad commissioner. Said commissioners shall be selected, so nearly as practicable, one from the southern, one from the central, and one from the northern part of the Territory.

§ 2. POWERS OF COMMISSIONERS.] Said commissioners shall have general supervision of all railroads in the Territory and shall inquire into any neglect or violation of the laws of this Territory by any railroad corporation, its officers, agents or (employes doing business therein, and shall from time to time carefully examine and inspect the condition of each railroad in the Territory, and the manner of its conduct and management, with reference to its safety and general relations to the public business of the Territory.

§ 3. DUTY OF COMMISSIONERS.] Whenever in the judgment of the railroad commissioners, it shall appear that any railroad corporation fails in any respect or particular to comply with the laws of the Territory, or its charter, or when, in their judgment, any repairs are necessary upon its road, or any addition to its rolling stock, or any addition or change in its station houses, or any change in the rates of passenger fare or its charges for transporting freight or transferring the same from one road or station to another, or any change in the manner of operating its road and conducting its business, is reasonable and expedient in order to promote security, convenience and accommodation of the public, said commissioners shall inform such railroad corporation of the improvements and changes which they deem to be proper, by notice in writing, to be served by leaving a copy thereof, certified by the commissioners' clerk, with any station agent, clerk or treasurer, or any director of said corporation, and a report of the proceedings shall be included in the report of the railroad commissioners to the legislature. Nothing in this section shall be construed as relieving any railroad company from their present responsibility or liability for damage to persons or property.

§ 4. REPORTS—WHAT TO CONTAIN.] The said railroad commissioners shall, on or before the first Monday in December in each year, make a report to the Governor of their doings for the preceding year, containing such facts, statements and explanations as will disclose the workings of the system of railroad transportation in the Territory, and its relation to the general business and prosperity of the citizens of the Territory; and such suggestions and recommendations in respect thereto as may to them seem appropriate. Said report shall also contain as to every railroad corporation doing business in this Territory:

1. The amount of its capital stock.
2. The amount of its preferred, if any, and the amount of its preferment.
3. The amount of its funded debt and the rate of interest.
4. The amount of its floating debt.

5. The cost and present value of its road and equipment, including permanent way buildings and rolling stock, all real estate used exclusively in operating the road, and all fixtures and conveniences for transacting its business. .

6. The estimated cash value of all property owned by such corporation, with a schedule of the same, not including lands granted in aid of its construction.

7. The number of acres originally granted in aid of construction of its road, by the United States or by this Territory.

8. Number of acres of such land remaining unsold

9. A list of its officers and directors with their respective places of residence.

10. Such statistics of the road and of its transportation business for the year, as may in the judgment of the commissioners be necessary and proper for the information of the Legislative Assembly or as may be required by the Governor. Such report shall exhibit and refer to the condition of such corporation on the first day of July of each year, and the details of its transportation business transacted during the year ending June 0th.

11. The average amount of tonnage that can be carried over each road in the Territory with an engine of given power.

§ 5. RAILROAD OFFICERS TO MAKE REPORT] To enable said commissioners to make such report, the president or managing officer of each railroad corporation doing business in this Territory, shall annually make to the said commissioners, on the 15th day of the month of September, such returns, in the form which they may prescribe, as will afford the information required for their said official report. Such returns shall be verified by the oath of the officer making them, and any railroad corporation whose returns shall not be made as herein prescribed by the 15th day of September shall be liable to a penalty of one hundred (100) dollars for each and every day after the 16th day of December, that such returns shall be willfully delayed or refused.

§ 6. PRINCIPAL OFFICER—SALARY.] The said commissioners shall hold their office at such place as they shall determine; they shall each receive a salary of $2,000 to be paid as the salaries of their territorial officers are paid, and shall be provided at the expense of the Territory with necessary office furniture and stationery, and they shall have authority to appoint a secretary who shall receive a salary of fifteen hundred (1,500) dollars per annum.

§ 7. OATH AND BOND.] The said commissioners and secretary shall be sworn to the due and faithful performance of the duties of their respective offices before entering upon the discharge of the same; and no person in the employ of any railroad cor-

1885—24

poration, or holding stock in any railroad corporation, shall be employed as secretary. Each of said commissioners shall enter into bonds, with security to be approved by the Governor, in the sum of ten thousand (10,000) dollars, conditioned for the faithful performance of his duties.

§ 8. POWER TO EXAMINE BOOKS.] The said commissioners shall have power, in the discharge of the duties of their office, to examine any of the books, papers or documents of any such corporation, or to examine under oath or otherwise, any officer, director, agent or employe of any such corporation. They are empowered to issue subpœnas and administer oaths in the same manner, and with the same power to force obedience thereto in the performance of their said duties, as belong and pertain to courts of law in this Territory, and any person who may willfully obstruct said commissioners in the performance of their duties. or who may refuse to give any information within his possession that may be required by said commissioners, within the line of their duty, shall be deemed guilty of a misdemeanor, and shall be liable, on conviction thereof, to a fine not exceeding one thousand ($1,000) dollars, in the discretion of the court, and the cost of such subpœnas and investigation, to be first paid by the Territory, on the certificate of said commissioners. Said commissioners shall have power, and it is hereby made their duty, in all cases where they find, on due investigation, that any rate char ed by any company or corporation is exorbitant, unjust or oppressive, to alter or lower the same, and fix a maximum; no railroad company shall charge or receive from any person a higher rate per ton per mile for one car load of freight than for a greater number of car loads per car.

§ 9. RAILROAD COMPANIES REQUIRED TO FURNISH CARS TO ALL PERSONS, ETC.] It shall be the duty of all railroad corporations doing business in this Territory, upon reasonable notice, to furnish suitable cars to any and all persons who may apply therefor for the transportation of any and all kinds of freight, and to secure and transport such freight with all reasonable dispatch, and provide and keep suitable facilities for the securing and handling of the same at any depot on the line of its road, and also to receive and transport in like manner the empty and loaded cars furnished by any connecting line of road, to be delivered at any station or stations on the line of its road, to be loaded or discharged, or reloaded and returned to the road so connecting, and for compensation it shall not demand or receive any greater sum than is accepted by it from any other connecting railroad for similar service.

§ 10 SHALL TRANSPORT GRAIN.] Any railroad company doing business in this Territory, when desired by any person wishing to ship grain over its road, shall receive and transport such grain in bulk within a reasonable time, and permit the same to be loaded either on its track adjacent to its depot, or at any warehouse or side track without distinction, discrimination or favor between one shipper and another, and without discrimination or distinction as to the manner in which such grain is offered for transportation, or as to the person, warehouse, elevator, or the place where or to which it may be consigned. Every railroad company shall permit connections to be made and maintained in a reasonable manner with its track, to and from any warehouse, elevator or mill adjacent to any station on its line, without reference to its size or capacity, where grain or flour is or may be stored; *Provided, however*, That such railroad company shall not be required to pay the cost of making and maintaining said connection, or of the siding or switch-track necessary to make the same; and *Provided, further*, That a majority of the commissioners appointed under this act shall direct such railroad to make such connection and siding. Grain shall also be received from wagons or sleighs in car load lots, the same as when offered from warehouses or elevators, allowing reasonable time for loading the cars, and the cars shall be placed in a convenient place, easy of access.

§ 11. SHALL NOT DISCRIMINATE.] No railroad corporation shall charge, demand or receive from any person, company or corporation, for the transportation of persons or property, or for any other service, a greater sum than it shall at the same time charge, demand or receive from any other person, company or corporation for a like service from the same place, and all concession of rates, rebates, drawbacks and contracts for special rates shall be open to and allowed to all persons, companies and corporations, and they shall charge no more for transporting from any point on its line than a fair and just proportion of the price it charges for the same kind of freight transported from any other point of equal distance within the Territory.

§ 12. CHARGES SHALL BE REASONABLE.] No railroad company shall charge, demand or receive from any company or corporation an unreasonable price for the transportation of persons or property, or for the handling or storage of freight, or for the use of its cars, or for any privilege or services afforded by it in the transaction of its business as a railroad corporation, and shall not demand the payment of freight beyond the point to which the goods or property is consigned by the shipper.

§ 13. PENALTY FOR EXTORTION.] Any railroad corporation which shall violate any of the provisions of this act as to extortion or unjust discrimination, shall forfeit for every such offense to the person, company or corporation aggrieved thereby, three times the actual damage sustained or overcharges paid by the said party aggrieved, together with costs of suit and a reasonable attorney's fee, to be fixed by the court, and if an appeal is taken from the judgment, or any part thereof, it shall be the duty of the appellate court to include in the judgment an additional attorney's fee for service in the appellate court or courts therefor. And in all cases where complaint is made in accordance with the provisions of section 14 hereinafter provided, that an unreasonable charge or regulation is made, the commissioners shall require a modified charge or regulation, such as they shall deem reasonable, and in all cases of a failure to comply with the recommendations of the commissioners, shall be embodied with the report of the commissioners to the Legislature, and shall apply to any unjust discrimination, extortion or over charge by said company, or other violation of law.

§ 14.   DUTY OF COMMISSIONERS ON COMPLAINT.]   Upon complaint of the mayor and alderman of any city, or board of county commissioners, or of the trustees, or supervisors of any town or township, of the freight tariff charged, or of any injustice to the public, growing out of any rule or regulation of a railroad company, it shall be the duty of the commissioners, in case they deem the case just and reasonable, to proceed to make examination, first giving the petitioners and corporation reasonable notice in writing of the time and place of entering upon the same. If upon examination it shall appear to said commissioners that the complaint of the petitioners is well founded, they shall so find, and shall inform the corporation operating such railroad of their adjudication within ten days, and shall also report their action to the Governor as provided in this act. All sleeping car companies, express companies and telegraph companies doing business in this Territory shall make such reports of their business as the railroad commissioners may require; and said commissioners shall have the same authority over and supervision of all sleeping car companies, express companies and telegraph companies doing business in this Territory, as over railroad corporations.

§ 15.   PROVISIONS OF THIS ACT TO GOVERN.]   All railroad companies operating any lines of road in this Territory are hereby declared subject to the provisions of this act, and the commissioners herein provided for are authorized and it is made their duty to enforce its provisions in the courts of this Territory; and it is made the duty of the district attorney, or in case of his neglect or refusal, the attorney general, to prosecute any and all violations of its provisions upon complaint being made by said commissioners.

§ 16.   THIS ACT HOW CONSTRUED.]   Nothing in this act shall be construed to estop or hinder any person or corporation from bringing suit against any railroad company for any violation of the laws of this Territory for the government of railroads.

§ 17. All acts and parts of acts inconsistent with this act are hereby repealed.

§ 18. This act shall take effect and be in force from and after its passage and approval.

Approved, March 6, 1885.

CHAPTER 127.

AN ACT to Amend an act entitled " An act to Provide for the Establishment of a Board of Railroad Commissioners, Defining their Duties and to Regulate the Receiving and Transportation of Freight on Railroads in this Territory," approved March 6, A. D. 1885.

Be it enacted by the Legislative Assembly of the Territory of Dakota :

§ 1. PROVISION REPEALED.] Section eight (8) of an act of the Legislative Assembly of this Territory, approved March 6, A. D. 1885, entitled "An act t · provide for the establishment of a Board of Railroad Commissioners, defining their duties and to regulate the receiving and transportation of freight on railroads in this Territory," is hereby amended by striking out the following words : " Said commissioners shall have power and it is hereby made their duty in all cases, where they find on due investigation that any rate charged by any company or corporation is exorbitant, unjust or oppressive, to alter or lower the same, and fix a maximum.

§ 2. This act shall take effect and be in force from and after its passage and approval.

Approved, March 13, 1885.

Roads.

HIGHWAY LABOR.

CHAPTER 128.

AN ACT to Amend Sections 12 and 21 of Sub-chapter II, of Chapter 112 of the Session Laws of 1883.

Be it enacted by the Legislative Assembly of the Territory of Dakota:

§ 1. PERSONS LIABLE.] Section 12 of sub-chapter II, of chapter 112 of the session laws of 1883, is hereby amended by striking out the word "sixty" and insert in lieu thereof the word "fifty" where the same refers to the age of persons liable to highway labor.

§ 2. HOURS OF LABOR.] Section 21, sub-chapter II of chapter 112 of the session laws of 1883, is hereby amended by striking out the word "ten" and inserting in lieu thereof the word "eight" where the same refers to the number of hours necessary to constitute a day's labor on the highway.

§ 3. This act shall take effect and be in force from and after its passage and approval.

Approved, March 10, 1885.

Revenue.

PERSONAL PROPERTY—WHERE TO BE ASSESSED.

CHAPTER 129.

AN ACT to Amend Section 17 of Chapter 28 of the Political Code, and for other purposes.

Be it enacted by the Legislative Assembly of the Territory of Dakota:

§ 1. That section 17 of chapter 28 of the Political Code entitled " Revenue " is hereby amended to read as follows : § 17. Property listed, assessed and taxed, when—where. All personal property is to be listed, assessed and taxed in the county where said property may be situated and kept on the first day of April of the then current year, and if the owner, his agent or person having charge of such property neglects to list it he will be subject to the penalty hereinafter provided.

§ 2. IN UNORGANIZED COUNTY.] When any personal property is situated and kept in any unorganized county of this Territory then such property shall be subject to taxation in the nearest organized county thereto and shall be listed and assessed by the assessor of said nearest organized county; and when said unorganized county borders upon two or more organized counties, then sald property shall be assessed and taxed in that organized county having the greatest extent of contiguous boundary line.

§ 3. MISDEMEANOR.] If any assessor or county commissioner shall enter into any contract, agreement or understanding with the owner or his agent of any personal property, whereby and pursuant to which such property is to be assessed at less than its cash value in consideration that the owner or owners of such property shall remove or cause to be removed said property for the purpose of taxation into the county of said assessor or commissioner, such assessor or commissioner, and the owner of such property, and all persons aiding or abetting such corrupt transaction and agreement shall be deemed guilty of a misdemeanor, and upon conviction thereof shall be punished by a fine of not less than five hundred dollars and by imprisonment in the county jail for not less than three months nor more than six months

§ 4. All acts and parts of acts inconsistent with this act are hereby repealed.

§ 5. This act to take effect and be in force from and after its passage and approval.

Approved, March 12, 1885.

TAX SALES IMPROPERLY MADE.

CHAPTER 130.

AN ACT to Amend Section 78 of Chapter 28 of the Political Code.

Be it enacted by the Legislative Assembly of the Territory of Dakota:

§ 1. INTEREST ALLOWED.] That section seventy-eight of chapter twenty-eight of the Political Code, is amended by striking out after the word "interest" in the fourth line of said section, the words "to which he would have been entitled had the land been rightfully sold," and insert in lieu thereof the words, "at the rate of twelve per cent. per annum from the date of sale."

§ 2. This act shall take effect and be in force from and after its passage and approval.

Approved, March 12, 1885.

COUNTY TO PURCHASE AT TAX SALE.

CHAPTER 131.

AN ACT Authorizing the County Treasurer in each of the Counties in this Territory at all tax sales thereafter to be made under the laws of this Territory, to bid off any or all Real Estate offered at said sales for the amount of the taxes due and unpaid thereon, in the name of the County in which said sale takes place, in case there are no other bidders for the same and to provide for the transfer or redemption thereof

Be it enacted by the Legislative Assembly of the Territory of Dakota:

§ 1. COUNTY TREASURER MAY PURCHASE—WHEN.] That the county treasurer of each county within this Territory is hereby authorized at all tax sales hereafter made under the laws of this Territory in case there are no other bidders offering the amount due, to bid off all or any real estate offered at said sale for the amount of taxes, penalty, interests and costs due and unpaid thereon in the name of the county in which the sale takes place, said county acquiring all the rights both legal and equitable that any other purchaser could acquire by reason of said purchase.

§ 2. REDEMPTION.] That in case the owner of said real estate or any person having any legal or equitable interest therein is desirous of redeeming said real estate from said county, they shall have the right so to do any time within two years from the date of sale by paying the amount of taxes, penalty, interest and cost of sale up to date of redemption, and upon the payment thereof the said county treasurer is hereby required to give to the person so redeeming a certificate of redemption and to mark upon the tax duplicate that is kept in his office opposite the description of said real estate where said description is entered upon said duplicate, the word "redeemed" and the date when the same was done.

§ 3. TREASURER MAY SELL CERTIFICATE.] That if any person is desirous of purchasing the interest of said county in said real estate acquired by reason of said county treasurer bidding the same off in the name of and for said county, he may do so by paying to said county treasurer the amount of the taxes, penalty, interest and costs of sale and transfer up to the date he so pays, and thereupon the said treasurer shall and it is hereby made his duty to assign and deliver to said purchaser the certificate of purchase held by said county for said real estate, which assignment and transfer shall convey unto said purchaser all rights of said county both legal and equitable in and to said real estate as much so as if he had been the original purchaser at said tax sale.

§ 4. CERTIFICATE OF PURCHASE TO COUNTY.] That whenever the county treasurer of any county shall bid off any real estate in the name of his county, he shall make out a certificate of purchase to said county just as he is required to do if the sale had been made to any other person, but he shall retain the same in his office until transferred as provided in section three of this act.

§ 5. CERTAIN TAXES NOT PAYABLE] That no amount due the Territory or any other fund, costs or treasurer's commission shall be payable by the county until redemption is made from such sale or the time for redemption has expired, or until the interest of said county has been transferred or assigned as provided in section three of this act.

§ 6. All acts or parts of acts inconsistent with this act are hereby repealed.

§ 7. This act to take effect and be in force from and after its passage and approval.

Approved, March 7, 1885.

1885—25

POSTPONING THE TIME WHEN TAXES OF 1884 BECOME DUE.

CHAPTER 132.

AN ACT Extending the Time in which Taxes shall Become Delinquent for the Year 1884.

Be it enacted by the Legislative Assembly of the Territory of Dakota :

§ 1. EXTENDED TO JUNE 1.] That the date on which taxes of all kinds levied for the year 1884 shall become delinquent and a penalty attach for non-payment is hereby extended to June 1, 1885, at the end of which time the same proceedings shall be had as would regularly be taken under the present law.

§ 2. This act shall not apply to taxes due from railroad and telegraph companies.

Approved, January 31, 1885.

School of Mines.

CHAPTER 133.

AN ACT to Locate, Establish and Endow a School of Mines for the Territory of Dakota.

Be it enacted by the Legislative Assembly of the Territory of Dakota :

§ 1. SCHOOL OF MINES ESTABLISHED.] That a School of Mines for the Territory of Dakota be established at Rapid City, in Pennington county, Dakota Territory. It shall be the object of such school of mines to furnish facilities for the education of such persons as may desire to receive special instruction in chemistry, metallurgy, mineralogy, geology, mining, milling, engineering, mathematics, mechanics, drawing, the fundamental laws of the United States, and the rights and duties of citizens ; *Provided,* That a tract of land of not less than five acres within the corporate limits of said Rapid City, or immediately adjacent to said corporate limits, be donated and secured to the Territory of Dakota in fee simple as a site for said Schoo! of Mines, within six months from the taking effect of this act, and the Governor of the Territory is hereby authorized and it is made his duty to see that a good and sufficient deed be made to the Territory for the same.

§ 2. TRUSTEES.] The Governor of the Territory, with the advice and consent of the council, shall appoint a board of trustees of said school of mines, to be composed of five persons, who shall, except as hereinafter provided, hold their office for a period of two years, and until their successors are appointed and qualified. Any three of said board of trustees shall constitute a quorum for the transaction of business, and the said board shall have such powers and perform such duties as are herein specified.

§ 3. OATH] Every trustee appointed shall, before he enters upon the duties of his office. take and subscribe an oath to support the constitution of the United States and Organic act of Dakota Territory, and to perform faithfully the duties of his office to the best of his ability and understanding.

§ 4. POWERS OF TRUSTEES.] That said board of trustees shall have the control and management of said school of mines, and of the property belonging thereto, subject to the laws of this Territory, and may provide all needful rules, regulations and by-laws for the government of said board, and for the government and management of said school of mines, not inconsistent with the laws of this Territory.

§ 5. AUTHORITY TO BUILD.] The board of trustees is hereby authorized and it is made its duty to begin at once the erection and construction of a suitable building for said school of mines, upon the ground specified in this act, as a site for the same, as soon as sufficient appropriation is secured for the erection thereof, and also to procure such machinery and other appliances as may be necessary to carry out the object and intention of said institution, and to promote the welfare thereof, whenever the funds provided for the support of said school of mines shall warrant the same; *Provided,* That all contracts connected with the erection and construction of said building shall be let to the lowest responsible bidder, after notice of the letting of said contract shall have been published in at least two newspapers located in the western part of the Territory, for at least thirty days before the letting of said contract, and the board may reject any or all bids and advertise anew.

§ 6. PUPILS.] The said school of mines shall be a place for instruction without charge, to all *bona fide* residents of this Territory, without regard to sex or color, and with the consent of said board, students from other states or territories may be admitted thereto, upon such terms and upon such rates for tuition as the board may prescribe.

§ 7. OFFICERS.] The said board at their first meeting, and biennially thereafter, shall elect one of their number president of such board, and shall also appoint a secretary and treasurer either from their own number or other suitable persons, as they may deem best, and prescribe their duties, and may, in their discretion, remove such secretary and treasurer; and the trustees hereby appointed shall hold their first meeting as soon as practicable after this act shall take effect. All meetings of said board shall be held at Rapid City, in the county of Pennington, in this Territory.

§ 8. GOVERNOR TO APPOINT.] The Governor of this Territory, with the advice and consent of the council, shall at each regular session of the Legislative Assembly of Dakota Territory, appoint suitable persons to fill all vacancies in said board of trustees, either by expiration of their term of office or otherwise, and any vacancies occuring in said board when [the] Legislative Assembly is not in session, may be temporarily filled by the Governor until the next meeting of the Legislative Assembly

§ 9. REPORT.] The board of trustees shall elect a president of the school of mines who shall bi-ennially on or before the 30th day of December in each year, make a report to the Governor of this Territory of the prosperity and condition of said school of mines, containing such statistical and other information pertaining thereto as may be deemed necessary and useful, and also a detailed statement of the receipts and disbursements of such institution.

§ 10. PROPOSALS FOR BUILDING.] Whenever any building is to be erected the board of trustees shall have authority to procure all necessary plans and specifications for such building, and it shall be their duty to advertise for proposals for the erection and completion of said building in such manner as they shall deem most advantageous, and shall let the contract for the erection of said building to the lowest responsible bidder. Such contractor in every case to give adequate security for the faithful performance of his contract; and the said board of trustees shall have authority to appoint a building superintendent, whose duty it shall be to superintend the construction of said building in compliance with the terms of the contract, and to perform such other duties as shall be prescribed by the said board of trustees, and such building superintendent shall receive such compensation for his services as the board of trustees shall determine, and such compensation shall be paid out of the building fund.

§ 11. BOND OF TREASURER.] The said board of trustees shall require the treasurer of the school of mines to give such bonds as may be deemed sufficient to protect such institution against loss of any funds which may come into his hands as such treasurer, conditioned for the safe keeping and faithful disbursement thereof, and the said treasurer of the school of mines shall not pay out any of the funds which shall come into his hands as such treasurer, except upon the order of the president of the school of mines, countersigned by the secretary thereof.

§ 12. FEES FOR ASSAYING.] It shall be lawful for the dean of the said school of mines, who shall be appointed by the board of trustees, to charge and collect such reasonable fees for any and all assays, analysis or mill-tests made at the school of mines, as the said board may prescribe, an account of which shall be kept by said dean and paid over monthly to the treasurer of said school of mines, which shall become a part of the school of mines fund.

§ 13. FUND TO BE USED—HOW.] The school of mines fund shall be used solely for the support of the school of mines and for no other purpose whatever.

§ 14. SUBORDINATE OFFICERS.] Said board of trustees shall have power to appoint a dean and such other instructors and officers as may be required, and fix the salaries of each and prescribe their several duties. They shall also have the power to remove said dean and any or all of said instructors or officers and appoint others in their stead. They shall prescribe the books of instruction to be used in said school of mines, and shall make all needful rules, regulations and by-laws necessary for the good government and management of the same.

§ 15. PUBLIC NOTICE OF OPENING.] As soon as said school of mines is prepared to receive pupils for instruction, the president of the board of trustees shall give notice of the fact to each county clerk in the Territory, and shall also publish said notice in at least one newspaper in each judicial district in said Territory.

§ 16. PER DIEM.] For performing the duties prescribed by this act each member of the said board of trustees shall be entitled to three dollars per day for the days actually and necessarily employed, and five cents for each mile necessarily traveled in attending meetings of said board.

§ 17. MEETINGS.] The board of trustees shall hold two regular meetings in each year on the first Tuesday of June and December, and special meetings of the board may be called upon the written order of the president, which order shall specify the object of the meeting. All financial matters, claims and accounts shall be disposed of at such board meetings. A true and faithful journal of all their proceedings, shall be kept, subject at any reasonable time to the inspection of any member of the board.

§ 18. BONDS TO BE ISSUED.] That for the purpose of providing funds to pay the cost of construction and erection of a main building of the school of mines at Rapid City, Dakota Territory, the territorial Treasurer is hereby authorized and empowered, and it is hereby made his duty to prepare for issue ten thousand dollars of territorial bonds, running for a term or period of twenty years, and payable at the option of the Territory after a term of ten years, and bearing interest at the rate of six per cent per annum with coupons attached, made payable semi-annually on the first day of July and January, of each year, at the Chemical National Bank in the city of New York. Such bonds shall be executed under the seal of the Territory by the Governor and Treasurer and shall be attested by the Secretary and shall be negotiated by the Treasurer of the Territory.

§ 19. PROPOSALS FOR BONDS.] It shall be the duty of the treasurer to receive sealed proposals for the purchase of said bonds, and upon request of the board of trustees, he shall give public notice for thirty days in two newspapers of general circulation, one of which shall be published in the city of New York, and said bonds shall be sold to the highest bidder for cash, at not less than par.

§ 20. PROVIDING FOR PAYMENT.] For the purpose of prompt payment of principal and interest of the bonds herein provided for, there shall be levied by the territorial board of equalization at the time the other taxes are levied and collected in the same manner that other territorial taxes are collected, such sums as shall be sufficient to pay such interest and exchange thereon, and after ten years from the first day of May, 1885, in addition thereto a sinking fund tax shall be annually levied sufficient to pay and retire said bonds at their maturity; and it shall be the duty of the territorial Treasurer to pay promptly on the first days of July and January of each year, such interest as shall then be due, and to purchase said bonds at their market value, and retire and cancel the same with the sinking fund tax as fast as the same shall be received, and no tax or fund provided for the payment of said bonds, either principal or interest, shall at any time be used for any other purpose.

§ 21. PAYMENT OF INTEREST.] If for any reason the territorial Treasurer shall not have in his hands sufficient funds herein provided to pay the interest upon such bonds when due, he shall pay such interest out of any unappropriated funds belonging to the Territory: and there is hereby appropriated and set apart out of the general funds of the Territory a sum sufficient to pay such interest on said bonds as may become due before the funds and taxes herein provided for can be made available; and it shall be made the duty of said Treasurer to pay such interest promptly, at the time it falls due, out of said funds.

§ 22. CERTAIN FUNDS TO BE REPLACED.] All moneys belonging to the territorial general fund, applied by said Treasurer in payment of the interest on such bonds, shall be replaced from the special tax levied to pay the same.

§ 23. APPROPRIATION.] There is hereby appropriated out of the territorial treasury all the funds realized by the sale of the bonds provided by this act; and the board of trustees shall, within ninety days after the passage of this act, proceed to secure and adopt plans, and begin the erection and construction of said building, with all the powers in the premises conferred by this act upon said board of trustees, or any of its officers.

§ 24. AUDITOR TO DRAW WARRANTS.] It shall be the duty of the Auditor of the Territory, upon the application of the board of trustees of the school of mines, or a majority thereof, to draw warrants upon the territorial Treasurer for the purpose of constructing said building, and for the purpose of carrying out the provisions of this act; *Provided, however*, That a good and sufficient deed in fee simple, free to the Territory, shall first be made for the tract of land hereinbefore specified.

§ 25. IN CASE OF DIVISION.] In case of a division of the Territory of Dakota, that part of said Territory in which said school of mines is located after such division, shall assume and pay all bonds and coupons existing at that time by reason of the erection of the building herein provided for.

§ 26. This act shall take effect and be in force from and after its passage and approval.

Approved, March 7, 1885.

Sheep Husbandry.

LIABILITY FOR DAMAGES OCCASIONED BY VICIOUS DOG.

CHAPTER 134.

AN ACT to Amend Section Seven of Chapter Sixty-three of the Laws of 1881, entitled "An act for the Protection and Encouragement of Sheep Husbandry and Providing Bounty for Wolf Scalps," approved February 14, 1881.

Be it enacted by the Legislative Assembly of the Territory of Dakota :

§ 1. OWNER OF DOG, LIABLE.] That section seven of "An act for the protection and encouragement of sheep husbandry and providing a bounty for wolf scalps," approved February 14, 1881, be and the same is hereby amended to read as follows : § 7. That any person keeping, owning or harboring a dog that shall chase, worry or kill sheep shall be liable for all damages committed by such dog upon any sheep, to the owner of such sheep, and shall not be entitled to any benefit from the laws exempting property from execution, but all property shall be subject to execution on judgment for such damages and costs.

§ 2. This act shall take effect and be in force from and after its passage and approval.

Approved, March 13, 1885.

Sheep Inspectors.

CHAPTER 185.

AN ACT to Provide for the Appointment of Sheep Inspectors.

Be it enacted by the Legislative Assembly of Dakota Territory :

§ 1. APPOINTMENT AND TERM OF OFFICE.] The county commissioners may, if they deem it expedient, appoint a sheep inspector who shall be a citizen of the county for which he is appointed, for each county containing two thousand sheep, who shall hold his office for two years unless sooner removed. And any inspector may act in an adjoining county having no inspector on request of the commissioners thereof.

§ 2. DUTIES OF SHEEP INSPECTORS.] It shall be the duty of the sheep inspector whenever he has knowledge or information that any sheep within his jurisdiction have the scab or any other malignant contagious disease, to inspect said flock and report in writing the result of his inspection to the county clerk of his county, to be filed by him for reference for the county commissioners, or any party concerned, and if so diseased once every four weeks thereafter to reinspect said flock and report in writing the result and treatment, if any, in the same manner until said disease is reported cured ; *Provided,* That in case of the removal of the flock six miles from the range of any other sheep, as hereinafter provided, he shall only make one inspection every three months.

§ 3. REPORT TO INSPECTOR OF ARRIVAL OF STOCK IN TERRITORY—

INSPECTION IN CASE OF FAILURE TO REPORT.] And upon the arrival of any flock of sheep into the Territory, the owner or agent shall immediately report them to the inspector of the county for inspection, and the inspector shall inspect and report as provided in section two, and in case of failure from any cause of owner or agent to report for inspection, a fine of one hundred dollars shall be imposed on said owner or agent for each offense by any court of competent jurisdiction, which fine when collected shall be paid into the county treasury for the use of the sheep inspectors' fund, and any judgment for such fine shall be a lien upon such flock.

§ 4. DUTIES OF OWNER OR AGENT OF DISEASED FLOCK.] The owner or his agent of any flock reported by the inspector to be so diseased, shall immediately herd them so that they cannot range upon or within one mile of any grounds accustomed to be ranged upon by any other sheep, or shall restrain them from passing over or traveling upon or within one mile of any public highway or road, and in case this cannot be done he shall immediately remove said sheep to a locality where they shall not be permitted to range within less than six miles of any other flock of sheep, and said sheep shall continue to be herded under the above restrictions, until upon inspection they shall be reported free from such disease.

§ 5. PENALTY FOR VIOLATION OF THIS ACT.] The owner or his agent or employes of any flock of sheep, requesting or about to be inspected, shall afford the inspector all reasonable facilities for making his inspection, and for every violation of any of the provisions of this act, said owner or his agent or his employes shall be fined not less than ten dollars nor more than three hundred dollars, and every separate day's offense shall constitute a separate offense, and the written report of an offense, made by an inspector under oath, shall be *prima facie* evidence of the commission of said offense, and any justice of the peace of the county in which the offense is committed shall have jurisdiction thereof, and the inspector shall *ex-officio* report all violations of the provisions of this act, of which he has knowledge.

§ 6 OATH AND BOND OF INSPECTOR.] Every inspector before entering upon the duties of his office, shall take the oath of office prescribed by law, and shall give bond to the Territory of Dakota in the sum of one thousand dollars, with good sureties, conditioned that he will faithfully perform the duties ot his office; such bond shall be approved by the county clerk who shall endorse upon every bond he shall approve as follows: "I am acquainted with the sureties herein, and believe them to be worth the amount of the sum of the within bond, over and above their just debts and liabilities."

§ 7. RECORD OF, AND SUITS UPON BOND.] Such bond, with the oath endorsed thereon, shall be recorded in the office of the regis-

1885—2d

ter of deeds for the county in which the inspector shall reside, and may be sued on by any person injured on account of the unfaithful performance of said inspector's duty; *Provided*, That no suit shall be so instituted after more than twelve months have elapsed from the time the cause of action occurred.

§ 8. RECORD OF OFFICIAL ACT OF INSPECTOR.] Every inspector shall keep a fair and correct record of all his official acts, and if required, give a certified copy of any record upon payment of the fees therefor, and in case of the inspector's death, resignation or removal said record shall be deposited with the register of deeds.

§ 9. FEES OF INSPECTION.] The inspector shall receive for his services four dollars per day while necessarily employed in inspecting; and for the first inspection an additional fee of one half cent for every sheep, when the flock inspected is five hundred or less, and for inspecting larger flocks two dollars and fifty cents for the first five hundred, and one-fourth cent each for the remainder of said flock, to be paid by the owner or his agent, and two cents per line of the words for any official report or document, *Provided*, If any person shall keep several separate flocks of sheep, and some flock or flocks be not infected with scab, the owner shall be required to pay only the fees for inspection of such inspected flock or flocks; and *Provided, further*, That when an inspection is made, and the result shall show no disease, the inspector shall give the owner a written statement to that effect, and shall be paid for said inspection as provided in section *fifteen* [nine] The inspector shall receive ten per cent. of all fines and penalties in cases in which he gives information of the offense, and his interest in the result shall not affect his competency as a witness, and all fines and penalties except as herein provided shall be paid to the county treasurer as part of the inspection fund of the county.

§ 10. BY WHOM NOTICE TO BE SERVED.] The notice herein shall be served by the inspector or the sheriff, or any constable of the county.

§ 11. AMOUNT OF FINE FOR FALSE REPORT BY INSPECTOR.] Whenever a sheep inspector shall willfully or falsely report any sheep subject to disease, he shall be subject to a fine of ten times the amount of the fees charged by him for the inspection, and if he shall willfully or falsely report any sheep inspected by him free from disease that are thus infected, he shall be subject to a penalty not exceeding three hundred dollars for each offense.

§ 12. FOR WHAT CAUSES INSPECTOR MAY BE REMOVED.] If any sheep inspector shall be found guilty of either of the offenses set forth in section eleven, or if on complaint in writing by any three wool growers of the county, the county commissioners, after allowing the inspector a fair hearing, shall be of opinion that he is competent to discharge intelligently and efficiently the duties of his office, or that having sufficient knowledge or information he has for any cause willfully or negligently failed to make the required inspection, or that he has needlessly made inspections for the purpose of securing fees, or that his reports have been influenced by favor or prejudice, or from any cause he has failed in the proper discharge of the duties of his office, it shall be the duty of said commissioner to declare said inspector's office vacant and to make a new appointment.

§ 13.   OWNERS TO DIP ON OWN PREMISES]   That every owner of sheep having scab or other malignant contagious disease shall dip or otherwise treat the same upon his own premises, *Provided, that* when he has more than one ranch or set of ranches and the diseased sheep are not upon the ranch where his dipping works or other facilities for treating the disease are situated, he shall have the right to drive through intermediate ranges, but in so doing shall consult the owners or occupants of said range as to where he shall cross the same, and in no case shall he enter another corral or water at his troughs or accustomed watering place with his diseased sheep without the written or otherwise expressed consent of the owner, and for every violation of the provisions herein, he shall be subject to a penalty of not exceeding one hundred dollars.

§ 14.   SHEEP INSPECTORS FUND—WHAT SHALL CONSTITUTE—HOW EXPENDED, ETC.]   That in each county there shall be levied and assessed annually a tax not exceeding in any one year, one-half of a mill upon the dollar of the assessed valuation of the sheep within the county, which shall be collected as other general taxes, and which, with the penalties herein provided, shall constitute a sheep inspector fund of the county, and which fund shall only be expended in the payment of the legal fees of the sheep inspector, and said fees shall only be paid by the county treasurer after they shall have been approved and allowed by the county commissioners in the same manner and form as claims against the county are approved and allowed by them; and from said fund the sheep inspector shall be paid not to exceed three dollars per day actually employed in making the annual round, which it is hereby made his duty to do, between the tenth of August and the tenth of December of each year, and three dollars per day for each day actually employed in making the inspection required by section two and three, and when he reports in substance no disease.

§ 15.   REPEALING CLAUSE.]   All acts or parts of acts in conflict with the provisions of this act are hereby repealed.

§ 16.   This act shall be in force and take effect from and after its passage and approval.

Approved, March 13, 1885.

Sheriff's Sales.

CHAPTER 136.

AN ACT to Amend Section 339 of the Code of Civil Procedure.

Be it enacted by the Legislative Assembly of the Territory of Dakota:

§ 1. POSTPONEMENTS.] That section three hundred and thirty-nine of the Code of Civil Procedure, be amended so as to read as follows: § 39 POSTPONEMENTS—When there are no bidders or when the amount offered is grossly inadequate, or when from any cause the sale is prevented from taking place on the day fixed, the sheriff may postpone the sale for not more than three days, without being required to give any further notice thereof, but he shall not make more than two such postponements, and such postponement must be publicly announced when and where the sale should have taken place.

§ 2. This act shall take effect and be in force from and after its passage and approval.

Approved, February 10, 1885.

Statistics.

CHAPTER 137.

AN ACT providing for the Collection and Compilation of the Statistics of the Territory of Dakota.

Be it enacted by the Legislative Assembly of the Territory of Dakota:

§ 1. ASSESSOR TO PROCURE STATISTICS.] It shall be the duty of the county or township assessor of each organized county of the Territory to obtain at each annual assessment of real and personal property in his county, the following statistics, to-wit: The assessed value of all real and other personal property in the county : The number of acres of land under cultivation, the number of acres and estimated yield in each kind of grain, and the total number of acres assessed in the county : The number of horses, cattle, hogs, and other live stock : The number of townships, and parts of townships, and the total areas of land and water in the county, and the male and female population of the county. The county or township assessor shall be required within thirty days after the date of the return of the said annual assessment, to transmit the statistics obtained as provided for in this section to the commissioner of immigration and *ex-officio* territorial statistician, who shall compile and preserve the same as required by law.

§ 2. STATEMENTS OF INDEBTEDNESS.] It shall be the duty of township, village, city, or county clerks, and county auditors to prepare certified statements on the first day of January and on the first day of June of each year, showing the amount of township, village, city and county indebtedness of all kinds ; giving the amount and character of all bonds issued, the term of years such bonds are to run, the interest payable on same, the date of issue, and the price paid for such bonds, and showing the amount and character of all floating and outstanding indebtedness. The said statements shall be transmitted on or before the fifteenth day of January and the fifteenth day of June of each year, to the commissioner of immigration and *ex-officio* territorial statistician for compilation and preservation as required by law.

§ 3. CORONER TO OBTAIN STATISTICS.] It shall be the duty of the coroner of each organized county of the Territory to obtain the following statistics, to-wit : The number of deaths, the ages and nativity of deceased, and the cause of their decease: The number of births, male and female, and the number of marriages, and nativity and ages of the parties contracting in marriage in the county for the six months each preceding the first day of January and the first day of June of each year, and to transmit the same within fifteen days thereafter to the commissioner of immigration and *ex-officio* territorial statistician for compilation and preservation as required by law.

§ 4. COMMISSIONER OF IMMIGRATION TO PROCURE.] The commissioner of immigration and *ex-officio* territorial statistician shall be required to furnish to the several officers herein named the necessary blanks, stationery, and postage, and the expenses incurred in procuring and furnishing the same shall be paid by the territorial Treasurer on the warrant of the territorial Auditor, which shall be issued on presentation of the sworn expense account of the commissioner of immigration and *ex-officio* territorial statistician, when approved by the Governor.

§ 5. This act shall take effect and be in force from and after its passage and approval.

Approved, March 13, 1885.

Summons.

SERVICE OF.

CHAPTER 138.

AN ACT to Amend Chapters Thirty-four and Thirty-five of the Session Laws of 1883, Relating to the Service of Summons and other Process in Justices and District Courts respectively.

Be it enacted by the Legislative Assembly of the Territory of Dakota :

§ 1. REPEALED.] That section two of chapter thirty-five of the session laws of 1883, approved March 9, 1883, be and the same is hereby repealed.

§ 2. REPEALED.] That section two of chapter thirty-four of the session laws of 1883, approved March 9, 1883, be and the same is hereby repealed.

§ 3. This act shall take effect and be in force from and after its passage and approval.

Approved, March 13, 1885.

TIME TO BE SPECIFIED IN SUMMONS.

CHAPTER 139.

AN ACT Amending Section 15 of the Justices Code.

Be it enacted by the Legislative Assembly of the Territory of Dakota :

§ 1. TIME SPECIFIED FOR APPEARANCE.] That section 15 of the Justices Code, is hereby amended so as to read as follows: " § 15.

The time specified in the summons for the appearance of the defendant shall in all cases be not less than three nor more than twelve days from the date of the service of the same."

§ 2. This act shall take effect and be in force from and after its passage and approval.

Approved, March 12, 1885.

Supreme Court.

CHAPTER 140.

AN ACT Amending Chapter (10) Ten of the Political Code.

Be it enacted by the Legislative Assembly of the Territory of Dakota:

§ 1. THREE TERMS ANNUALLY.] That chapter ten (10) of the Political Code be amended so as to read as follows: " Chapter ten —terms of supreme court—three terms annually." There shall be held three terms annually of the supreme court, as follows: One term at Bismarck commencing on the first Tuesday of February, one term at Yankton commencing on the second Tuesday of May and one term at Deadwood commencing on the first Tuesday of October.

§ 2. This act shall take effect and be in force from and after its passage and approval.

Approved, March 13, 1885.

Telegraph Lines, Etc.

RIGHT OF WAY—REPEAL OF CERTAIN LAWS.

CHAPTER 141.

AN ACT to Repeal Chapter One Hundred and Eight (108) of Chapter Sixty; Chapter One Hundred and Ten (110) and One Hundred and Sixteen (116).

Be it enacted by the Legislative Assembly of the Territory of Dakota:

§ 1. TAX COMMISSION REPEALED.] That chapter one hundred and eight (108) of the session laws of eighteen hundred and eighty-three, entitled a joint resolution providing for the appointment of a tax commissioner is hereby repealed.

§ 2. FISH COMMISSIONER REPEALED.] That chapter sixty of the session laws of 1883, entitled an act to stock with food-fishes the waters of Dakota, and to protect the same and for other purposes, is hereby repealed.

§ 3. RIGHT OF WAY TO CERTAIN LINES] There is hereby granted to the owners of any telegraph or telephone lines operated in this Territory, the right of way over lands and real property, in this Territory, and the right to use public grounds, streets, alleys and highways in this Territory, subject to control of the proper, municipal authorities as to what grounds, streets, alleys or highways said lines shall run over or across, and the place the poles to support the wires are located; the right of way over real property granted in this act may be acquired in the same manner and by like proceedings as provided for railroad corporations.

§ 4. TELEPHONE ACT REPEALED.] That chapter one hundred and ten (110) of the session laws of 1883, entitled an act to amend chapter one hundred and thirty-two (132) of the general laws passed at the territorial session of the Legislative Assembly of this Territory, are hereby repealed.

§ 5. TAXATION OF TELEGRAPH COMPANIES REPEALED.] That chapter one hundred and thirty-two of the session laws of 1881, entitled "an act to provide for the payment of taxes by telegraph companies" and granting the right and power to use highways and roads to telegraph companies, is hereby repealed.

§ 6. WHEAT COMMISSION REPEALED.] That chapter one hundred and sixteen (116) of the session laws of 1883, entitled "an act regulating the grading and weighing of wheat, and for other purposes in the Territory of Dakota" is hereby repealed.

§ 7. This act shall take effect and be in force from and after its passage and approval.

Approved, March 13, 1885.

Timber Acreage.

CHAPTER 142.

AN ACT to Provide for Ascertaining the Acreage of Timber in Dakota Territory.

Be it enacted by the Legislative Assembly of the Territory of Dakota:

§ 1. DUTY OF ASSESSORS] All assessors within this Territory are authorized and it is hereby made their duty to determine and report each year the acreage of timber within their respective districts. Such report shall indicate separately the acreage of natural and cultivated or planted forests, averaging four feet or over in height, and shall also specify the kind of trees. Such data shall be taken and reported by such assessor without extra salary or charge.

§ 2. This act to take effect and be in force from and after its passage and approval.

Approved, March 12, 1885.

1885—27

Townships.

REPEALING JUDICIAL DISTRICT ROADS.

CHAPTER 143.

AN ACT to Repeal Sections Sixty-four, Sixty-five, Sixty-six, Sixty-seven and Sixty-eight of Chapter Two of Chapter One Hundred and Twelve of the Session Laws of Eighteen Hundred and Eighty-three.

Be it enacted by the Legislative Assembly of the Territory of Dakota :

§ 1. CERTAIN PROVISIONS REPEALED.] That sections sixty-four, sixty-five, sixty-six, sixty-seven, sixty-eight of chapter two of chapter one hundred and twelve of the session laws of eighteen hundred and eighty-three are hereby repealed.

Approved, March 13, 1885.

PROVIDING FOR ISSUE OF CIVIL TOWNSHIP BONDS.

CHAPTER 144.

AN ACT Allowing Town Supervisors to Issue Bonds.

Be it enacted by the Legislative Assembly of the Territory of Dakota :

§ 1. SUPERVISORS TO ISSUE BONDS.] That whenever a petition shall be presented to the board of supervisors of any of the organized· towns in the Territory, or that may hereafter be organized, bearing the signatures of two-thirds of the legal voters of such township, (of which fact that such petition bears the signature of said majority of such legal voters, the last registered poll list of such town shall be *prima facie* evidence,) praying for a certain amount of money to be raised, not to exceed five per centum of the taxable valuation of said town, as shown by the last assessment roll, nor in any case more than five thousand ($5,000) dollars, for the construction of any public road or roads, ditch or ditches, embankments, levees, or any similar work over any lands within said township, the said supervisors shall issue and sell the bonds, with coupons attached, of such township, for and in the amount specified in such petition; said bonds to run not longer than twenty (20) years, and to draw a rate of interest not exceeding ten (10) per centum per annum, payable annually. Said bonds shall not be sold or disposed of for less than their par value. Said town shall provide for the payment of the said bonds and the interest thereon by sufficient taxation to meet the same.

§ 2. FUNDS—HOW USED.] The money obtained from the sale of said bonds shall be used under the direction of the supervisors of said town in the construction of the work for which the bonds were issued, and in the purchase of such tools and machinery, or as shall have been prayed for in said petition, and any other that the supervisors may deem advisable for the prosecution of said work.

§ 3. BONDS TO BE RECORDED.] The bonds herein provided for shall be signed by the chairman of the board of supervisors of such town, and be countersigned by town clerk, who shall file and record the petition upon which the said bonds were issued, and shall keep a record showing the action of the board of supervisors in the premises, and also a record showing the amount, date of issue, to whom issued, rate of interest and date of maturity of said bonds.

§ 4. FUNDS—HOW DISBURSED.] All money *devided* [derived] from the sale of such bonds shall be paid into the town treasurer of such *term* [town,] who shall pay the same out on the order of the chairman of the board of supervisors, countersigned by the town clerk.

§ 5. This act to take effect and be in force from and after its passage and approval.

Approved, March 13, 1885.

Tree Planting.

CHAPTER 145.

AN ACT to Promote the Planting of Forest Trees upon the Prairies of the Territory of Dakota.

Be it enacted by the Legislative Assembly of the Territory of Dakota.

§ 1. BOUNTY FOR.] That every person planting one acre or more of prairie land within five years after the passage of this act, with any kind of forest trees, except black locust and cottonwood, and successfully growing and cultivating for three years, shall be entitled to receive for ten years thereafter an annual bounty of two dollars for each acre so planted and cultivated, to be paid out of the territorial treasury, but such bounty shall not be paid any longer than such grove of trees is maintained and kept in growing condition

§ 2. BENEFITS OF LAW, HOW SECURED.] Any person wishing to secure the benefits of this act shall, within three years after planting such grove of trees, and annually thereafter, file with the county auditor or clerk of the county in which the same is located, a correct plat of the land describing the section or fraction thereof on which such grove has been planted or cultivated, and shall make due proof of such planting and cultivation as well as of the title to the land, by oath of the owner and the affidavit of two householders residing in the vicinity, setting forth the facts in relation to the growth and cultivation of the grove of trees for which such bounty is demanded. The several county auditors or clerks shall, on or before the first Monday of August of each year, forward to the territorial Auditor a certified list of all the lands and tree planting reported and verified to them in compliance with this act, with the name and postoffice address of the respective owners thereof; *Providing,* This act shall not apply to any railroad company for planting of trees within two hundred feet of its track, for the purpose of making a snow fence, nor to any trees planted upon land held, entered and acquired under the timber culture laws of the United States.

§ 3. AUDITOR TO ISSUE WARRANTS.] If the territorial Auditor shall find that the provisions of this act have been duly complied with, he shall issue to the several applicants entitled thereto, his warrant upon the territorial Treasurer for the bounty so earned.

§ 4. This act shall take effect and be in force from and after its passage and approval.

Approved, March 13, 1885.

Trials.

ISSUES AND MODE OF.

CHAPTER 146.

AN ACT to Amend Section Two Hundred and Thirty-six of the Code of Civil Procedure.

Be it enacted by the Legislative Assembly of the Territory of Dakota :

§ 1. Issue, how tried.] That section two hundred and thirty-six of the Code of Civil Procedure of the Territory of Dakota, be and the same is hereby amended so as to read as follows : " Section two hundred and thirty-six." An issue of law must be tried by the court or by the Judge. An issue of fact for the recovery of money only, or of specific real or personal property, must be tried by a jury, unless a jury trial be waived, as provided in section two hundred and sixty-five.. Every other issue is triable by the court which, however, may order the whole issue or any specific question of fact involved therein, to be tried by a jury or may refer it as provided in sections two hundred and seventy-one and two hundred and seventy-two.

§ 2. This act shall take effect and be in force from and after its passage and approval.

Approved, March 12, 1885.

ISSUES AND MODE OF TRIALS.

CHAPTER 147.

AN ACT amending Section Two Hundred and Thirty-seven of the Code of Civil Procedure.

Be it enacted by the Legislative Assembly of the Territory of Dakota:

§ 1. ISSUES OF FACT HOW AND WHEN TRIED.] That section two hundred and thirty-seven of the code of civil procedure be and same is hereby amended so as to read as follows: § 237. All issues of fact, triable by a jury, or by the court, must be tried before a single judge. Issues of fact must be tried at a regular term of the district court, when the trial is by jury, otherwise at a regular or special term, as the court may by its rules prescribe. Issues at law must be tried at regular or special term of the district court, or by the court in vacation, or judge at chambers. If by the court in vacation, or judge at chambers, the same may be heard, tried and determined in any county of the district, within which the action is brought and judgment thereon entered in the proper county, upon the giving by either or any party, of the notice prescribed by section two hundred and thirty-eight of the code of civil procedure: but in such case no note of issue need be filed: and any judgment, final decision or actual determination, made upon such trial and hearing, may be appealed from in the same manner and subject to the same rules and provisions, as in cases of other appeals from actual determinations and final decisions of any regular or special terms of the district courts of this Territory.

§ 2. This act shall take effect and be in force from and after its passage and approval.

Approved, March 9, 1885.

Vacancies in Office.

CHAPTER 148.

AN ACT to amend Chapter 22 of the Political Code.

Be it enacted by the Legislative Assembly of the Territory of Dakota :

§ .1 How TO FILL VACANCIES.] That section nine of chapter twenty-two of the political code be and the same is hereby amended by adding thereto the following: "And in case a majority of the officers before described do not agree as to the appointment of a person to fill said vacancy, the county treasurer shall be called in and shall act as an additional member of said board to fill said vacancy."

Approved, February 26, 1885.

Verifications.

CHAPTER 149.

AN ACT to amend Section 126 of the Code of Civil Procedure.

Be it enacted by the Legislative Assembly of the Territory of Dakota :

§ 1. VERIFICATION, WHAT TO STATE.] That section one hundred and twenty-six (126) of the code of civil procedure be and the same is hereby amended so as to read as follows: § 126. The verifications must be to the effect that the same is true to the knowledge of the person making it, except as to those matters stated upon information and belief and as to those matters he believes it to be true, except where it is made by any person other than a party to the action, in which case it must be to the effect that the same is true to the best knowledge, information and belief of the person making it : and such verification must be by the affidavit of party, or if there be several parties united in interest and pleading together by one at least of such parties acquainted with the facts, if such party be within the county where the attorney resides and capable of making the affidavit. The affidavit may also be made by the agent or attorney if the party is absent from the county in which such attorney resides or is not a resident thereof, and when the pleading is verified by any other person than the party he shall set forth in the affidavit the reasons why it is not made by the party. When a corporation is a party the verification may be made by any officer thereof : and when the Territory or any officer thereof in its behalf is a party, the verification may be made by any person acquainted with the facts. The verification may be omitted when an admission of the truth of the allegation might subject the party to prosecution for felony, and no pleading can be used in a criminal prosecution against the party as proof of a fact admitted or alleged in such pleading.

§ 2. This act shall take effect and be in force from and after its passage and approval.

Approved, March 13, 1885.

University.

SALE OF LIQUORS.

CHAPTER 150.

AN ACT to Prevent the Sale of Intoxicating Liquors within a Distance of Three Miles of the Dakota University, in the City of Vermillion, County of Clay and Territory of Dakota, except for Medicinal and Mechanical Purposes.

Be it enacted by the Legislative Assembly of the Territory of Dakota:

§ 1. UNLAWFUL TO SELL.] It shall not be lawful for any person by himself, agent or otherwise, to sell in any quantities, intoxicating liquors at any place, room, building, or premises, within three miles of the Dakota University, in the city of Vermillion, county of Clay ; and no license to sell liquors within said limits shall be issued by the authorities of either the county of Clay or the city of Vermillion ; *Provided, however,* This act shall not be so construed as to prohibit any druggist from selling liquors for medicinal or mechanical purposes.

§ 2. PERSON BUYING TO SIGN HIS NAME.] Every person buying liquors for medicinal or mechanical purposes shall sign his name in a book, to be kept by each druggist in said city for that purpose.

§ 3. PENALTY.] Every person selling intoxicating liquors in violation of the provisions of this act, shall be deemed guilty of a misdemeanor, and upon conviction thereof, shall be punished by a fine of not less than one hundred dollars nor more than three hundred dollars for the first offense, and not less than three hundred dollars for the second offense and each and every offense thereafter, or by imprisonment in the county jail not less than thirty days for the first offense, and not less than sixty days for the second offense, or by both such fine and imprisonment, in the discretion of the court.

§ 4. DISTANCE, HOW CALCULATED.] For the purpose of calculating and ascertaining the distance of said three miles from said Dakota University, the starting point shall be the middle point of the east front line of the main building of said University at the surface of the ground as said building now stands.

§ 5. GIVING AWAY PROHIBITED.] The giving away of intoxicating liquors, or any other shift or device, to evade the provisions of this act, shall be deemed and held to be an unlawful selling within the provisions of the same.

§ 6. FINES, HOW DISPOSED OF.] All fines collected under the provisions of this act shall be paid over to the county treasurer to the credit of the general school fund of the county of Clay, and all property, real and personal, except that absolutely exempt belonging to the person convicted, and all furniture, liquors, glasses, bottles, kegs and barrels in the custody of any person so selling intoxicating liquors, shall be liable to seizure and sale, to pay any fine against such person so selling intoxicating liquors.

§ 7. This act shall take effect and be in force from and after the first day of July, A. D. 1885.

Approved, March 15, 1885.

1885—28

Weights and Measures.

CHAPTER 151.

AN ACT to Provide a Standard of Weights and Measures for the Territory of Dakota, and for other purposes.

Be it enacted by the Legislative Assembly of the Territory of Dakota:

§ 1. STANDARD TO BE KEPT BY TREASURER.] The treasurer of the Territory shall procure and keep in his office at the capitol of the Territory, the following standards of weights and measures, which shall conform in every *practical* [practicable] particular to the United States standards of weights and measures, to-wit: One bushel; one half bushel; one peck; one half peck; one quart; one wine gallon; one wine half gallon; one wine quart; one wine pint; one wine gill. Said measures shall be made of copper, or other suitable and substantial material; also one surveyors chain thirty-three standard feet in length; one yard measure; one foot measure and one inch measure; also one one hundred pound weight; one fifty pound weight; one twenty-five pound weight; one ten pound weight; one one pound weight; one half pound weight; one quarter pound weight; one one-eighth of a pound; one one-sixteenth of a pound or one ounce weight; one set of apothecaries weights from one pound to one grain; one set of troy weights from one pound to one ——— besides such other scales, beams and balances as shall be necessary to test other weights by these standards, which measures, weights, scales, beams and balances are hereby declared to be the legal standards of weights and measures for this territory. The said territorial treasurer shall be charged with the custody, and accountable to the Territory for the proper use and care of the same. Said standards shall be used only for testing the standards provided for in section 2 of this act, and said treasurer shall keep a record of all county weights, measures, beams and balances marked and tested by him.

§ 2. COUNTY COMMISSIONERS TO PURCHASE DUPLICATE.] The county commissioners of each county are hereby authorized to purchase such duplicates of the above enumerated weights and measures as they may deem necessary for the use of their respective counties in carrying out the following provisions of this act, which duplicates shall be paid for by the county and be delivered to the sheriff, who is hereby declared to be the sealer of weights and measures for the county, and may appoint such deputies as he may consider necessary in different parts of the county who shall possess the same powers and perform the same duties under this act as the sheriff may, and may furnish such deputies with such duplicates as the county commissioners may be willing to provide for their separate use, or may allow them to use those provided for himself. Each and every such sealer and deputy sealer of weights and measures, shall give a bond to the county of not less than double the cost of the duplicates furnished him conditioned that he will safely keep and care for such duplicates, and in good condition will turn them over to his successor, and upon said bond shall take and subscribe oath of office of substantially the same form as that administered to other county officers.

§ 3. SHERIFF TO MAKE TEST.] The sheriff as *ex-officio* sealer of weights and measures shall in the month of July in each year, test by his duplicates all scales, weights and measures found by him in his county, used as provided in section 4 of this act, and shall give the person in charge thereof a certificate of the correctness thereof, if found to be correct, and if found to be incorrect he shall cause the same to be made correct if it can so be done, and if not he shall mark the same "condemned." He shall keep a record of all such certificates issued by him and of all his transactions under this act. For testing any measure, weight or scale as provided in this section, he may charge the owner or person in charge the sum of fifty cents; *Provided*, That when any scale is tested the certificate shall cover the weights used with scale and the sealer shall not be allowed to charge more than fifty cents for testing each scale and its several weights.

§ 4. COMMISSIONERS TO PRESCRIBE.] The county commissioners of each county shall prescribe, by resolution to that effect, what kinds and quantities of goods, wares, merchandise, grain, live stock and produce may be sold or exchanged with or without the use of the standard weights and measures and tested scales, and may amend such resolution at any regular meeting; which resolution and amendments shall be entered in the minutes of their meeting and published as part of their proceedings, and it shall be unlawful for any person, firm or corporation by themselves or any representative to use any scale, weight or measure for computing the quantity of any goods, wares, merchandise, grain, live stock or produce to be bought or sold by him or them in any greater quantity than that allowed by the board of county commissioners of the county without having the same conform to the standard provided for by this act, and having the same tested as provided for in section 3 of this act, or under the conditions named in section 6.

§ 5. COMPLAINTS.] Any person believing any dealer is violating any of the provisions of this act or any subsequent resolution of the board of county commissioners made by authority hereof may make complaints in writing to any sealer or deputy sealer and deposit with him five (5) dollars, setting forth the particular facts of such violation, and that he has reason to believe that the same are true Upon such complaint such sealer or his deputy shall forthwith test the scale, weights or measures respecting the matter complained of by his duplicates and if found to conform thereto he may convert the five (5) dollars so deposited by the complainant to his own use as his fees for such service If he find that any of the matters complained of be true he shall return the five (5) dollars to the complainant and it shall be his duty to forthwith arrest the person in charge of such scales, and bring him to trial before any justice of the peace in the county, and upon conviction such person, whether the owner or not, shall be guilty of a misdemeanor and punishable in the discretion of the court. In all such cases the sealer or deputy sealer making the test shall make and swear to the complaint in court and shall be entitled to the same fees as allowed officers making arrests upon a warrant, besides the sum of one dollar for making the test. Any sealer may upon his own view of violation of the provisions of this act, or any subsequent resolution made by the board of county commissioners of his county, arrest and bring to trial such offender in the manner above provided.

§ 6. DUTY OF DEALER.] It shall be the duty of every person, firm or corporation who desire to use any scale, weight or measure for computing the quantity of any goods, wares, merchandise, produce, grain or live stock, to be bought or sold by him or them in greater quantity than those provided in the resolutions of the county commissioners of his county, to send by mail a notice to any sealer to test such scales, weights or measures, and it shall be the duty of any sealer receiving such notice to test such scale, weights or measures within ten days and during such time before the same is tested the same may be used for such purpose, and the user shall be liable only for damages in a civil action.

§ 7. This act as to section 1, shall take effect from and after its passage and approval; as to sections 2, 3, 4, 5, 6 and 7, shall take effect and be in force in each county in this Territory upon a resolution to that effect adopted by a majority of the board of county commissioners thereof.

Approved, March 13, 1885.

SUPPLEMENT

TO

LAWS OF 1885. DAKOTA TERRITORY

NOXIOUS WEEDS.

AN ·ACT to Prevent the Spread of Noxious Weeds in the Territory of Dakota.

Be it Enacted by the Legislative Assembly of the Territory of Dakota :

§ 1. Every person and every corporation shall destroy upon all lands which he or she shall occupy, all weeds of the kinds known as Canada thistle, cockle burr and mustard, at such time and in such manner as shall effectually prevent their bearing seed ; such time and manner of destroying such weeds shall be prescribed by township boards of supervisors or by board of county commissioners in counties which shall not be organized into townships, and the same shall be published at least two weeks in some newspaper published in the county, not less than two weeks before the time so prescribed ; *Provided,* That if there be no newspaper published in the county, then written notices of the same shall be posted the same as election notices are posted, in lieu of such publication. Every overseer of highways of every township or county shall also in like time and manner destroy all such weeds that may grow either on the highway of his road district or on any unoccupied land therein, which the occupant thereof shall refuse or neglect to so destroy. For so doing such overseer shall have such compensation, payable out of the township treasury or county treasury as the township board of supervisors or board of county commissioners, upon the presentation of his account therefor, verified by his oath, and specifying by separate items the charges on each piece of land, describing the same, shall deem reasonable; and the respective accounts so paid, except for the destruction of such weeds upon the highways, shall be placed on the next tax roll of the township or county as the case may be, in a separate column headed: "For destruction of weeds," as a tax against the lands upon which such weeds were destroyed, and be collected as other taxes, and the entry of such tax on the tax roll shall be conclusive evidence of the liability of the land so taxed to such tax.

§ 2. If the occupant of any such lands or any such overseer shall fail to destroy such weeds as so required, such occupant or overseer shall forfeit not less than five dollars nor more than fifty dollars. The chairman and each supervisor of every township, or the chairman and each commissioner of counties not organized into townships, shall prosecute promptly for every such forfeiture which he shall have reason to believe to have been incurred.

§ 3. That an act entitled "An act to prevent the spread of noxious weeds in the counties of Union, Clay, Lincoln and Cass," be and the same is hereby repealed.

§ 4. This act shall take effect and be in force from and after its passage and approval.

Approved March 12, 1885.

SPECIAL LAWS.

Counties.

ADAMS AND BROWN COUNTIES—DIVISION OF.

CHAPTER 1.

AN ACT creating the County of Adams and for Other Purposes.

Be it enacted by the Legislative Assembly of the Territory of Dakota:

SECTION 1. The following described territory, to-wit: Commencing at the northeast corner of township one hundred and twenty-four (124) north, range sixty (60) west, thence west on the township line between townships one hundred twenty-four (124), and one hundred and twenty-five (125), to the northwest corner of township one hundred and twenty-four (124), north, range sixty-five (65) west, thence south on range line between ranges sixty-five (65) and sixty-six (66) to the southwest corner of township one hundred and twenty-one (121), north range sixty-five (65) west, thence east on township line between townships one hundred and twenty (120), and one hundred twenty-one (121) to the southeast corner of township one hundred and twenty-one (121) north, range sixty (60)west, thence north on range line between ranges fifty-nine (59) and sixty (60) to the place of beginning, shall be and the same is hereby declared to be the county of Adams.

§ 2. That the county of Adams as hereby created is declared to be liable for such portion of the legal indebtedness of the county of Brown, existing at the time of the taking effect of this act, as the assessed valuation for the year A. D., 1884, of the property situated in the county of Adams as herein created bears to the whole of assessed valuation of the county of Brown for the year A. D., 1884, as shown by the assessment rolls of the said county for the year A. D., 1884, and the cash assets in the hands of the county treasurer of said county of Brown at the time of taking effect of this act, shall be turned over to the county treasurer of the county of Adams in proportion as the assessed valuation of all property in the county of Adams bears to the whole assessed valuation of the county of Brown for the year A. D , 1884. And it is hereby made the duty of the county treasurer of the county of Brown to turn over such portion of the money in his hands as above provided.

§ 3   All unpaid taxes a ainst all kinds of property situated in that portion of the county of Brown which by the provisions of this act is created into the county of Adams shall belong to and be collected by the county of Adams.

§ 4. If by the provisions of this act any school township or townships shall be divided, each portion shall be liable for its proportion of the entire debt of said school township or townships, based on the assessed valuation of all property in said tonwship or townships for the year A. D., 1884; the assets of said township or townships so divided shall be apportioned to the parts divided in proportion to the assessed valuation in each part so divided.

§ 5. It shall be the duty of the county commissioners of the county of Adams, and county of Brown, to meet at the court house in the village of Columbia, in said Brown county, on the first Monday in June, A D., 1885, to equalize and provide for the assumption of the debts of the county of Brown.

§ 6. It is hereby made the duty of the register of deeds of the county of Adams as herein created, within thirty days after the county of Adams shall be organized according to law, to commence and transcribe from the records of the county of Brown all instruments therein recorded in any manner relating to property situated in the county of Adams as herein created, in proper books for that purpose, and it is hereby made the duty of the officers of Brown county to allow the register of deeds of the county of Adams to have access to the records of Brown county for the purpose of making such transcripts. The register of deeds of Adams county shall be allowed the same fees for making such transcript as are allowed by law for recording the same, to be paid by the county of Adams; the register of deeds shall also make a transcript of all unpaid tax lists, tax sales, redemption from tax sales and assessment rolls, against all property situated in the county of Adams, as herein defined, and for his services he shall be allowed a reasonable compensation to be fixed by the county commissioners of Adams county, and paid by the county of Adams. The register of deeds of Adams county shall certify to all transcripts, so made, and deliver them to the proper officers of the county of Adams, and take their receipts therefor; and the said transcribed records shall have the same force and effect for all purposes as the original records.

§ 7. The county seat of the county of Adams as herein created is hereby temporarily located in the town of Aberdeen, subject to removal by a majority vote at the next general election.

§ 8. The county commissioners of the county of Adams shall meet at the city hall, in the city of Aberdeen, on Monday the 18th day of May, A. D., 1885, at twelve (12) o'clock noon, and qualify according to law, and proceed to organize said county of Adams according to law, by appointing the county officers of said county and carrying out the provisions of this act.

§ 9. All that portion of Brown county not within the limits of the county of Adams as hereby created, shall be and remain the county of Brown.

§ 10. The officers of Brown county elected at the last general election, including the county commissioners of said county who hold over by non-expiration of their term of office, shall be and remain the officers of Brown county; *Provided*, Such of them as reside within the limits of Adams county as herein created, shall, within thirty days from the time this act shall take effect, remove and reside within the limits of Brown county. The chairman of the board of county commissioners, the clerk of the district court, and the superintendent of public schools shall meet at the county seat of the county of Brown, at the expiration of thirty days from the time of this act taking effect, and fill all vacancies in the board of county commissioners of the county of Brown, and all other vacancies in any of the county offices shall be filled by the board of county commissioners.

§ 11. The county of Brown as herein defined shall have five county commissioners.

§ 12. The question of the division of the county of Brown, as set forth in this act, shall be submitted to the legal voters of Brown county, as it now exists, at a special election to be held in said county on the third Tuesday, the 21st day of April, A. D. 1885; notice of said election to be given by the county clerk of Brown county for at least thirty days prior to said election; and in addition thereto, this act shall be published in at least three of the newspapers published in the county of Brown for four successive issues prior to said election, to be designated by the clerk of the county of Brown. The said election, in all manner not expressly provided for in this act, shall be governed in the same manner as required by law in conducting general elections; the ballots used in said special election shall be in the following form, to-wit: "For division of Brown County; Yes;" or "For division of Brown County; No;" and may be either written or printed, or part written and part printed.

§ 13. If, upon a canvass of all votes cast at said special election, it shall appear that a majority of the votes cast at said special election were cast "For division of Brown county, Yes," then all that portion of territory described in section one of this act, shall be and is hereby constituted and created the county of Adams

§ 14. The county clerk, the chairman of the board of county commissioners, the district attorney, the county treasurer, the clerk of the district court, the judge of the probate court, and the sheriff of Brown county, are hereby constituted a board of canvassers to canvass the vote cast at the special election herein provided for, a majority of whom shall constitute a quorum and are authorized to proceed with said canvass, and it is hereby made their duty to meet at the office of the county clerk in the village of Columbia, in the county of Brown, and the Territory of Dakota, within ten days from the date of said special election, and proceed to canvass the vote cast at said special election. They shall organize by electing one of their number chairman, and one of their number secretary, and shall enter the minutes of their proceedings at length upon the county commissioner's record of the county of Brown. They shall make an abstract of all the votes cast at said special election, and transmit a certified abstract of the same, under seal to the secretary of the Territory of Dakota; and if they shall find that a majority of all the votes cast in the county of Brown, at said special election were cast "for the division of Brown county, Yes" they shall furnish a certified transcript of all the votes so cast to each of the county commissioners of the county of Adams hereinafter mentioned, to be by the sheriff of the county of Brown delivered and served upon each of the county commissioners hereinafter named of the county of Adams, personally, which shall be authority for the county commissioners of the county of Adams hereinafter named, to meet at the time and place specified in section eight of this act, and proceed to organize the county of Adams according to law.

§ 15. That John A. Honlahan, Stephen Wade, C. J. C. McLeod, James D. Reeves and Dr. A. Grant, be and are hereby appointed county commissioners of the county of Adams and shall hold their offices until the next general election.

§ 16. If upon a canvass of all the votes cast at the special election provided for in this act, it shall appear that a majority of all the votes cast at said special election were for the division of Brown county, "No," then this shall be of no force and effect, but if upon said canvass it shall appear that a majority of all the votes so cast were "For the division of Brown county, Yes," then this act shall be and remain in full force and effect.

§ 17. All acts and parts of acts in conflict with the provisions of this act are hereby repealed.

§ 18. This act shall take effect and be in force from and after its passage and approval.

Approved, March 13, 1885.

Counties.

COUNTY AUDITORS IN BROWN AND OTHER COUNTIES.

CHAPTER 2.

AN ACT to Amend Chapter One of the Special Laws of 1883, Relating to County Auditors.

Be it enacted by the Legislative Assembly of the Territory of Dakota:

§ 1. That chapter one of the special laws of 1883, approved March 9, 1883, be amended so as to create the office of county auditor in the counties of Brown, Day, Grant, Codington, Deuel, Sargent, Ransom and Dickey.

§ 2. The county auditors appointed under the provisions of this act shall hold their offices until their successors are duly elected in 1886 and qualified under the general laws of the Territory the same as other county officers.

§ 3. In the counties above mentioned the register of deeds shall not hold the office of county auditor during the time in which he is register of deeds.

§ 4. This act shall take effect on its passage and approval.

Approved, March 13, 1885.

1885—29

BOUNDARIES OF BILLINGS AND OTHER COUNTIES.

CHAPTER 3.

AN ACT to Define the Boundaries of Billings, Villard, Dunn and Wallace Counties.

Be it enacted by the Legislative Assembly of the Territory of Dakota :

§ 1. The boundaries of the county of Billings are hereby designated and established as follows, to-wit: Beginning at the point where the line between towns one hundred and forty-four (144) and one hundred and forty-five (145) north, intersects the boundary line between the territories of Dakota and Montana; thence south along said boundary line to the line between towns one hundred and thirty-two (132) and one hundred and thirty-three (133) north; thence east along said town line to the line between ranges one hundred and one (101) and one hundred and two (102) west; thence north along said range line to the line between towns one hundred and forty-four (144) and one hundred and forty-five (145) north; thence west along said town line to the place of beginning; and the territory included within such boundaries shall be and constitute the said county of Billings.

§ 2. The boundaries of the county of Villard are hereby designated and established as follows, to-wit: Beginning at the point on the line between towns one hundred and forty-four (144) and one hundred and forty-five (145) north, where the same is intersected by the line between ranges one hundred and one (101) and one hundred and two (102) west; thence south along said range line to the line between towns one hundred and thirty-two (132) and one hundred and thirty-three (133) north; thence east along said town line to the line between ranges ninety-seven (97) and ninety-eight (98) west; thence north along said range line to the line between towns one hundred and forty-four (144) and one hundred and forty-five (145) north; thence west along said town line to the place of beginning; and the Territory included within such boundaries shall be and constitute the said county of Villard.

§ 3. The boundaries of the county of Dunn are hereby designated and established as follows, to-wit: Beginning at a point on the line between towns one hundred and forty (140) and one hundred and forty-one (141) north, where the same is intersected by the line between ranges ninety-seven (97) and ninety-eight (98) west, thence east along said town line to the line between ranges ninety-three (93) and ninety-four (94) west; thence north along said range line to the line between towns one hundred and forty-eight (148) and one hundred and forty-nine (149) north; thence west along said town line to the line between ranges ninety-seven (97) and ninety-eight (98) west; thence south along said range line to the place of beginning; and the territory included within such boundaries shall be and constitute the said county of Dunn.

§ 4. The boundaries of the county of Wallace are hereby designated and established as follows, to-wit: Beginning at the point where the line between ranges ninety-three (93) and ninety-four (94) west, intersects the line between towns one hundred and forty-eight (148) and one hundred and forty-nine (149) north; thence north along said range line to the middle of the channel of the Missouri river; thence along said channel in a northerly and westerly course to the line between ranges one hundred and one (101) and one hundred and two (102) west; thence south along said range line to the line between towns one hundred and forty-eight (148) and one hundred and forty-nine (149) north; thence east along said town line to the place of beginning; and the territory included within such boundaries shall be and constitute the said county of Wallace.

§ 5. This act shall take effect and be in force from and after its passage and approval.

Approved, March 10, 1885.

BLAINE COUNTY CREATED.

CHAPTER 4.

AN ACT Creating the County of Blaine and for other Purposes.

Be it enacted by the Legislative Assembly of the Territory of Dakota:

§ 1. That all t at district of country included within the following boundaries, to-wit:—Beginning at the southeast corner of township one hundred and fifty-five (155) range fifty-seven west, and running north on range line between range fifty-six (56) and fifty-seven (57) to the north east corner of township one hundred and fifty-eight (158), thence west to the northwest corner of one hundred and fifty-eight (158) in range sixty-one (61), thence south on range line between ranges sixty-one (61) and sixty-two (62), to the southwest corner of township one hundred and fifty-five (155), range (61) sixty-one, thence east on the township line between townships one hundred and fifty-four (154) and township one fifty-five (155), to the place of beginning; shall be and the same is hereby declared to be and the same is constituted the county of Blaine.

§ 2. SPECIAL ELECTION. That for the purpose of carrying out the provisions of section one of this act, it is hereby made the duty of the county auditor of Walsh county in this Territory, to call a special election within the limits of the boundaries of the county of Walsh, to be held at the several precincts within the county of Walsh, not later than the first Tuesday in May, A. D., 1885, and shall cause three notices to be posted in each of said precincts at least twenty days prior to the election, which said notices shall state where the polls shall be, the day of the week, the day of the month and the hour at which the polls shall be opened, and closed, and the purpose for which the election is called. . The ballots to be used by the electors within the county of Walsh shall have printed or written or partly printed and partly written "for division of Walsh county—'No, or yes,'" as the case may be. The judges of election shall make returns to the county auditor of Walsh county, showing how many votes were cast for county division "No," for county division "Yes." The county commissioners of Walsh county, shall together with the county auditor of the county, meet at the county seat of Walsh county within ten days from the day of election, to canvass the votes of the several precincts. And the county auditor of Walsh county shall make certified abstracts of the votes cast at said election, and forward the same to the Secretary of the Territory, and one to the Governor of the Territory and if the Governor and Secretary shall find that a majority of all the votes at said election have been cast in favor of such division, then it shall be the duty of the Governor to issue a proclamation to that effect. And then and thereafter the district described in section one shall constitute, and be known as the county of Blaine, and shall be organized as other counties are organized, upon proper petition, and that the county of Blaine shall be attached to the county of Walsh for judicial purposes.

§ 3. All acts or parts of acts in conflict with this act are hereby repealed.

Approved, March 13, 1885.

TO REIMBURSE BROWN COUNTY FOR CARE OF PAUPERS.

CHAPTER 5.

AN ACT to Appropriate Money to Reimburse Brown County for the Payment of Money for Taking Care of Certain Paupers therein Named.

Be it enacted by the Legislative Assembly of the Territory of Dakota :

§ 1. That there is hereby appropriated out of the funds of the territorial treasury, not otherwise appropriated, the sum of four hundred and fifty dollars and ninety-six cents for the following purposes, viz: One hundred and four dollars and thirty-one cents to reimburse Brown county for money paid out in the case of Mrs. Feecenhouse, a pauper residing in town 125 of range 66, and also the sum of three hundred and forty-six dollars and sixty-five cents paid out by Brown county in the case of William Carlson, a pauper residing in township 123 of range 66, making in the aggregate an appropriation for the purposes named, the sum of four hundred and fifty dollars and ninety-six cents.

§ 2. The money herein appropriated shall be paid out to the county treasurer of Brown county, or order, upon the presentation to the territorial Treasurer of the proper vouchers, showing that such sums of money was paid out by said county for the purpose above stated.

§ 3. This act shall take effect and be in force from and after its passage and approval.

Approved, March 9, 1885.

FIXING PAY OF COMMISSIONERS OF CUSTER AND PENNINGTON
COUNTIES

CHAPTER 6.

AN ACT Fixing the Per Diem and Mileage of the County Commissioners of
Custer and Pennington Counties while Necessarily Engaged in County
Business.

Be it enacted by the Legislative Assembly of the Territory of Dakota:

§ 1.   That the county commissioners of Custer and Pennington
counties shall each be allowed for the time they shall be necessarily employed in the duties of their office, the sum of five dollars
per day and ten cents per mile for the distance necessarily traveled
in attending the meetings of the board, and when engaged in
other official duties, to be paid out of the county general fund.

§ 2.   All acts and parts of acts inconsistent with this act are
hereby repealed so far as they apply to the said counties of Custer
and Pennington.

§ 3.   This act shall take effect and be in force from and after
its passage and approval.

Approved, February 26, 1885.

GOVERNMENT ROADS IN CHARLES MIX COUNTY.

CHAPTER 7.

AN ACT in Relation to the United States Government Bridge across Chotean
Creek, and to the Government Road in the Counties of Charles Mix and
Bon Homme.

Be it enacted by the Legislative Assembly of the Territory of Dakota:

§ 1.   That the road made through Bon Homme county and
Charles Mix county, together with the bridges therein, are herein
made a public highway in said counties, and said highway is

hereby subject to any and all general laws in force in said counties relating to public highways and bridges.

§ 2. It is the duty of the county commissioners of said counties to maintain and keep in repair the bridge upon the highway across Choteau creek ; each county being liable for the maintainance and repairs of that portion of said bridge within its own boundary. The sums raised by the said counties respectively to carry out the provisions of this act, shall be levied as other bridge and road taxes.

§ 3. This act shall take effect and be in force from and after its passage and approval.

Approved, March 13, 1885.

SALARY OF SUPERINTENDENT OF SCHOOLS FOR CASS AND GRAND FORKS COUNTIES

CHAPTER 8.

AN ACT to Repeal Chapter Thirty-six of the Session Laws of 1883.

Be it enacted by the Legislative Assembly of the Territory of Dakota :

§ 1. That chapter thirty-six (36) of the special laws of 1883, entitled an act to fix the salary of the superintendent of public schools in and for Cass county, Dakota Territory, be and the same is hereby repealed.

§ 2. The county superintendents of schools in and for the counties of Grand Forks and Cass will be entitled to such fees and compensation as now allowed or may be hereafter allowed superintendents of other counties for like services.

§ 3. This act shall be in force and effect from and after its passage and approval.

Approved, March 4, 1885.

COUNTY AUDITOR IN CASS, WALSH, GRAND FORKS, LINCOLN, TRAILL AND PEMBINA COUNTIES,

CHAPTER 9.

AN ACT Regulating the Term of Office of Auditor in the Counties of Cass, Walsh, Grand Forks, Lincoln, Traill and Pembina.

Be it enacted by the Legislative Assembly of the Territory of Dakota :

[§ 1.] That in the counties of Pembina, Walsh, Grand Forks Lincoln, Traill and Cass, wherein county auditors have been heretofore elected in pursuance of chapter 1 of the special laws of 1883, the county auditors so elected shall continue to hold their respective offices until the general election of county officers in November, 1886.

[§ 2.] That this act shall apply and take effect only in such of the above counties as have elected auditors for the term of two years at the annual election of 1883.

[§ 3.] That all auditors elected at the annual election of 1883, who have taken oath and given bond for a term of two years only, from the time of their said election, shall, at the expiration of said time for which they were elected, again qualify for the term of one year, or until the term of office hereby extended expires.

[§ 4.] All acts or parts of acts in conflict with this act are hereby repealed.

[§ 5.] This act to be in force and effect from and after its passage and approval.

Approved, March 12, 1885.

CLAY AND LINCOLN COUNTIES INCLUDED IN ACT FOR FIVE COMMISSIONER DISTRICTS.

CHAPTER 10.

AN ACT to Amend Chapter Thirty-three of the Special Laws of 1883, relating to County Commissioners.

Be it enacted by the Legislative Assembly of the Territory [of Dakota :]

§ 1. That section five of chapter thirty-three of the special laws of 1883, entitled "An act to provide for the division of counties into five commissioners districts and the appointment and election of commissioners therefor, and amending section fifteen of chapter twenty-one of the Political Code," be and the same is hereby amended by striking out all of the provisions in said section five of said act.

§ 2. The provisions of said act are hereby expressly extended and made to apply to the counties of Clay and Lincoln in this Territory.

§ 3. This act to take effect and be in force from and after its passage and approval.

Approved, February 26, 1885.

CAVALIER COUNTY—BOUNDARIES OF.

CHAPTER 11.

. AN ACT Defining the Boundaries of Cavalier County, and for other Purposes.

Be it enacted by the Legislative Assembly of the Territory of Dakota :

§ 1. All that district of country included within the following boundary lines shall be and the same is hereby constituted and declared to be the county of Cavalier, viz: Beginning at the southeast corner of township 159 north, range 57 west; thence
1885—30

north to the international boundary on the line running between ranges 56 and 57; thence west on the international boundary line to a point where said line is intersected by the line running between ranges 62 and sixty-three (63); thence south to the southwest corner of township 159 north, range 62 west; thence east on the township line between townships 158 and 159 to the place of beginning, shall be and remain the county of Cavalier.

SPECIAL ELECTION—DUTY OF AUDITOR OF PEMBINA COUNTY.

§ 2. That for the purpose of carrying out the provisions of section one of this act, it is hereby made the duty of the county auditor of the county of Pembina, in this Territory, to call a special election within the limits of the boundaries of the said county of Pembina, as now constituted, to be held at the several precincts within said county, not later than the twelfth day of May, 1885, and shall cause three notices to be posted in each of the several precincts within said county at least twenty days prior to said election, which said notices shall state where the polls shall be— the day of the week, the day of the month, and the hour at which said polls shall be opened and closed, and the purpose for which the election is called. The ballots to be used by the electors within the county of Pembina shall have printed or written or partly printed or written, "For division of Pembina county, No" or "Yes," as the case may be. The judges of election shall make a return to the county auditor of Pembina county, showing how many votes were cast for county division "No," for county division "Yes." The county commissioners shall, together with the county auditor of the county, meet at the county seat of Pembina county within ten days from the day of election to canvass the votes of the several precincts, and the county auditor of Pembina county shall make certified abstracts of the vote of the county of Pembina, and if a majority of all the votes cast at said election have been cast in favor of such division, then and thereafter the district described in section one shall constitute and be known as the county of Cavalier.

§ 3 In case a majority of the voters of Pembina county fail to vote for the division of Pembina county as provided in this act, then the boundaries of Cavalier county shall be as follows: Beginning at the southwest corner of township (159) one hundred and fifty nine, range (59) fifty-nine; thence north to the international boundary line; thence west along said international boundary line to a point where it is now intersected by the range line between ranges 64 and 65; thence south on said range line between ranges 64 and 65 to the southwest corner of township 159, range 64; thence east on the township line between townships 159 and 158 to the place of beginning; and the question of county seat location shall be submitted to the voters at the next annual election ; a majority of all the votes cast shall decide.

§ 4.   All acts and parts of acts in conflict with this act are hereby repealed.

Approved, March 13, 1885.

DAY AND MARSHALL COUNTIES—BOUNDARIES OF.

CHAPTER 12.

AN ACT Creating the County of Marshall and defining the Boundaries of Day County.

Be it enacted by the Legislative Assembly of the Territory of Dakota :

§ 1.   That the northern tier of townships of the county of Clark are hereby detached from said county of Clark, and the same are hereby attached to and made a part of the county of Day, and the boundaries of said county of Day are hereby declared to be as follows, to-wit: Commencing at the northeast corner of township 124 north of range 54 west, of the fifth principal meridian, running thence west on the north line of said tier of townships to the northwest corner of township 124 north, of range 59 west, thence south along the west said tier of townships to the southwest corner of township 120 north, of range 59 west, thence east along the same line of said tier of townships to the southeast corner of township 120 north, of range 54 west, thence north along the east line of said tier of townships to the northeast corner of township 124 north, of range 54 west, and the jurisdiction of said county of Day shall, upon the taking effect of this act, extend over all the district embraced in the above boundaries.

§ 2.   That all that portion of Day county as now defined lying north of the township line, between townships 124 and townships 125, shall be and the same is hereby declared to be the county of Marshall.

§ 3.   That the county of Marshall is hereby declared to be liable for such proportion of the legal indebtedness of the county of Day, existing at the date of the approval of this act, as the assessed valuation for the year A. D., 1884, of the property taken from the county of Day bears to the whole assessed valuation of Day county for the year A. D., 1884, as shown by the assessment rolls of said Day county, and the cash assets in the treasury of Day county at the time said Marshall county is organized according to law, shall be turned over to the treasurer of the county of Marshall in the proportion that the assessed valuation of said Marshall county bears to the whole valuation of Day county as shown by the assessment of the year A. D., 1884, and it is made the duty of the treasurer of Day county to turn over the money on hand as above provided.

§ 4. All unpaid taxes for the year A. D., 1884, assessed against that portion of Day county which, by the provisions of this act, becomes Marshall county, shall belong to and be collected by the county of Marshall.

§ 5. All that portion of territory detached from the county of Clark under the provisions of this act, is hereby charged with its proportion of the entire indebtedness of Clark county, based on the assessment of Clark county for the year A. D. 1884.

§ 6. If the provisions of this act shall divide any school township, each portion shall be liable for its proportion of the entire debt of said school township, based on the assessment of the year A. D., 1884, and shall receive its just proportion of the assets of such school township, based on the last annual assessment thereof.

§ 7. It shall be the duty of the county commissioners of D:y, Clark and Marshall counties to meet at the court house in the village of Webster, in said county of Day, on the first Monday in June, A. D., 1885, to equalize and provide for the assumption of the debt of Day and Clark counties.

§ 8. The officers of said county elected at the last general election, including the county commissioners who hold over by reason of non-expiration of their term of office, shall be and remain, in case of the division of said Day county, as provided in this act, said officers of said Day county, *Provided*, That they shall elect to remove, and reside within the limits thereof, if not already residents.

§ 9. The register of deeds, clerks of court, judges of probate, and county treasurers of Day and Marshall counties, respectively, shall within thirty days after the said county of Marshall shall be organized according to law, transcribe all the records of deeds, mortgages and other instruments, judgments and mechanics liens and other records; also duplicate of the assessment roll and tax list for the year A. D., 1884, from the books of said officers, respectively, in the counties of Clark and Day, pertaining to their respective counties, and such transcribed records shall have the same force and effect for all purposes as original records, and such registers of deeds, clerks of court and probate judges, shall be paid by their respective counties, fifty per cent. of such fees as are provided by law, for recording original instruments of the same character, except the county treasurer, who shall be allowed four (4) dollars per day for all services performed by him in carrying out the provisions of this section

§ 10. The said county of Marshall is hereby attached to the county of Day for judicial purposes.

§ 11. A special election shall be held in the counties of Day and Marshall as constituted in the preceding sections of this act, on the second day of May, A. D., 1885. That it shall be the duty of the sheriff of Day county, as heretofore organized, to give fifteen days notice of such election by publication for two successive weeks, in two weekly newspapers printed in said county, and that the election precincts, polling places and judges of election at such special election, shall be the same as at the last general election in Day county, *Provided*, If any such shall not be present at the opening of the polls, judges may be chosen as provided by law at general elections, and *Provided, further*, That any elector residing in that portion of Clark county attached to Day county by the provisions of this act, may vote at such election, at such polling place in Day county as heretofore organized, as may be nearest his place of residence; that said election, except as herein otherwise expressly provided, shall be governed in all things as provided by law for general elections. The ballots used at said election shall be as near as may be of one of the following forms: "For the division of Day county, Yes," or "For the division of Day county, No." If a majority of the legal votes cast at said election shall be in favor of the division of Day county, then the said counties of Day and Marshall shall be established and constituted as provided in the preceding sections of this act.

§ 12. That the register of deeds, judges of the probate court, and clerk of the district court of Day county, shall meet at the office of the register of deeds of said county, on the ninth day of May, A. D., 1885, and canvass the vote cast at said special election, that the judges of election of the several precincts shall make their returns in time to enable said canvassers to canvass the vote cast at said election on the ninth day of May, A. D., 1885; that said canvassers shall canvass the vote cast at said election, as provided by law, and they shall make three certified abstracts of the votes cast at the several precincts, at said election, and they shall immediately forward one of said abstracts to the Governor of the Territory of Dakota, and one of said abstracts to the Secretary of said Territory, and the Governor and Secretary of said Territory shall proceed to canvass the vote cast at the said election as soon as they shall receive said abstracts, and if a majority of the votes ca t at said election shall be in favor of the division of Day county then it shall be the duty of the Governor within twenty (20) days to organize the said county of Marshall according to law.

§ 13. All acts and parts of acts inconsistent herewith are hereby repealed.

§ 14. This act shall take effect and be in force from and after its passage and approval.

Approved, March 10, 1885.

TRANSCRIBING RECORDS IN EDMUNDS AND McPHERSON COUNTIES.

CHAPTER 13.

AN ACT to provide for Transcribing the Records in Edmunds and Mc-Pherson Counties.

Be it enacted by the Legislative Assembly of the Territory of Dakota:

§ 1. That the records of transfers affecting the title to real and personal property in townships 121, 122, 123 and 124, range 66, Edmunds county, shall be transcribed from the records of Brown county by the register of deeds of said Edmunds county, and shall become a part of the records of said Edmunds county.

§ 2. That the record of transfers affecting the title to real and personal property in townships 125, 126, 127 and 128, range 66, McPherson county, shall be transcribed from the records of Brown county by the register of deeds of said McPherson county and shall become a part of the records of said McPherson county.

§ 3. Said records when transcribed shall be of full force and effect, as fully as if said transfers had been originally recorded in said Edmunds and McPherson counties, and shall be public notice from and after the date of said transcript; and said transcript shall be paid for out of the treasuries of said Edmunds and Mc-Pherson counties at the legal rates; *Providing, however,* That the board of county commissioners of the respective counties of Edmunds and McPherson may contract and let the transcribing of said records at any rates less than the legal rates.

§ 4. This act shall be in force from and after its passage and approval.

Approved, March 13, 1885.

DEFINING THE BOUNDARIES OF EDMUNDS AND McPHERSON COUNTIES.

CHAPTER 14.

AN ACT to Define the Boundary lines of Edmunds and McPherson Counties.

Be it enacted by the Legislative Assembly of the Territory of Dakota:

§ 1. The county of McPherson shall be bounded and described as follows: Beginning at the intersection of the seventh standard parallel with the range line between ranges sixty-five (65) and sixty-six (66); thence west along the seventh standard parallel to its intersection with the range line between ranges seventy-three (73) and seventy-four (74); thence south along said range line between ranges seventy-three (73) seventy-four (74), to the sixth (6) standard parallel; thence east along said sixth (6) to the southeast corner of township one hundred and twenty-five (125) of range sixty-six (66); thence north along the range line between ranges sixty-five (65) and sixty-six (66) to the seventh standard parallel the place of beginning.

§ 2. The county of Edmunds shall be bounded and described as follows: Beginning at the intersection of the sixth (6) standard parallel with the range line between ranges sixty-five (65) and sixty-six (66); and thence west along the sixth (6) standard parallel to its intersection with the range line between ranges seventy-three (73) and seventy-four (74); thence south along said range lines between ranges seventy-three (73) and seventy four (74) to its intersection with the fifth (5) standard parallel; thence east along said 5th standard parallel to the southeast corner of township one hundred and twenty-one (121), of range sixty-six (66); thence north along the range line between ranges sixty-five (65) and sixty-six (66) to the sixth (6) standard parallel the place of beginning.

§ 3. All acts and parts of acts inconsistent with this act are hereby repealed.

§ 4. This act shall take effect and be in force from and after its passage and approval.

Approved, February 6, 1885.

CREATING EDDY COUNTY AND DEFINING ITS BOUNDARIES.

CHAPTER 15.

AN ACT Creating the County of Eddy, Defining its Boundaries and Defining the Boundaries of the County of Foster, and for other purposes.

Be it enacted by the Legislative Assembly of the Territory of Dakota :

§ 1. That all that district of country included within the following boundary lines, shall be and the same is hereby constituted and declared to be the county of Eddy, viz: Beginning at the southeast corner of township number one hundred and forty-eight (148) north, of range sixty-two (62), west of the fifth principal meridian, running thence north along the line between ranges sixty-one (61) and sixty-two (62) west, to the northeast corner of township number one hundred and fifty (150) north, of range number sixty-two (62) west, thence west and along the line between townships one hundred and fifty (150) and one hundred and fifty-one (151) *west*, [north], to the northwest corner of township number one hundred and fifty (150) north, of range number sixty-seven (67) west, thence south along the line between ranges number sixty-seven (67) and sixty-eight (68) west, to the southeast corner of township number one hundred and forty-eight (148) north, of range number sixty-seven (67) west, and thence along the line between townships number one hundred and forty-seven (147) and one hundred and forty-eight (148) north, to the southeast corner of township number one hundred and forty-eight (148) north, of range sixty-two (62) west.

§ 2.
That all that district of country included within the following boundary lines shall be and the same is hereby constituted and declared to be the county of Foster, viz: Beginning at the southeast corner of township number one hundred and forty-five (145) north, of range number sixty-two (62) west of the fifth principal meridian, thence north along the line between ranges number sixty-one (61) and sixty-two (62) west to the northeast corner of township number one hundred and forty-seven (147) north, of range number sixty-two (62) west, thence west and along the line between townships numbers one hundred and forty-seven (147) and one hundred and forty-eight (148) north, to the northwest corner of township number one hundred and forty-seven (147) north, of range number sixty-seven (67) west, thence south along the line between ranges number sixty-seven (67) and sixty-eight (68)

west, to the southwest corner of township number one hundred and forty-five (145) north, of range number sixty-seven (67) west, and thence east along the line between townships number one hundred and forty-four (144) and one hundred and forty-five (145) north, to the southeast corner of township number one hundred and forty-five (145) north of range number sixty-two (62) west.

§ 3. That the county seat of Foster county shall be and remain at the village of Carrington, situated in section number nineteen (19), township number one hundred and forty-six (146) north, of range number sixty-six (66) west, in said county of Foster, until changed according to law, and the county seat of the county of Eddy shall be and remain at the village of New Rockford, situated in section number thirty-two (32), township one hundred and forty-nine (149) north of range number sixty-six (66) west, in said county of Eddy, until changed according to law.

§ 4. That the question of the creation of the county of Eddy and the division of the county of Foster as provided in section number (1) and two (2) of this act shall be submitted to the legal voters of the said counties of Foster and Eddy, as constituted and defined by this act, at a special election, to be held as provided in the next section of this act.

§ 5. That a special election shall be held in the counties of Foster and Eddy, as constituted and defined in this act, on the thirty-first day of March, A. D. 1885 ; that it shall be the duty of the county clerk of Foster county, as now organized, to give fifteen (15) days' notice of such special election, by publication for two (2) successive weeks next preceding said election in two (2) weekly newspapers, one of which newspapers shall be published in the county of Foster and one of which shall be published in the county of Eddy ; that the election precincts, polling places and judges of election at said special election shall be the same as at the last general election in Foster county ; *Provided,* That the said polling places shall be within the limits of said counties of Foster and Eddy, as herein defined, and that special ballot boxes shall be provided by said clerk for said special election ; *And provided further,* That if any of such judges shall not be present at the opening of the polls, other judges may be chosen as provided by law at general elections.

§ 6. That said election, except as herein otherwise expressly provided, shall be governed in all things as provided by law for general elections ; that the ballots used at said special election shall be in one of the following forms : "For the creation of Eddy county and the division of Foster county, Yes," or "For the creation of Eddy county and the division of Foster county, No ;" and that if a majority of the legal votes cast at said special election upon the

1885—31

question submitted shall be in favor of the creation of Eddy county and the division of Foster county, then said county of Eddy shall be deemed created and the said county of Foster shall be divided as provided in this act.

§ 7. That the county clerk, judge of probate and county treasurer of Foster county, or a majority of them, shall meet at the office of said county clerk on the first Monday after said special election and canvass the votes cast at said special election; that he judges of election of the several voting precincts shall make their election returns to said county clerk in time to enable said canvassers to canvass the votes cast at said election on the said first Monday after said election; that said canvassers shall canvass the votes cast at said election as provided by law, and they shall make three certified abstracts of the votes cast in the several precincts at said election, and they shall immediately forward one of said abstracts to the Governor of the Territory of Dakota and one of said abstracts to the Secretary of said Territory, and one abstract shall be filed as a public record with the county clerk of Foster county. The Governor and Secretary of said Territory shall proceed to canvass the votes cast at said special election as returned in said abstracts, as soon as they shall receive said abstracts; and if a majority of the votes cast at said election upon the question submitted shall be in favor of the creation of the county of Eddy and the division of the county of Foster, the Governor shall within ten days thereafter appoint three (3) commissioners for the said county of Eddy, residing therein, and shall appoint two (2) commissioners for the county of Foster, residing therein; that said commissioners so appointed for the county of Eddy shall, except as herein otherwise provided, proceed to organize said county of Eddy.

§ 8. That the register of deeds and the clerk of the District Court of the county of Eddy respectively, shall without delay transcribe all the records of deeds, mortgages, and other instruments and judgments, and mechanics' liens, and other records, from the books of said office in the county of Foster, and such transcribed records shall have the same force and effect for all purposes as the original records; and said register of deeds and clerk of the District Court shall be paid by the county of Eddy for transcribing such records, such fees as are provided by law for recording original instruments of the same character.

§ 9. That the indebtedness of the county of Foster, existing at the time of the passage of this act, except the sum of twenty-one hundred dollars ($2100), to be paid exclusively by the county of Foster, shall be assumed and paid by the counties of Foster and Eddy in the proportion that the assessed valuation in 1884 of the property in each county shall bear to such indebtedness.

§ 10. That all taxes heretofore assessed or levied upon property situated within said counties of Foster and Eddy shall be collected by the treasurer of Foster county, and that said taxes shall be applied in liquidation of the proportion of the indebtedness of Foster county herein assumed by Eddy county; *Provided*, That all school moneys belonging to school townships situated within the county of Eddy, shall be paid by the treasurer of Foster county to the treasurer of Eddy county.

§ 11. That in case any school township shall be divided by the division of said Foster county, then that part of such school township as may lie in either of said counties as herein provided, to be created or defined, shall be annexed to and become a part of the school township which may lie next east of it.

§ 12. That all acts and parts of acts inconsistent with this act are hereby repealed.

§ 13. That this act shall take effect and be in force from and after its passage and approval.

Approved, March 9, 1885.

DIVIDING EMMONS COUNTY AND CREATING WINONA.

CHAPTER 16.

AN ACT to Divide the County of Emmons and Create the County of Winona.

Be it enacted by the Legislative Assembly of the Territory of Dakota:

§ 1. That all that district of country included within the following boundary lines, to-wit: Beginning at the middle of the main channel of the Missouri river, where the eighth (8) standard parallel intersects said channel; thence east along said parallel line to the northeast corner of township one hundred and thirty-two (132) north, of range seventy-four (74) west; thence south along the eastern boundary line of Emmons county to the southeast corner of said county of Emmons; thence west along the southern boundary line of said county of Emmons to the middle of the main channel of the Missouri river; thence north along the middle of the main channel of the Missouri river to the place of beginning, shall be, and the same is hereby declared to be, and is constituted the county of Winona.

§ 2.   That for the purpose of carrying out the provisions of
section one of this act, it is hereby made the duty of the county
clerk of Emmons county, of this Territory, to call a special election in the county of Emmons, on the thirtieth day of March, A.
D. 1885, to be held in said county, at which election there shall
be two polling places, one in the town of Williamsport; and the
county clerk of said county shall give notice of such election by
causing to be posted in five of the most public places in said
county, ten days before election, written or printed notices, which
notices shall state the time when the election will be held, where
the polls will be, the time when the polls will be opened and
closed, and the purpose for which the election is called.

§ 3.   The ballots to be used by the electors shall have printed
or written, or partly written or printed, " For division of Emmons
county— Yes, or No ; " and it is hereby made the duty of the
county commissioners of the county of Emmons, at least ten days
before the day of election, to appoint three electors, residing in
the election precinct for which they are appointed, judges of election for each of said polling places, and two electors possessing
the same qualifications, clerks of election for each of said polling
places.   And it is made the duty of the county clerk to make out
under his hand and official seal, a notice to each of the persons
so appointed judges and clerks, and serve the same upon each of
them personally, within five days after they are appointed.   And
if the county commissioners shall neglect or fail to appoint such
judges and clerks of election, or if for any cause judges and
clerks of election are not present at the polling places at the hour
designated in the notices for the opening of the polls, the electors
present may choose from among their number three persons to
act as judges of election, and the judges so chosen may appoint
two electors clerks of election for that polling place.

§ 4.   The polls shall be open at 9 o'clock a. m., and be kept
open until four o'clock p. m.; and immediately upon the closing
of the polls it shall be the duty of the judges to proceed to canvass the votes cast, which canvass shall be completed before any
adjournment of the board ; and when the canvass is made, the result thereof shall be certified under their hands to the county
clerk of Emmons county, and the poll boxes and ballots cast shall
also be delivered to the county clerk of said county and be by
him safely kept until thirty days after the result of the election is
made known.

§ 5.   And it is hereby made the duty of the county clerk of said
county of Emmons, within five days after said election is held to
canvass the returns received from the judges of election, and by
proclamation declare the result of the election, and under his official seal certify the result to the Governor of this Territory.

§ 6. The laws of this Territory declaring the qualifications of electors and governing general elections shall apply to the election hereby authorized to be held in all matters not provided for herein.

Approved, March 12, 1885.

FENCE LAW FOR FALL RIVER, CUSTER, PENINGTON, LAW-RENCE, ETC.

CHAPTER 17.

AN ACT to Establish a Fence Law in the Counties of Fall River, Custer, Pennington, Lawrence, Butte, Harding, Burdick, Ewing, Bowman and all of Billings and for other purposes

Be it enacted by the Legislative Assembly of the Territory of Dakota.

§ 1. That in the counties of Fall River, Custer, Pennington, Lawrence, Butte, Harding, Burdick, Ewing, Bowman, and all of Billings, a fence constructed as hereinafter described shall be sufficient and lawful.

§ 2. Posts or other uprights of reasonable strength and firmness in position, not more than thirty-two feet distant from each other, with two suitable stays between posts, nearly equally dividing such space into three parts, with three strands of ordinary barbed fence wire, well stretched and firmly fastened to such posts, uprights and stays, with the upper strand not more than forty-eight, nor less than forty-two inches above the general surface of the ground thereunder, and the lower strand shall not be more than eighteen, nor less than twelve inches above the general surface of the ground thereunder, and the middle strand shall nearly equally divide the space between the upper and lower strand.

§ 3 Any other kind of a fence or barrier, as effective for the purposes of a fence as that provided in section 2 of this act, is hereby declared sufficient and lawful; *Provided,* That all corral fence exclusively for purposes of inclosing stacks is outside of any lawful inclosure shall not be less than sixteen feet distant from such stacks so inclosed; shall be substantially built with posts not more than eight feet distant from each other, and with not less than five strands of barbed fence wire, shall be not less than five feet high; and *Provided, further,* That any other kind of a fence equally as effectual for the purpose of a corral fence may be made in lieu thereof.

§ 4   Any person owning or having in charge any horses, mules, asses, cattle, sheep, or goats, or any such animals, which shall breach through, over or under any lawful fence, not the property of the owner of such offending animals, shall be liable to the party having sustained injury by reason of such breaching, to be recovered in civil action before any court of competent jurisdiction, and it shall be sufficient in any such action, that it was a lawful fence where the breach was made, and the proceedings shall be the same as in other civil actions except as herein modified.

§ 5.   Any person owning or having in charge in either of said counties, any swine which shall trespass upon the lands or premises of another, including premises in towns, villages and cities, whether such lands or premises are fenced or not fenced, such person owning or having in charge such trespassing swine shall be liable to any party sustaining such injury for all damages he may sustain by reason of such trespassing, to be recovered in a civil action before any court having jurisdiction thereof, and the proceedings shall be the same in all respects as in other civil actions, except as herein modified ; *Provided*, That if such trespassing swine shall be restrained, the person so restraining the same shall be entitled to one (1) dollar for each of such swine so restrained, distinctly as a compensation for such restraining.

§ 6.   The parties sustaining damages done by such trespassing animals as mentioned in sections 4 and 5, before commencing action thereon, shall notify the owner or person having in charge such offending animals of such damages and the probable amount thereof, provided he knows to whom such offending animals belong, and that the owner or person in charge, reside and is within the county.

§ 7.   The party suffering damages done by offending animals as mentioned in sections 4 and 5 of this act, may retain and keep in custody such offending animals until the damages, other sums provided for herein, and costs are paid, or until sufficient security be given for the same, and when any animals are restrained as herein authorized, the person restraining the same shall without unnecessary delay notify the owner or person in whose custody the same was at the time the trespass was committed, of the seizure of such animals, provided such owner or person who had the same in charge is known to be the person making such seizure, and by him known to be, and reside, within the county.

§ 8.   For serving notice as provided in sections six and seven of this act, the person making such service shall be entitled to the same fees and mileage allowed a sheriff in serving a summons.

§ 9. Upon the trial of an action under the provisions of this act the plaintiff shall prove the amount of damages sustained and the amount of expenses incurred, for restraining and keeping the offending animals, if such have by him been restrained, and any judgment rendered for damages, other sums provided for, costs and expenses against the defendant, shall be a lien upon the animals having committed the damages, and they may be sold and the proceeds applied to the satisfaction of the judgment.

§ 10. If upon trial it shall appear that the defendant is not the owner or person in charge of such offending animals he shall be discharged and the suit may proceed against the defendant whose name is unknown, and if at the commencement of the action the plaintiff does not know the name of the owner or keeper of such offending animals, he may bring a suit against a defendant unknown. In such case service shall be made by publishing a copy of the summons with a notice stating the nature of the action in a newspaper, if there be one published in the county, and if not, by posting copies of the summons and notice in three public places in the county in either case not less than ten days previous to the day of trial.

§ 11. After judgment shall have been rendered against the defendant unknown as aforesaid, the offending animals or so many of them as may be necessary, shall be sold as in other civil actions and after said judgment and costs have been satisfied, if there is a surplus of money, it shall be placed in the hands of the county treasurer, and if the defendant does not appear and call for the same within six months from the day of sale, it shall be placed into the school fund, for the use of the public schools of the county.

§ 12. Taking or attempting to take, or advising or assisting in the taking from the possession of any person having them in charge, without the consent of such person, except by due course of law, any animals restrained and held by virtue of section 7 of this act, is hereby declared a misdemeanor, and upon conviction thereof shall be punished by a fine not to exceed fifty dollars or by imprisonment in the county jail not to exceed thirty days, or by both fine and imprisonment at the discretion of the court.

§ 13. In all actions under and by virtue of the provisions of this act, wherein the amount of damages claimed does not exceed twenty-five (25) dollars, the judgment of the court having original jurisdiction thereof shall be final, provided either party to such suit shall be entitled upon demand therefor, to a jury trial.

§ 14. No property shall be exempt from seizure and sale under execution upon judgment obtained under and by virtue of the provisions of this act, except those exemptions made absolute.

§ 15. All actions under the provisions of this act, unless commenced within six months from the date of alleged damages are hereby declared barred by statute of limitations.

§ 16. Chapter 78 of the laws of 1881, and amendments thereto, and all acts and parts of acts containing the provisions of this act, so far as to their application to the counties herein named, are hereby repealed.

§ 17. This act shall take effect and be in force from and after its passage and approval.

Approved, March 12, 1885.

FAULK COUNTY—COUNTY SEAT.

CHAPTER 18.

AN ACT to amend Section one, Chapter Nineteen, of laws of 1883, Providing for vote to change County Seat in said County

Be it enacted by the Legislative Assembly of the Territory of Dakota :

§ 1. That section one, of chapter nineteen of the laws of 1883, be amended by adding at the end thereof the following: That until the county seat of said county has been located by a vote of the people at a not greater distance than one mile from a depot to which a railroad is finished and cars running, said county of Faulk may change its county seat at any general or annual election if a majority of the legal voters of the county at such election shall vote for any one place, and the county commissioners of the county shall submit said vote upon a petition of a majority of the qualified voters of the county. Said election and proceedings under this act shall be conducted as provided in chapter 21 of the political code, except as herein provided, and after said county seat is so located within one mile of a depot to which a railroad is finished and cars running it may thereafter be changed as provided in section seven (7) of chapter 21 of the political code.

§ 2. All acts and parts of acts inconsistent with this act are hereby repealed, so far as it relates to Faulk county.

§ 3. This act to take effect and be in force from and after its passage and approval.

Approved, March 12, 1885.

ROAD IN GRAND FORKS COUNTY.

CHAPTER 19.

AN ACT to establish and Maintain a road on Forest River in Grand Forks and Walsh Counties, Dakota.

Be it enacted by the Legislative Assembly of the Territory of Dakota :

§ 1. That there is hereby established in the county of Grand Forks and Walsh in the Territory of Dakota, a winter road on the south side of the Forest river whose courses shall be determined as hereinafter provided.

§ 2. Said road shall commence on the east line of the township of Inkster in Grand Forks county and thence proceeding easterly by the most practicable route to the village of Minto in said county of Walsh.

§ 3. It shall be the duty of the supervisors of each township through which said road passes to lay out and maintain the same.

§ 4. Said road when so laid out shall be maintained as a road from the 1st day of December to the first day of April in each year.

§ 5. It shall be unlawful to use the same for road purposes except as provided in the preceding section.

§ 6. All acts or parts of acts inconsistent herewith, are hereby repealed.

§ 7. This act being deemed of immediate importance shall take effect from and after its passage and approval.

Approved, February 26, 1885.

1885—32

SALARY OF COUNTY TREASURER AND REGISTER OF DEEDS
IN GRAND FORKS COUNTY.

CHAPTER 20.

AN ACT entitled "An act Prescribing the Duties and Regulating the Salaries
of the County Treasurer and Register of Deeds for Grand Forks County,
D. T."

Be it enacted by the Legislative Assembly of the Territory of Dakota:

§ 1.　The county treasurer within and for the county of Grand
Forks, Territory of Dakota, shall discharge such duties as are now
provided by law, not inconsistent with this act, and such other
duties as are hereinafter provided.

§ 2.　He shall receive all moneys directed by law to be paid *by*
[to] him as such treasurer, and shall pay the same out only upon
the order of the proper authority.　All moneys belonging to the
county shall be paid out only upon the order of the board of
county commissioners, signed by the chairman thereof and attested
by the county auditor.　All moneys due the Territory, arising
from the collection of taxes or other sources, shall be paid upon a
draft of the territorial Auditor, drawn in favor of the territorial
Treasurer, a duplicate copy of which the territorial Auditor shall
forward to the county auditor who shall preserve the same and
credit the county treasurer with the amount thereof.

§ 3.　There is hereby created a board of auditors for said county
which board shall consist of the county auditor, the chairman of
the county commissioners and the clerk of the District Court of
said county, whose duty it shall be to examine and audit the accounts, books and vouchers of the treasurer, and to account and
ascertain the kind, description and amount of funds in the treasury of said county or belonging thereto, at least three times in
each year, without previous notice to the treasurer, and make report thereof, and of their acts and doings in the premises, to the
board of county commissioners at their next meeting after such
examination, and to publish the result of such examination in one
or more newspapers in the county, and also to witness and attest
the transfer and delivery of accounts, books, vouchers and funds
by any outgoing treasurer to his successor in office, and report the
same to the board of county commissioners at their next meeting.

§ 4.　All the funds of said county shall be deposited by the
county treasurer in one or more designated National bank or

banks in said county, on or before the first day of each month, in the name of the county ; such bank or banks shall be designated by the said board of auditors, after advertising in one or more newspapers published in the county, for at least two weeks, for proposals and receiving proposals, stating what security would be given to said county for such funds so deposited, and what interest on monthly balances of the amount deposited, upon condition that said funds with accrued interest shall be held subject to draft and payment at all times on demand ; *Provided,* That the amount deposited in any bank shall not exceed the assessed capital stock of said bank.   Every payment to the county treasurer of funds deposited in such bank shall be made on a warrant of the chairman of the board of county commissioners, duly attested by the county auditor.

§ 5.   The treasurer shall keep the books of his office in such way and manner as to show plainly and accurately every receipt and disbursement or payment daily, and on the same day on which such receipts and payments, or either of them actually occurs, and no unfinished business shall be kept or entered upon loose memorandum or slips of paper, and the said treasurer's books shall be balanced plainly and accurately every business day.   Before any National bank shall be designated as such depository, such bank shall deposit with such treasurer a bond payable to the said county and signed by not less than five freeholders of said county as sureties, which bond shall be approved by the county commissioners, and shall be in such amount as said board shall direct, in a sum not less than the amount of funds deposited in such bank at any one time.

§ 7. [6.]   The board of auditors shall be entitled to three dollars for each day actually employed in the discharge of their duties under this act, not to exceed thirty days in any one year.

§ 8. [7.]   Whenever any portion of the funds of the county is deposited in any National bank or banks in the manner as provided in this act, such county treasurer and the sureties on his bond shall be exempt from all liabilities thereon by reason of the loss of any such deposited fund from the failure, bankruptcy or any other act of such bank to the extent and amount of such funds in the hands of such bank at the time of such failure or bankruptcy.

§ 9. [8.]   On the last day of December and July in each year, the treasurer shall make settlement with and shall exhibit his accounts since the last settlement, balanced to said day, to the board of county commissioners and county auditor, showing all the moneys received and disbursed by him since his last settlement, and the balance remaining in his hands.   The books, accounts and vouchers of the treasurer and all moneys remaining in the treasury, shall at all times be subject to the inspection and examination of the board of county commissioners or any committee thereof.

§ 10. [9.] The treasurer and auditor of said county, conjointly shall make out and cause to be published in the official newspaper of the county a statement of the exact amount of money in the treasury of said county, on the last day of December and July in each year, particularly specifying in such settlement the amount to each particular fund, together with all other property, bonds, securities, claims and assets belonging to the county in the custody or under control of such treasurer.

§ 11. [10] The county treasurer for said county shall receive as full compensation for his services as county treasurer in lieu of all fees now allowed him by law, a salary of two thousand dollars per annum to be paid out of the county general fund in monthly payments upon an order from the county auditor. The said treasurer shall also be allowed a sufficient sum for clerk hire to be fixed by the county commissioners, not to exceed the sum of two thousand dollars in any one year, to be paid as herein provided for the payment of the salary of the county treasurer.

DUTIES OF REGISTER OF DEEDS.

§ 12. [11] The register of deeds for the county of Grand Forks, D.T., shall discharge such duties as is required of him under the laws of this Territory, and such other duties as herein provided for.

§ 13. [12.] The register of deeds within and for the county of Grand Forks and Territory of Dakota, in lieu of all fees now allowed him by law, shall receive a compensation of fifteen hundred dollars per annum, to be paid in monthly installments out of the general county fund by an order from the county auditor of said county. The board of county commissioners of said county shall allow a sum sufficient to pay necessary clerk hire for the office of register of deeds not to exceed in the aggregate for such clerk hire in addition to the salary herein allowed for the register of deeds, the sum of two thousand dollars per annum, to be paid to said clerk or clerks in the same manner as the salary of the register of deeds is paid.

§ 14. [13] The register of deeds shall charge and collect the same fees as now allowed by law for filing and recording any and all records and papers to be filed and recorded in the office of register of deeds, which fees so received shall on the first day of every month, except when the first day shall be a Sabbath day, then on the second day, be by said register of deeds turned over to the county treasurer of said county, to be placed to the credit of the general county fund, taking the receipt of said county treasurer for the same, and it is hereby made the duty of the county treasurer to receive such sum or sums, and to give his receipt therefor and to credit the amount so received to the general county fund. The register of deeds shall also, upon the first day of each month, make and file, with the county auditor of said county a certified copy of a detailed statement in writing under oath, showing the date of the receipt in his office of every such instrument or paper required to be filed or recorded in his office, from whom received, the kind of instrument or paper to be so filed or recorded and the regular fees allowed by law for the same, the aggregate total of said fees to tally with the amount turned into the county treasurer, and the county auditor shall thereupon charge up said amount against the county treasurer. The original copy of the report herein provided to be made to the county auditor shall be kept in the office of the register of deeds in a properly ruled book, and the board of county commissioners shall provide said register of deeds with the necessary record for the same.

§ 15. [14] The failure to comply with any of the provisions of this act by any of the officers herein named shall be a misdemeanor, and upon conviction thereof, the offender shall be fined in a sum of not less than ($100.00,) one hundred dollars, nor more than five hundred dollars, and removed from office.

§ 16. [15] All acts and parts of acts inconsistent with this act, so far as the same may apply to the county of Grand Forks, are hereby repealed.

§ 17. [16] This act shall also apply to the counties of BonHomme and Brown, and that where the county auditor appears in said bill, it shall apply to and mean county clerk in the said counties of Bon Homme and Brown.

§ 18. [17] This act shall take effect and be in force from and after its passage and approval.

Approved, March 13, 1885.

GARFIELD COUNTY—BOUNDARIES OF,

CHAPTER 21.

AN ACT to create the County of Garfield and Define its Boundaries.

Be it enacted by the Legislative Assembly of the Territory of Dakota :

§ 1. That the county of Garfield is hereby created and established of, and including, the territory within the following described boundaries, to-wit: Beginning at a point on the town line between towns one hundred and fifty-two (152) and one hundred and fifty-three (153) north, where the same is intersected by the line between range eighty-six (86) and eighty-seven (87) west; thence south on the said range line to the middle of the main channel of the Missouri river, thence along the middle of said channel in a westerly course to the line between ranges ninety-one (91) and ninety-two (92) west; thence north on the said range line to the line between towns one hundred and fifty-two (152) and one hundred fifty-three (153) north; thence east on said town line to the place of beginning.

§ 2. This act shall take effect and be in force from and after its passage and approval.

Approved, March 13, 1885.

GRANT AND ROBERTS COUNTIES– BOUNDARIES OF.

CHAPTER 22.

AN ACT to Correct and Define the Boundary Line between the Counties of Grant and Roberts.

Be it enacted by the Legislative Assembly of the Territory of Dakota :

§ 1. That the boundary line between the counties of Grant and Roberts shall be the township line between township one hundred and twenty-one (121) and township one hundred and twenty-two (122.)

§ 2. All acts or parts of acts in conflict herewith are hereby repealed.

§ 3. All assessments of real and personal property heretofore made in conformity with this act are hereby legalized.

§ 4 This act shall take effect from and after its passage and approval.

Approved, February 2, 1885.

KIDDER COUNTY—BOUNDARIES OF.

CHAPTER 23.

AN ACT to define the Boundaries of Kidder County.

Be it enacted by the Legislative Assembly of the Territory of Dakota:

BOUNDARIES OF KIDDER COUNTY.

§ 1. The county of Kidder shall be bounded and described as follows: Beginning at the sout' east corner of township one hundred and thirty-seven, between ranges sixty-nine and seventy, thence north on said line to the eleventh standard parallel; thence west along said parallel to the range line between ranges seventy-four and seventy-five; thence south on said range line to the southwest corner of township one hundred and thirty-seven; thence east along the ninth standard parallel to the place of beginning.

§ 2. The following named persons: S. S. May, Robert Allison and E. J. Moore, are hereby appointed commissioners for calling and holding an election within the Territory embraced in range 74, townships 137,–138,–139,–140,–141,–142,–143 and 144. The commissioners shall call said election and appoint the time and place for holding the same as soon as may be after the passage and approval of this act. They shall give at least twenty days notice of holding said election and no person shall vote at said election except persons who have resided within the townships above described prior to the passage of this act.

§ 3. Returns of said election shall be made in triplicate; one shall be filed with the county clerk of Kidder county, one with the county clerk of Burleigh county, and one with the secretary of the Territory.

§ 4. This act shall take effect from and after its passage and approval.

Approved, March 10, 1885.

KIDDER COUNTY—BOUNDARIES OF.

CHAPTER 24.

AN ACT to Amend an Act entitled "An Act Defining the Boundaries of Kidder County.

Be it enacted by the Legislative Assembly of the Territory of Dakota :

§ 1. That the portion of Kidder county segregated from Burleigh county lying in range seventy-four (74) west, shall not be released of its just and equitable proportion of the bonded indebtedness of said Burleigh county, at the date of the passage of this bill, and that said county of Kidder shall assume and pay said indebtedness.

§ 2. That within sixty days after the passage and approval of this act, the county commissioners of said Kidder county shall meet the county commissioners of Burleigh county, in the city of Bismarck, and the said commissioners of the two counties shall constitute a joint board of commissioners whose duty it shall be to ascertain the amount of the bonded indebtedness to be assumed by the county of Kidder, as provided in section one of this act ; the assessment of Burleigh county for the year eighteen hundred and eighty-four being taken as the basis of valuation, and when so ascertained the commissioners of said county of Kidder shall, and are hereby authorized to execute and deliver to the board of county commissioners of Burleigh county, for such share of the bonded indebtedness so ascertained, bonds of the county of Kidder with interest coupons attached, bearing the same rate of interest, due and payable at the same time as the bonds of Burleigh county, against which they are to be issued.

§ 3. The bonds to be issued under and by virtue of this act shall be printed upon bond paper, signed by the chairman of the board of county commissioners of the county of Kidder and attested by the official seal and signature of the county clerk thereof, and shall be numbered consecutively in their respective series, and recorded by the county clerk in a book kept for that purpose.

§ 4. All acts and parts of acts in conflict with this act are hereby repealed.

§ 5. This act shall take effect and be in force from and after its passage and approval.

Approved, March 10, 1885.

COLLECTION OE DELINQUENT TAXES IN LAWRENCE, PEN-
NINGTON, CUSTER, FALL RIVER AND BUTTE COUNTIES.
[SEE SUPPLEMENTARY ACT.]

CHAPTER 25.

AN ACT Supplementary to Chapter 28 of the Political Code Entitled "Revenue" and to Authorize the Bringing of suits for the Recovery of Delinquent Taxes, and to Regulate Proceedings therein.

Be it enacted by the Legislative Assembly of the Territory of Dakota :

§ 1.   MAY COLLECT TAX BY ACTION.]   At any time after the annual tax sale has closed; if any real property remains unsold for
want of bidders thereof or any taxes remain unpaid, the county
treasurer is hereby authorized and empowered, when so directed
by the board of county commissioners, in lieu of the private sale
provided by section 69 of chapter 28 of the political code, to institute a civil action in the district court of his county or subdivision, in his own name as treasurer of his county for the collection
of such taxes from the party or parties liable therefor, against the
real property chargeable therewith.   In such action the treasurer shall include taxes remaining unpaid and delinquent for any
previous year or years, and all delinquent taxes for whatever
year, against whomsoever assessed that are a lien upon the real
property sought to be charged in the action, and that can properly be united in the same action.

§ 2.   TREASURER MAY BRING ACTION AGAINST UNKNOWN OWNER.]
Where the real property appears assessed against any owner or the
title of a subsequent owner of such property appears of record, the
treasurer may bring the action against either or both at his own
option, and in cases where the property appears assessed to
an unknown owner, and the title of no subsequent owner appears
of record, he may bring the action against an unknown owner,
and all persons having an interest in the property shall be pre-
sumed to have notice of such action and the proceedings therein.

§ 3.   ACTION HOW BEGUN.]   This action shall be begun by the
service of a summons in like manner as in other civil actions, and
in the case of non-residents and of unknown defendants, service
of the summons shall be made by publication upon the same proceedings and in like manner as are provided in the code of civil
procedure for non-resident and unknown defendants having or
claiming an interest in or lien upon real property.

1885—33

§ . COSTS.] In every judgment recovered under this act, the same costs shall be taxable as in ordinary civil actions, and in addition thereto, the sum of one dollar in each case for the treasurer for his certificate of the tax entry, and it shall be the duty of the county attorney to prosecute all such suits when directed so to do by the board of county commissioners without any additional fees therefor, *Provided, however,* That none of these taxable costs shall be demanded of the treasurer of the county in advance, but shall be payable when collected by the treasurer.

§ 5. COMPLAINT—FORM OF.] In the action brought by the treasurer, the complaint may be in the following form, and shall be legally sufficient; (title of court,) (name of plaintiff) vs. (name of defendant.) The plaintiff complains and alleges, that the defendant is indebted to the plaintiff in the sum of $——, (naming the total amount due the territorial, county and other funds,) for taxes, with five per cent. penalty added thereto, for the non-payment thereof, and interest thereon, at the rate of one per cent per month from (date of delinquency) and ——cents cost of advertising, which said taxes were duly assessed and levied upon the (real or personal) property of the defendant, to-wit: (describe the property as assessed) for the fiscal year (naming the year). (For taxes for a previous year and additional paragraph may be added in similar form.) That the taxes aforesaid, with penalty, interest and costs are a lien upon the real property before described. Wherefore the plaintiff prays judgment against said defendant for the sum of $——, with penalty and interest as aforesaid, and costs of suit, and that the lien of said taxes may be enforced against said real property, and the same be condemned to be sold to satisfy plaintiff's judgment. [*Signature of Attorney*]. In case of an unknown owner or of personal tax chargeable as a lien on real property or where the defendant is sued in a representative capacity, or in other causes presenting peculiar circumstances the complaint shall contain such additional allegations as such circumstances may require.

§ 6. EVIDENCE] In the trial of any action brought under this act, a certificate in the following form, signed by the treasurer and under the seal of the county, shall be *prima-facie* evidence of the due assessment and levy of the tax, and that it is due and delinquent. " I hereby certify that the following is a correct transcript of entry on the duplicate tax list of —— county now in my hands for collection " (name description of real property, personal tax to different funds, totals, remarks.) That the above tax became delinquent on (date), has since been advertised for sale at a cost of $——, and not sold for want of bidders, and remains unpaid.

(COUNTY SEAL.)

(TREASURER.)

§ 7. ACTIONS –HOW GOVERNED.] These actions shall be governed by the rules and practice of the code of civil procedure, and judgment may be taken as in such code provided, either in term time or vacation. Where issue is joined the cause shall at once, on request of the plaintiff, be placed by the clerk on the calendar for trial, without serving or filing note of issue or notice of trial, and shall be given precedence in the district court next after criminal business Such issue shall be triable by the court, subject to its power to send any or all of the issues to be tried to a jury, as provided in the code of civil procedure.

§ 8. AFTER PAYMENT—TREASURER TO PAY COSTS.] Upon the payment of any taxes after suit shall have been brought, or the payment or collection thereof after judgment, the treasurer shall pay therefrom the costs and make distribution of the balance as provided by law.

§ 9. INTEREST ON JUDGMENT.] All judgments obtained under the provisions of this act, shall bear interest at the rate of thirty [per cent.] per annum until paid.

§ 10. ENFORCING JUDGMENT.] Upon the recovery of judgment in any case brought under this act, the same may be enforced by execution, in like number as now provided in the code of civil procedure for cases of judgment requiring the sale of property, and the proceedings throughout shall be the same as in such cases except that in all cases arising under this act, execution shall be directed to the treasurer of the county in which the property to be sold is situated, instead of to the sheriff, and the treasurer shall discharge all and singular the duties in and about the receipt of said execution, the advertisement and sale of the real property directed to be sold thereunder, the conduct of the sale, the execution of certificate of purchase, return of execution and report of sale, and any other duties now required of the sheriff in the sale of real property on execution, in the same manner as the same are required by law to be performed and discharged by the sheriff in the case of sale of real property by him under writs of execution, requiring the sale of real property. The proceedings of the treasurer in the premises, to be reported to the court upon return of the execution, and be subject to review and confirmation by the court, in like manner as sheriff's sale of real property on execution. The premises sold by the treasurer shall be subject to redemption in like manner upon the same terms and conditions, and within the same period, as provided for ordinary sales of real property on execution. *Provided, however*, That during the period allowed for redemption, and until redemption is made the treasurer's certificate of purchase shall bear interest at the rate of thirty per cent. per annum.

§ 11. HIGHEST BIDDER.] In any sale upon execution under

this act, the person who offers to pay the amount due on any parcel of land, for the smallest portion of the same is to be considered the highest bidder: Such portion to be chosen in like manner as provided for sales made by the treasurer under ordinary tax sales in section sixty-three (63) of chapter twenty-eight (28) of the political code.

§ 12. WHEN COUNTY TO PURCHASE.] If in any instance there should be no bidders willing to give the full amount of the judgment, penalty, interest and costs for any real property advertised and offered for sale then it shall be the duty of the treasurer, when directed by the board of county commissioners, to bid for such real property in the name of the county of which he is treasurer, for the amount of judgment, interest and costs accrued, and certificate shall issue to such county in like manner as to any other purchaser; *Provided, however,* That no costs or treasurers' commission, shall be payable by the county until redemption is made from such sale, or the time for redemption has expired. *Provided, further,* That all property purchased by any county, under the provisions of this act, shall be offered for sale to the highest bidder, by the treasuer, at each annual tax sale, until the same is sold.

§ 13. EXPIRATION OF REDEMPTION.] At the expiration of the period allowed for redemption, if no redemption shall have been made, the treasurer must make the purchaser, or the party entitled thereto, a deed of the real property sold, which deed shall be in the usual form of deeds made by the sheriff after sale under execution on a judgment directing the sale of real property, and shall have the same force and effect.

§ 14. FEES OF TREASURER.] For his services in attending and conducting any sale under this act, the treasurer shall be allowed the following fees; for advertising and attending sale and returning execution, one (1) dollar; for executing certificate of purchase, one (1) dollar; for execution of deed, one (1) dollar; the last item to be be paid by the grantee in the deed; the other items to be taxed as accrued costs in making sale.

§ 15. PURCHASER'S PRIVILEGES.] The purchaser at any sale as aforesaid, or his assignee, may pay any tax becoming delinquent before redemption from his purchase has been made, and thereafter no redemption can be made from him without paying the amount due on his certificate of purchase, with interest at the rate of thirty per cent. per annum from the date thereof, and such other liens held by him as are now required to be paid in making redemption from sales on ordinary execution, and in addition thereto, the amount of such subsequent tax paid by him with interest from date of his payment thereof, at the rate of thirty per cent. per annum.

§ 16. Limitation of action.] The same limitation shall apply to the bringing of action to impeach any deed made under the provisions of this act, and the same pre-requisites be enforced against the party bringing such action, as in case of deed executed by the treasurer on ordinary tax sale made by him in section seventy-five (75) of chapter twenty-eight (28) of the political code.

§ 17. No defense.] In actions brought under the provisions of this act, it shall be no defense thereto that the land described has not been advertised or offered at the tax sale or that a public tax sale for any year has not been held, or that there were irregularities in the conduct of the sale or the advertisement thereof, or in the assessment and levy of the tax; nor shall any defense be admissable or any relief granted against the tax sought to be enforced, except such as may have been heretofore permitted under the existing revenue laws of the Territory.

§ 18. Penalties remitted.] It is further provided that any parties paying their delinquent taxes prior to October 1st, 1885, for the year 1883, and all previous years, shall have remitted to them all penalties and interest due on the same.

§ 19. · This act shall be in force and effect from and after its passage and approval, but no proceedings for the sale of property under the provisions thereof, shall take place prior to November 1st, 1885.

Approved, March 3, 1885.

SUPPLEMENTARY TO CHAPTER 25.

CHAPTER 26.

AN ACT Supplementary to an Act entitled "An act Supplementary to Chapter 28 of the Political Code, entitled 'Revenue.'" Approved March 3, 1885.

[*Be it enacted by the Legislative Assembly of the Territory of Dakota :*]

§ 1. That the provisions of section eighteen of an act entitled an act supplementary to chapter 28 of the Political Code, entitled Revenue, and to authorize the bringing of suits for the recovery of delinquent tax: s and to regulate proceedings *proceedings* therein, approved, March 3, 1885, shall apply only to and be in force in the counties of Lawrence, Pennington, Custer, Fall River and Butte.

§ 2. This act shall take effect and be in force from and after its passage and approval.

Approved, March 13, 1885.

TO LOCATE THE COUNY SEAT OF LA MOURE COUNTY.

CHAPTER 27.

AN ACT to Enable the Voters of La Moure County to Locate the County Seat.

Be it enacted by the Legislative Assembly of the Territory of Dakota:

§ 1. That at the next general election in the year one thousand eight hundred and eighty-six (1886) the qualified voters of La Moure county, Territory of Dakota, are hereby empowered to vote upon the location of the county seat of said county, by ballot, and for this purpose each voter may designate on his ballot the place of his choice for county seat of said county, in manner following, to-wit: "For county seat, ————————" the name of the place to be either written or printed in the foregoing blank.

§ 2. The said election for county seat shall be governed by the law relating to general elections, and returns of said vote for county seat shall be made by the officers appointed under and pursuant to said general election law, in the various voting precincts, to the county clerk, as therein provided, who shall proceed with other officers as therein directed to ascertain the result of said vote, and shall truly certify the same to the county commissioners of said county, said certificate to be duly filed of record by said commissioners.

§ 3. That the place having the majority of the votes polled for county seat at such election, shall be the county seat of said county and if it shall appear that a majority of the votes polled for county seat were cast for some place other than the present county seat, the county commissioners of said county shall assemble at their usual place of meeting within ten days after the issuing of the certificate mentioned in the last preceding section, and shall give immediate public notice in accordance with the result of the vote, of the change of county seat by publication at least once in all the newspapers published in said county ; and it shall be the further duty of said commissioners to make provision for the further removal of the public records and public offices of the county, and to remove the same within thirty days after the publication of such notices to the place named therein as the future county seat.

§ 4. All acts or parts of acts in conflict herewith are hereby repealed.

§ 5. This act to take effect and be in force from and after its passage and approval.

Approved, March 13, 1885.

ENLARGING THE COUNTY OF McHENRY

CHAPTER 28.

AN ACT to Annex Certain Townships to the County of McHenry, Dakota Territory, and Making them a Part of said County.

Be it enacted by the Legislative Assembly of the Territory of Dakota:

§ 1. That townships numbered one hundred and fifty-one (151), one hundred and fifty-two (152), one hundred and fifty-three (153), one hundred and fifty-four (154), one hundred and fifty-five (155), one hundred and fifty-six (156), north of range eighty-one (81) west, are hereby attached to and made a part of McHenry county, and that the jurisdiction of McHenry county shall extend over the same.

§ 2. This act shall take effect and be in force from and after its passage and approval.

Approved, March 13, 1885.

TAXES COLLECTED BY THE TREASURER OF MINER COUNTY.

CHAPTER 29.

AN ACT to Repeal Section Five (5) of Chapter Thirty-one (31) of the Session Laws of 1883.

Be it enacted by the Legislative Assembly of the Territory of Dakota:

§ 1. That section five (5) of chapter thirty-one (31) of the session laws of 1883 of this Territory, be and the same is hereby repealed.

§ 2. That the treasurer of Miner county is hereby authorized and required to retain all moneys collected for that portion of Miner county out of which Sanborn county was created, and that said treasurer of Miner county is hereby directed to apply said money so collected by him to the payment of any indebtedness incurred by Miner county previous to the division of said county, said payment to be made by said treasurer as directed by the board of county commissioners of said Miner county.

Approved, February 29, 1885.

McLEAN COUNTY—BOUNDARIES OF.

CHAPTER 30.

AN ACT to Define the Boundaries of the County of McLean.

Be it enacted by the Legislative Assembly of the Territory of Dakota:

§ 1. That the county of McLean shall include all the territory within the following described boundaries, to-wit: Beginning at the southeast corner of town 143 north, range 80 west; thence west along the line between towns 142 and 143 north, to the middle of the channel of the Missouri river; thence following the middle of the channel of said river in a northwesterly direction to the town line between ranges 84 and 85 west; thence north along

the line between ranges 84 and 85 west, to the northwest corner
of town 147 north, range 84 west; thence east along the line between towns 147 and 148 north, to the northeast corner of town
147 north, range 80 west; thence south along the line between
ranges 79 and 80 to the place of beginning, adding to the said
county of McLean as now constituted, towns 143 and 144 north,
range 80 west, and fractional township 143 north, range 81 west;
Provided, however, That a majority of the legal voters of said towns
143 and 144 north, range 80 west, and fractional township 143
north, range 81 west, present and voting at an election called for
that purpose, shall vote in favor of being transferred to McLean
county.

§ 2. The board of county commissioners of the county of Burleigh are empowered and it is hereby made their duty to provide
for and call a special election to be held in the said townships 143
and 144 north, range 80 west, and fractional townships 143 north,
range 81 west, on the first Monday in April, 1885, at which election the legal voters of said townships shall vote in favor of or
against said townships being annexed to and made a part of said
McLean county. The ballots used at such election shall have
written or printed on them the words: "For annexation to Mc-
Lean county, Yes," or "For annexation to McLean county, No."
If a majority of ballots cast at said election shall be in favor of
annexation to McLean county, then said townships become and be
a part of said McLean county. It shall also be the duty of the
commissioners of Burleigh county to give not less than fifteen
days' notice of such election, by causing to be posted in three conspicuous places in each of said townships affected by this act,
written or printed notices of said election, which notices shall designate the time and place or places of holding said election, and
otherwise conform to the law providing for notices for election.
Said county commissioners of Burleigh county shall establish one
or more voting places in said townships, as in their opinion may
seem necessary, and appoint judges of election and make such
other provisions for said election as are required for general elections. The returns of said elections shall be made in the manner
provided for general elections, and the county clerk of Burleigh
county shall within ten days after such election returns are canvassed, make two certified copies of the same, one of which said
copies shall be spread at length upon the deed records of Burleigh
county, and the other of said copies delivered to the register of
deeds of McLean county, who shall record the same in the deed
records of said county, the recording of which said returns in the
respective counties named in this act shall be full and complete
notice of the result of said election.

1885—34

§ 3. This act shall take effect and be in force from and after its passage and approval.

Approved, March 12, 1885.

MERCER AND OLIVER COUNTIES—BOUNDARIES OF.

CHAPTER 31.

AN ACT to Define the Boundaries of the Counties of Mercer and Oliver and for other purposes.

Be it enacted by the Legislative Assembly of the Territory of Dakota:

§ 1. All that district of country in the Territory of Dakota included within the following boundary lines, to-wit: Commencing at a point in the middle o! a channel in the Missouri river where it is intersected by the boundary line between ranges number eighty-three and eighty-four, and running thence south to the boundary line between townships numbered one hundred and forty-three and one hundred and forty-four, thence west on said boundary line to the eastern boundary line of range number ninety-one, thence north on the line dividing ranges numbered ninety and ninety-one to the middle of the channel of the Missouri river, where it is intersected by said line, thence following the middle of the channel of said Missouri river to the place of beginning, is hereby constituted and declared to be the county of Mercer.

§ 2. That all the district of country included within the following boundary lines shall be and the same is hereby constituted and declared the county of Oliver, to-wit: Beginning at a point in the middle of the channel of the Missouri river on the northern boundary line of the county of Morton and running thence west on said boundary line which is also the tenth standard parallel to the eastern boundary line of Williams county, thence north along the said eastern boundary line of Willi.ms county which is the eastern boundary line of range number eighty-eight, to the point where it intersects the boundary line between townships numbered one hundred and forty-three and one hundred and forty-four, thence east upon this said line to the boundary line between ranges number eighty-three and eighty-four, thence north upon this said line to the middle of the channel of the Missouri river, thence following the downward course of the said river in the middle of the channel to the place of beginning, and the town of Raymond is hereby constituted the seat of government of said county of Oliver until changed according to law, and Henry Sawyer, H. E. Fisher and Lewis Connolly are hereby constituted commissioners of said county of Oliver until their successors are duly elected and qualified according to law.

§ 3. The counties, the boundaries of which are defined by this act, shall be attached to the county of Morton for judicial purposes. .

§ 4. This act shall not take effect until the same shall have been submitted to the legal voters of the counties of Mercer and Oliver as constituted and defined by this act at a special election to be held as provided in the next section of this act.

§ 5. That a special election shall be held in the counties of Mercer and Oliver as constituted and defined by this act on the second Tuesday of April A. D. 1885, which is the fourteenth day thereof. That it shall be the duty of the county clerk of Mercer county as now organized to give fifteen days notice of such special election by posting written notices thereof in a public place at each of the polling places constituted as hereinafter required, and by publishing the same for two weeks next preceding the said election in the *Stanton Pilot*, a weekly paper published at Stanton, in said county of Mercer.

§ 6. There shall be established by the county commissioners of Mercer county, as now organized, three polling places, each in the counties of Mercer and Oliver, as created and bounded by this act, and at such places as shall best accommodate the voters thereof. The said county commissioners of Mercer county, as now organized, shall appoint three judges of election for each voting precinct hereby constituted. The said judges of each precinct shall elect two clerks for that precinct and shall open the polls for said special election at ten o'clock A. M, on the day on which said special election is called, and close the same at four o'clock P. M. of that day, and in all other matters, except as hereinafter provided, shall conduct the election as any general election.

§ 7. The ballots used in the special election as provided by section five of this act, shall be in one of the following forms: "For the division of Mercer county and the creation of Oliver county, Yes," and "For the division of Mercer county and the creation of Oliver county, No;" and if a majority of the legal votes cast at said special election shall be for the division of the county of Mercer and the creation of the county of Oliver, then the county of Oliver shall be deemed created and the county of Mer er divided and their respective boundaries be as defined in sections one and two of this act.

§ 8. The judges of election of the several voting precincts for the special election provided by this act, shall make their returns of said election to the Secretary of Dakota Territory, and shall forward the same returns without delay as soon as they are completed, to the said Secretary of Territory, who, with the Governor of the Territory, shall canvass the votes cast at said special election as soon as the returns of the same are received, and within ten days notify the county clerk of Mercer county of the result, and if a majority of the votes cast at said election upon the questions submitted shall be in favor of creating the county of Oliver and the division of the county of Mercer, then the Governor shall within ten days thereafter notify the three commissioners for the county of Oliver as provided in section two of this act, who shall proceed to organize the said county according to law

§ 9. That the register of deeds of the county of Oliver upon the organization of said county, shall without unnecessary delay, transcribe the records of deeds, mortgages and other instruments from the books of said office in the county of Mercer, and such transcribed records shall have the same force and effect for all purposes as the original records, and the said register of deeds shall receive as compensation for transcribing such records such fees as are provided by law for recording original instruments of the same character.

§ 10. The special election as provided by section five of this act shall not be invalidated by the neglect of the county clerk of Mercer county to give proper notice thereof, or the neglect of the judges of election in any voting precinct.

§ 11. That should the county clerk of Mercer county neglect to give notice of said special election as required by this act, or the county commissioners neglect to establish voting precincts or appointing judges of election as required by this act, then the legal voters may assemble at the voting precincts as established at the last election in said county of Mercer as it now exists, and elect their own judges and proceed with said election as hereinbefore provided.

§ 12. This act to take effect upon its passage and approval.

Approved, March 12, 1885.

RAMSEY AND BENSON COUNTIES—BOUNDARIES OF.

CHAPTER 32.

AN ACT to Define the Boundaries of Ramsey and Benson Counties, and for other Purposes.

Be it enacted by the Legislative Assembly of the Territory of Dakota.

§ 1. That all that territory described as follows, to-wit: Beginning at the intersection of the thirteenth standard parallel with the range line between ranges 60 and 61; thence north on the range line between ranges 60 and 61 to the northeast corner of township 154; thence west on the township line between townships 154 and 155 to the northwest corner of township 154; thence north on the range line between ranges 61 and 62 to the northeast corner of township one hundred and fifty-eight; thence west on the township line between townships 158 and 159 to the northwest corner of township 158, between ranges 64 and 65; thence south on the ran e line between ranges 64 and 65 to the southwest corner of township 157; thence west on the township line between townships 156 and 157 to the intersection of said line with the ninth guide meridian; thence south along said ninth guide meridian to its second intersection with the Mauvaise Coulee; thence along the center of said Mauvaise Coulee to its intersection with the township line between townships 153 and 154; thence east on the township line between townships 153 and 154 to the range line between ranges 65 and 66; thence south on the range line between ranges 65 and 66 to the intersection of said range line with the 13th standard parallel; thence east on the 13th standard parallel to the south shore of Devils Lake; thence easterly along the south shore of Devils Lake to the southeastern extremity of said lake; thence east to the range line between ranges 61 and 62; thence north on the range line between ranges 61 and 62 to the 13th standard parallel; thence east on said 13th standard parallel to the place of beginning, shall be, and the same is hereby constituted, the county of Ramsey.

§ 2. That all that territory described as follows, to-wit: Beginning at the intersection of the 13th standard parallel with the range line between ranges 65 and 66; thence east on the 13th standard parallel to the south shore of Devils Lake; thence easterly along the south shore of Devils Lake to the southeastern extremity of said lake; thence east on the range line beween ranges

61 and 62 ; thence south on the range line between ranges 61 and 62 to the township line between townships 150 and 151 ; thence west on the township line between townships 150 and 151 to the range line between ranges 71 and 72 ; thence north on the range line between ranges 71 and 72 to the township line between townships 156 and 157 ; thence east on the township line between townships 156 and 157 to the ninth guide meridian ; thence south on the 9th guide meridian to its second intersection with the Mauvaise Coulee ; thence south along the center of said Mauvaise Coulee to its intersection with the township line between townships 153 and 154 ; thence east along said township line to the range line between ranges 65 and 66 ; thence south on said range line to its intersection with the 13th standard parallel, shall be and the same is hereby constituted, the county of Benson.

§ 3. SPECIAL ELECTION TO VOTE UPON ANNEXATION.] *Provided, however,* That the portion of Benson county hereby proposed to be atta hed to Ramsey county shall not be so attached unless the question of annexation shall first be submitted to a vote of the electors living in said portion proposed to be attached to Ramsey county, and it is hereby made the duty of the county clerk of Ramsey county to call said election within sixty days after the passage and approval of this act ; said election to be conducted in accordance with the laws governing elections. In case a majority of the legal voters of said portion voting shall vote in favor of said annexation, then this act shall be of full force and effect. The form of ballots shall be, " For annexation, Yes," " For annexation, No." All expenses of said election shall be paid by Ramsey county.

§ 4. All taxes levied for the year 1884 on that portion of Benson county hereby sought to be attached to Ramsey county shall be paid to the county treasurer of Benson county for the sole use and benefit of said Benson county.

§ 5. This act shall take effect and be in force from and after its passage and approval.

Note by the Secretary of the Territory.

The foregoing act having been presented to the Governor for his approval, and not having been returned to the House of Representatives, the house of the Legislative Assembly in which it originated, within the time prescribed by the Organic Act, has become a law without his approval.

JAMES H. TELLER,
Secretary of the Territory.

FIVE COMMISSIONER DISTRICTS IN RICHLAND, FAULK, HYDE
AND SARGENT COUNTIES.

CHAPTER 33.

AN ACT to provide for County Commissioners in the Counties of Richland,
Faulk, Hyde and Sargent.

Be it enacted by the Legislative Assembly of the Territory of Dakota:

§ 1.　That the counties of Richland, Faulk, Hyde and Sargent
shall have five county commissioners, whose powers and duties
shall be the same as now provided by law.

§ 2.　It is hereby made the duty of the clerk of the district
court, the judge of probate and the county superintendent of
schools of said counties to meet at the county seat of their respective counties on or before the first day of May, 1885, and proceed
to lay off their county into five commissioner districts which shall
contain as near as practicable an equal number of voters as evi-
denced by the votes p lled therein at the general election of 1884;
due regard being had to population and extent of territory, and
the division shall so be made that no polling precinct shall lie or
be in more than one commissioners district; the counties shall also
be so divided where practicable, that no two of the commissioners
of any county now holding offic: will be residents of one commissioner district.

§ 3.　Said officers whose duty it is hereby made to lay out and
so divide their respective counties shall order, and it is hereby
made their duty to order, an election in each of commissioner districts not already represented by the present board of county
commissioners, for the purpose of electing a commissioner for
such district; such election to be held on or before the first day of
June, 1885, upon a notice of not less than fifteen days, such notice
to be published twice in a weekly paper published in the county,
if one be published therein, and by posting such notices in five
conspicuous places in each commissioner district, and such notice
to also contain the time and place of holding such election, *Provided,*　That where in such division of commissioner districts, two
members of the present board of commissioners shall reside in
one commissioner district, one of such commissioners shall, by order of the said officers so authorized to make such division, be declared to represent one of the commissioner districts adjoining the
one in which such commissioner reside, and in such case the dis-

trict declared to be represented by one of the present board of commissioners shall hold no election for commissioner until the expiration of the term of the commissioner so declared to represent such district.

§ 4. All commissioners elected under this act shall hold their office until the next general election in 1886, except where they are elected to fill vacancy caused by the expiration of the term of office of any commissioner now holding office, in which case he shall hold for a period of two years next ensuing the annual or general election at which he is elected, and no commissioner of any county provided for by this act hereafter elected, shall be elected to hold for a longer period than two years next ensuing his election.

§ 5. The said officers hereby authorized to subdivide their respective counties as aforesaid, shall receive such fees for their services rendered herein as shall be allowed by the commissioners of their respective counties.

§ 6. This act shall take effect and be in force from and after its passage and approval.

Approved, March 12, 1885.

RICHLAND COUNTY—BOUNDARIES OF.

CHAPTER 34.

AN ACT to Change the Boundary Line of the County of Richland, and for other Purposes.

Be it enacted by the Legislative Assembly of the Territory of Dakota:

§ 1. That all that territory lying and being within the following boundary lines, to-wit: Commencing at the southeast corner of the county of Richland; thence in a southernly direction up the main channel of the Bois De Sioux river, along the boundary line of the State of Minnesota to a point where the same is intersected by the southern boundary line of township one hundred and twenty-nine (1 9) north; thence westward along said boundary line and onward to a point at the northeast corner of Day county; thence directly northward to the southern boundary line of said county of Richland; thence eastward along said southern boundary line to the place of beginning, including all that portion of townships one hundred and twenty-nine (129) north, ranges forty-seven (47), forty-eight (48), forty-nine (49), fifty (50), fifty-one (51) and fifty-two (52), not heretofore forming a part of said county of Richland, be and the same is hereby attached to and made a part of said county of Richland.

§ 2. That all taxes now assessed on said tract of land shall be collected and paid into the treasury of Roberts county.

§ 3. The county seat of government for the county of Roberts, Dakota Territory, is hereby established at the village of Wilmot in said county, and shall not be moved therefrom except by a vote of the people and in accordance with the general laws of the Territory.

§ 4. This act shall take effect and be in force from and after its passage and approval.

Approved, March 9, 1885.

LEGALIZING THE LOCATION OF THE COUNTY SEAT OF SANBORN COUNTY.

CHAPTER 35.

AN ACT Entitled an Act to Legalize the Location of the County Seat of Sanborn County.

Be it enacted by the Legislative Assembly of the Territory of Dakota:

§ 1. That the acts of the county commissioners of Sanborn county in declaring the town of Woonsocket duly elected county seat of Sanborn county at the general election of 1884, is hereby legalized.

§ 2. That the town of Woonsocket is hereby declared to be the permanent county seat of Sanborn county, subject to removal under the provisions of section seven, chapter 21, of the Code of Civil Procedure.

§ 3. This act shall be in full force and effect on and after its passage and approval.

Approved, March 12, 1885.

1885—35

SPINK COUNTY—COUNTY SEAT.

CHAPTER 36.

AN ACT to Relocate the County Seat of Spink County, Dakota.

Be it enacted by the Legislative Assembly of the Territory of Dakota :

§ 1. That the county seat of Spink cuunty, Dakota, is hereby removed from its present location and located at Ashton, Spink county, Dakota, situated on section thirty-five, township number one hundred and eighteen north of range sixty-four west.

§ 2. That within thirty days after the passage and approval of this act, the board of county commissioners of said county shall provide suitable offices at said Ashton for all the officers of said county, and all of said officers shall immediately thereafter remove all the records, files and documents pertaining to their respective offices to the places so provided at said Ashton, and shall thereafter hold their respective offices thereat ; *Provided,* That the county commissioners of said county shall expend no moneys in procuring the offices mentioned in this section except the annual rental thereof, which shall not exceed the sum of five hundred dollars.

§ 3. That in case said board of commissioners shall fail or refuse to provide suitable offices for any of said county officers at said Ashton within the time limited in the foregoing section, then each of said county officers shall provide for himself a suitable office at said Ashton, and shall immediately remove his office to said Ashton and shall thereafter keep the same thereat, and the expense incurred in providing such office and removing thereto shall be a charge against the said county of Spink ; *Provided,* That the entire rent per annum for the said county offices shall not exceed the sum of five hundred dollars.

§ 4. That the county clerk of said county shall within ten days after the passage and approval of this act, call a special meeting of the board of commissioners of said county for the purpose of enabling said board to carry into effect the provisions of this act.

§ 5. That the county seat of said Spink county may be removed from said Ashton if at the general election in 1886 a majority of all the votes cast shall be in favor of any other town, but if no town receive a majority of all the votes cast at said election then the said Ashton shall be and remain the permanent county seat of Spink county, unless afterwards removed in the manner provided by section seven of chapter twenty-one of the Political Code of Dakota.

§ 6. That all acts or parts of acts not consistent with this act are hereby repealed.

§ 7. That this act shall take effect and be in force from and after its passage and approval.

Approved, March 10, 1885.

COUNTY AUDITORS FOR SPINK AND OTHER COUNTIES.

CHAPTER 37.

AN ACT Providing for Appointing Auditors for the Counties of Spink, Stutsman, Barnes, Burleigh, Nelson, Brookings and Miner.

Be it enacted by the Legislative Assembly of the Territory of Dakota:

§ 1. That the board of county commissioners, county treasurer, and judge of probate, respectively, of the counties of Spink, Stutsman, Barnes, Morton, Burleigh, Nelson, Brookings and Miner, are hereby authorized to appoint an auditor for their respective counties, who shall hold his office till the first Monday in January, 1887, and until his successor is elected and qualified.

§ 2. That the special law creating the office of county auditor in the counties of Pembina, Walsh, Grand Forks, Lincoln, Traill, Cass and Richland, approved, March 9, 1883, chapter one, section one to twenty, inclusive, shall apply and prescribe the duties of the auditors of the counties of Spink, Stutsman, Barnes, Morton, Burleigh, Nelson, Brookings and Miner.

§ 3. This act to take effect and be in force from and after its passage and approval.

Approved, March 13, 1885.

STANTON COUNTY—BOUNDARIES OF.

CHAPTER 88.

AN ACT to Create and Define the Boundaries of the County of Stanton, and for other purposes.

Be it enacted by the Legislative Assembly of the Territory of Dakota:

§ 1. All that district of country included within the following boundary lines shall be, and the same is hereby constituted and declared the county of Stanton, viz: Beginning at the southeast corner of township one hundred and thirty-seven (137) north, of range sixty-nine (69) west, thence west between townships one hundred and thirty-seven (137) and one hundred and thirty-six (136) to the southwest corner of township one hundred and thirty-seven (137) north, of range seventy-one (71) west, thence north between range seven-one (71) and seventy-two (72) to the northwest corner of township one hundred and forty-four (144) north, of range seventy-one (71) west, thence east between townships one hundred and forty-four (144) and one hundred and forty-five (145) north, to the northeast corner of township one hundred and forty-four (144) north, of range sixty-nine (69) west, thence south between ranges sixty-nine (69) and sixty-eight (68) to the point of beginning, shall be and the same is hereby declared to be, and is constituted the county of Stanton.

§ 2. *Provided, however,* That the portion of Kidder county and the portion of Stutsman county hereby proposed to be segregated shall not be cut off unless the question of segregation shall be first submitted to a vote of the people of Kidder county, and also to the voters of that part of range sixty-nine (69) proposed to be detached from Stutsman county, at a special election called for that purpose, by giving at least fifteen (15) days notice of the same by posting such notices in each election precinct as already established; or if in such portion of either county proposed to be segregated no election precinct is already established, then it shall be the duty of the board of county commissioners at their first meeting after the passage of this act to appoint therein an election precinct, and it is hereby made the duty of the county commissioners of the counties of Kidder and Stutsman to call said election within sixty (60) days after the passage and approval of this act, and in case of a neglect or refusal of said commissioners to call said election, then it shall be the duty of the county clerks of said counties to call said election.

§ 3. In case a majority of the legal voters of said Kidder county and of said range sixty-nine (69) voting, shall vote in favor of said segregation, then this act shall be in full force and effect. It shall be the duty of the respective boards of county commissioners of Kidder and Stutsman counties to meet at their respective county seats within ten (10) days after said election to canvass said vote, and in case of refusal of said board to canvass said vote within the ten (10) days, then the respective county clerks are hereby authorized and empowered to appoint three freeholders of the county to act as a board of canvassers, who shall canvass the vote as now provided by law. The form of the ballot shall be: " For division, Yes." " For division, No." All expenses of said election shall be paid by the county of Stanton.

§ 3. [4.] All acts and parts of acts in conflict with this act are hereby repealed.

§ 4. [5] This act shall take effect and be in force trom and after its passage and approval.

Approved, March 13, 1885.

TRAILL COUNTY—COMMISSIONERS DISTRICT.

CHAPTER 39.

AN ACT Dividing the County of Traill, Dakota Territory, into Commissioner Districts

Be it enacted by the Legislative Assembly of the Territory of Dakota :

§ 1. The county of Traill is divided in county commissioner districts in the following manner: District number one (1) shall consist of the civil townships of Belmont, Caledonia and Elm River.

§ 2. District number two (2) shall consist of the civil townships of Eldorado, Hillsboro, Kelso and Bousack.

§ 3. District number three (3) shall consist of the civil townships of Irvin, Buxton and Norway.

§ 4. District number four (4) shall consist of the civil townships of Morgan, Mayville and Blanchard,

§ 5. District number five (5) shall consist of the civil townships of Garfield, Boseville, Norman and Galesburg.

§ 6. H C. Smette is hereby continued in office as county commissioner of the old district No. 2, till the expiration on January 1st, 1886, of the term for which he was elected and no longer. At the annual election in 1885 a commissioner shall be elected from district number four (4) in this act, who shall serve for three years from and after January 1st, 1886.

§ 7. If at any time hereafter the boundaries of the county of Traill are changed by division of said county or any addition thereto, then it shall be the duty of the board of commissioners of said county to divide said county into commissioner districts other than the foregoing.

§ 8. All acts and parts of acts in conflict with this act are hereby repeale l.

§ 9. This act shall take effect and be in force from and after its passage and approval.

Approved, March 13, 1885.

TURNER COUNTY - COUNTY SEAT.

CHAPTER 40.

AN ACT providing for the Location of the County Seat of Turner County Dakota Territory.

WHEREAS, The county seat of the county of Turner heretofore located at Swan Lake, by an act of the Legislative Assembly of the Territory of Dakota entitled "an act to organize the county of Turner, Hutchison, Hanson, and Buffalo and for other purposes," and approved January 13th, 1871, and, WHEREAS, At the general elections held in the years 1882 and 1884 the village of Parker received a majority of all the votes cast at such elections for the county seat in said county of Turner and, WHEREAS, The present location of the county seat of said Turner county at Swan Lake is wholly unfitted for court and county uses and purposes by reason of the village having become depopulated and no suitable buildings being therein situated to be used for such purpose; *Therefore,*

Be it enacted by the Legislative Assembly of the Territory of Dakota:

§ 1. That at the annual election to be held in the year 1885, the voters of said Turner county may designate upon their ballots the place of their choice for county seat of said county. And the place receiving a majority of the votes so cast at such election shall be the county seat of said Turner county, subject to be changed as provided by law for the removal of county seats from their permanent locations.

§ 2. That the county seat of said Turner county be and the same is hereby located at Parker in said county, subject to be changed as herein provided. *Provided, however,* That the county commissioners shall expend no money of the county in erecting county buildings at the village of Parker until such election has been had.

§ 3. All acts and parts of acts in conflict with this act are hereby repealed.

§ 4. This act shall take effect and be in force from and after its passage and approval.

Approved, February 26, 1885.

UNION COUNTY—BONDS.

CHAPTER 41

AN ACT to repeal Sections Eighteen, Nineteen, Twenty and Twenty-one in relation to road tax and road Supervisors of, "An Act, entitled An Act to Authorize and Empower the County of Union in the Territory of Dakota to issue Bonds to be used in Refunding and paying off its Outstanding Indebtedness and for the Payment of the same," Approved, March 9th, 1883.

Be it enacted by the Legislative Assembly of the Territory of Dakota:

§ 1. That sections eighteen, nineteen, twenty and twenty-one of "an act entitled an act to authorize and empower the county of Union, Territory of Dakota, to issue bonds to be used in refunding and paying off its outstanding indebtedness and for the payment of the same, are hereby repealed

§ 2. This act shall take effect and be in force from and after its passage and approval.

Approved, March 13, 1885.

WARD COUNTY—BOUNDARIES OF.

CHAPTER 42.

AN ACT Creating the County of Ward, Defining its Boundaries, and for other Purposes.

Be it enacted by the Legislative Assembly of the Territory of Dakota:

§ 1. All that tract of land included within the following boundary lines shall be and the same is hereby constituted and declared the county of Ward, to-wit: Beginning at the northeast corner of township number one hundred and fifty-seven (157) north of range eighty-two (82) west; thence south along the range line between ranges eighty-one (81) and eighty-two (82) to the southeast corner of township number one hundred and fifty-three (153) north of range eighty-two (82) west; thence west along the township line between townships number one hundred and fifty-two and one hundred and fifty-three (153) to the southwest corner of township number one hundred and fifty-three north of range eighty-seven (87) west; thence north along the range line between ranges eighty-seven (87) and eighty-eight (88) to the northwest corner of township number one hundred and fifty-seven north of range eighty-seven (87) west; thence east along the township line between townships number one hundred and fifty-seven (157) and one hundred and fifty-eight (158) to the place of beginning; and the jurisdiction of said county of Ward shall upon the taking effect of this act extend over all that district of country embraced within the boundaries herein described.

§ 2. CERTAIN BOUNDARY DEFINED.] That the south boundary of Ward county shall be the north boundary of Stevens county.

§ 3. COUNTY SEAT.] The county seat of said Ward county shall be and is hereby located at Burlington on section two (2) in township number one hundred and fifty-five (155) north of range numbered eighty-four west; *Provided,* That such location may be changed by vote of the qualified electors of said county as now provided by law in such cases.

§ 4. GOVERNOR TO APPOINT COMMISSIONERS, ETC.] It shall be the duty of the Governor upon the passage of this act to select and appoint three commissioners for the said Ward county. The commissioners so appointed shall be empowered and it is hereby made their duty after having duly qualified, to appoint all the officers of said Ward county as provided in the Code of this Territory ; and the said county commissioners and the officers so appointed by them shall each and all of them hold their several offices and discharge the duties thereof until the next general election, and until their successors are elected and qualified as provided in the general laws of the Territory.

§ 5. Prior to the taking effect of the preceding provisions of this act, the question of division of Stevens county and the creation of Ward county shall be submitted to a vote of the electors of Stevens county and of the territory affected, at a special election to be held at such time and at such places as may be designated by the Governor of the Territory of Dakota; *Provided, however,* That such election shall be called and held within sixty days from the passage of this act.

§ 6. The Governor of the Territory shall appoint the necessary judges and officers to conduct such election and to certify the returns thereof to the Governor, who shall, if the majority of the voters in said territory vote for the division of said county of Stevens and the creation of said county of Ward, declare the county of Ward duly created ; and he shall be further authorized and empowered to appoint three commissioners to serve as herein before provided, or may cause the selection of such commissioners and other county officers to be submitted to a vote of the people at such time and places as he may designate. Such election to be called and held within six months from the passage of this act, and the returns of said election shall be by the officers thereof, duly certified to the Governor, who shall, upon the coming in of such returns, issue to the persons elected to the respective offices, certificates of election therefor.

§ 7. The expenses of such elections shall be born by the county of Ward upon its organization, and it is made the duty of the commissioners thereof to reimburse the Territory of Dakota for any and all expense incurred in the creation and organization of said county, as well as to cause a full record of all election returns and other records pertaining to the organization of the county filed with the Governor, to be certified to the county clerk of said Ward county, to be by him recorded in the records of said county.

§ 8. All acts or parts of acts in conflict with this act are hereby repealed.

§ 9. This act shall take effect and be in force from and after its passage.

Note by the Secretary of the Territory.

The foregoing act having been presented to the Governor for his approval, and not having been returned to the House of Representatives, the house of the Legislative Assembly in which it originated, within the time prescribed by the Organic Act, has become a law without his approval.

JAMES H. TELLER,
Secretary of the Territory.

WELLS COUNTY, BOUNDARIES OF

CHAPTER 43.

AN ACT defining the boundaries of the County of Wells.

Be it enacted by the Legislative Assembly of the Territory of Dakota:

BOUNDARIES OF WELLS COUNTY.

§ 1. All that portion of the Territory of Dakota included within the following boundary lines to-wit: Beginning at the southeast corner of township number one hundred and forty-five (145) north of range number sixty-eight (68) west, and thence running west along the line between township one hundred and forty-five (145) and township one hundred and forty-four (144) to the southwest corner of township one hundred and forty-five (145) north, of range number seventy-three (73) west, thence north and along the line between ranges number seventy-three (73) and seventy-four(74) to the northwest corner of township number one hundred and fifty (150) north, of range seventy-three west, thence east and along the line of township one hundred and fifty (150) and one hundred and fifty-one (151) north, to the northeast corner of township one hundred and fifty (150) north, of range sixty-eight (68) west, thence south and along the lines between ranges sixty-seven (67) and sixty-eight (68) to the place of beginning. And the jurisdiction of said county of Wells shall upon the taking effect of this act, extend over all the district embraced in the foregoing boundaries.

§ 2. All acts or parts of acts in any way conflicting with the provisions of this act, are so far declared void and of no effect.

§ 3. This act shall take effect and be in force from and after its passage and approval.

Note by the Secretary of the Territory

The foregoing act, having been presented to the Governor for his approval and not having been returned to the Council, the House of the Legislative Assembly, in which it originated, within the time prescribed by the Organic Act, has become a law without his approval

JAMES H TELLER.
Secretary of the Territory.

ROADS IN YANKTON, TURNER AND CLAY COUNTIES.

CHAPTER 44.

AN ACT to establish a Public Highway on the County Line between Yankton and Turner and Yankton and Clay Counties.

Be it enacted by the Legislative Assembly of the Territory of Dakota:

§ 1. That there be and is hereby established a public highway on the county line between Yankton and Turner, and Yankton and Clay counties, with legal width of highway, described as follows, to-wit: Commencing at the northeast corner of Yankton county, thence south on the county line between Yankton and Turner and Yankton and Clay counties to where the said county line intersects the Missouri river, the road to be one-half on each side of said county line.

§ 2. This act shall take effect and be in force from and after its passage and approval.

Approved, March 10, 1885.

YANKTON COUNTY—REMISSION OF TAXES.

CHAPTER 45.

AN ACT to authorize the County Commissioners of Yankton County to Remit Certain Taxes.

Be it enacted by the Legislative Assembly of the Territory of Dakota:

§ 1. That the County Commissioners of the county of Yankton in said Territory be and they are hereby authorized and empowered to remit the whole or any part of the railroad taxes assessed or attempted to be assessed in said county in the years 1872, 1873, 1874 and 1875 as they may deem proper.

§ 2. This act shall take effect and be in force from and after its passage and approval.

Approved, March 12, 1885.

Division and Admission.

JOINT RESOLUTION.

CHAPTER 46.

Be it resolved by the Council and House of Representatives of the Territory of Dakota :

That there shall be appointed a joint committee, consisting of five from the Council and seven from the House, being one from each legislative district, whose duty it shall be to carefully and thoroughly consider the relation of this Territory to the general Government, and to report from time to time to their respective Houses what action they deem it advisable that this Legislature should take to secure division of the Territory and the admission of the southern half; and the further action it should take to convince the people of the Territory and the Congress of the United States that the people of Dakota are unalterably opposed to its admission as a whole.

Approved, January 30, 1885.

JOINT RESOLUTION AND MEMORIAL FOR DIVISION AND ADMISSION.

CHAPTER 47.

A JOINT RESOLUTION and Memorial to the Congress of the United States, Praying for the Division of Dakota and for the Admission of the Southern Portion of said Territory as a State.

To the Honorable the Congress of the United States :

The Legislative Assembly of the Territory of Dakota respectfully represents: That the people of this Territory earnestly desire the passage of the bill, now pending in the House of Representatives, providing for the admission of the southern portion

of Dakota as a state and praying for the creation of a separate
territory from the northern portion thereof, dividing the same on
the seventh Standard Parallel according to government survey,
or the 46th parallel of north latitude in the discretion of congress.

The desire for division is so universal, and the reasons for it so
apparent, that the people of this Territory have believed, and
still believe, that this measure of justice cannot be refused them.

The probable division of the Territory has been considered in
territorial conventions of both political parties at every meeting
for the last thirteen years and these conventions in almost every
instance without a dissenting voice, have invariably declared in
favor of division.

The Legislative Assembly of the Territory has repeatedly me-
morialized your honorable body for division.

Public institutions have been located and built with a view to
division.

Conventions have been held in each section to promote division and delegations have been appointed to go to the capital of
the United States to labor for division.

The people of the Territory have employed every possible form
of respectful petitions for division.

The population and area of the Territory justify division, and
refusing it leaves both sections in an unsettled condition and op-
erates to the serious disadvantage of both. The area of the Territory is greater than the united areas of New Hampshire, Ver-
mont, Massachusetts, Rhode Island, Connecticut, New York, New
Jersey, Pennsylvania, Delaware, and Maryland.

The population of the Territory, as shown by its vote, by the
public lands occupied, by its postal and internal revenues, and by
its banking and other business interests, is not less than 450,000,
and there is good reason for believing it amounts to 500,000.

The population of the southern portion, for which admission is
asked, cannot now fall much short of 300,000, and will very soon
exceed that figure.

The climate, surface and soil of the Territory are as well adap-
ted to agricultural pursuits and the ordinary industries of the
north as are the climate, surface and soil of Illinois or Iowa.

The people of the Territory have as great a regard for the
rights of others, and smart as keenly under a sense of injustice, as
those of any other territory or state: The revenues paid into the
United States treasury by the people of Dakota, and all statistics
attainable, prove that the population and material interests of
the Territory are sufficiently great to justify this consideration at
your hands.

No difficulty can arise as to the apportionment of the public debt
of the Territory, as it was wholly created for the erection of public
buildings, and the bonds clearly show for what purpose issued.

Those issued for public buildings in that part of the Territory
south of the forty-six h parallel should be paid by the southern
division of the Territory, and those issued for public buildings
erected in the north should be paid by the northern division of
the Territory.

The union of the two sections in one state would be unnatural and
would lead to endless difficulties.

The division prayed for is wise. It will quiet unrest, prevent
difficulties and misunderstandings, which will arise if it is not
granted and will promote the interests of both sections.

And although the people of all Dakota are earnestly in favor of
admission of the southern half as a state, still they will hail with
joy division only, and if asking for admission of the southern
half as a state will in any manner delay division, then we
earnestly request division, without the admission prayed for, at
the earliest possible time.

And for your favorable consideration hereof your memorialists
will ever pray.

Resolved, That a copy of the above and foregoing memorial,
signed by the President of the Council and Speaker of the House,
and attested by their chief clerks, be sent to the President of the
United States senate, the Speaker of the House of Representatives
of the United States, and to our delegate in Congress, the Honorable John B. Raymond

Approved, February 2, 1885.

Executive Office.

FOR THE EMPLOYMENT OF CLERKS.

CHAPTER 48.

AN ACT to Provide for Payment of Clerical work in the Executive Office.

Be it enacted by the Legislative Assembly of the Territory of Dakota:

§ 1. That the territorial Auditor be authorized to furnish such
clerical assistance as may be necessary to the executive office, the
same to be paid out of the receipts of said Auditor's office, not to
exceed five hundred dollars in any one year.

§ 2. That this act shall take effect and be in force from and after its passage and approval.

Approved, March 13, 1885.

Iroquois.

TO PROHIBIT THE SALE OF LIQUORS.

CHAPTER 49.

AN ACT to Prohibit the Sale or Licensing of the Sale of Intoxicating Liquors, within a mile of the portions of Iroquois and Denver, lying in Kingsbury County, Dakota.

Be it enacted by the Legislative Assembly of the Territory of Dakota :

§ 1. It shall not be lawful to sell or to license the sale of intoxicating liquors to be sold within one mile of that part of the villages of Iroquois and Denver, lying in the county of Kingsbury, in the Territory of Dakota, at any time or during which no license is granted in said county. Any license granted contrary to the provisions of this act shall be void, and any person violating the provisions hereof shall be subject to the prosecution provided for, and penalties imposed, by the laws now and hereafter in force on the subject of intoxicating liquors, and the general laws shall apply whenever applicable for the enforcement of the provisions of this act.

Approved, March 13, 1885.

Townships.

CIVIL TOWNSHIPS IN NORTH DAKOTA.

CHAPTER 50.

AN ACT to Amend an act entitled An Act to Provide for the Organization of Civil Townships and the Government of the same.

Be it enacted by the Legislative Assembly of the Territory of Dakota :

§ 1. That section 2 of chapter 1 of an act entitled "An act to provide for the organization of civil townships and the government of the same," approved, March 9, 1883, be and the same is hereby amended by inserting after the word "territory" the following: "And the board of county commissioners of any county lying north of the forty-sixth parallel of latitude west of the Missouri river may unite not less than four congressional townships into one civil township, or may add not more than three congressional townships to any congressional township already organized as a civil township, when petitioned by a majority of the legal voters affected thereby, if in the opinion of the said board of commissioners the best interests of said townships be subserved thereby.

§ 2. This act shall take effect from and after its passage and approval.

Approved, March 13, 1885.

TITLES OF SPECIAL AND PRIVATE ACTS, JOINT RESO-
LUiIONS AND MEMORIALS PASSED BY THE
LEGISLATURE OF 1885, AND NOT PUBLISHED IN
THIS VOLUME.

AN ACT to vacate certain portions of the city of Canton, Lincoln
county, Dakota Territory.

AN ACT to amend " An act authorizing the county of Roberts to
fund its outstanding indebtedness."

AN ACT to amend " An act to incorporate the city of Chamberlain "

AN ACT amendatory of an act to incorporate the city of Grand
Forks, D. T.

AN ACT to amend the charter of the city of Grafton, and for other
purposes.

AN ACT to amend an act entitled "An act to incorporate the city
of Valley City, Barnes county, D. T.," and legalizing the
incorporation of the city and declaring its status.

AN ACT to amend section 82 of article 7 of an act entitled an act
to incorporate the city of Grand Forks, Dakota Territory.

AN ACT to amend the charter of the city of Ashton.

AN ACT changing the corporate limits of the city of Redfield.

AN ACT to amend "an act to incorporate the city of Aberdeen, in
the Territory of Dakota."

AN ACT to amend an act entitled "An act to incorporate the village of Valley Springs," passed by the 13th legislative assembly of the Territory of Dakota.

AN ACT to amend the charter of the city of Steele, Dakota Territory.

AN ACT to appeal subdivision 2 of section 12 of an act entitled an
act incorporating the city of Deadwood.

AN ACT to amend section 72 of an act entitled an act incorporating the city of Deadwood.

AN ACT supplementary to an act approved March 13, 1883, entitled "An act to amend an act entitled "An act to incorporate the city of Bismarck," approved February 15, 1875.

AN ACT to amend section fourteen (14) of the city charter of the
city of Hillsboro, Traill county, Dakota.

AN ACT to amend the charter of the city of Vermillion and an
act amending said charter.

1885—37

AN ACT to amend an act incorporating the city of Larimore, Dakota, passed February 20, 1883.

AN ACT to amend an act entitled "An act to incorporate the city of Chamberlain."

AN ACT to amend the act to incorporate the village of Parker, Turner county, Dakota, and define its boundaries, approved March 9, 1883.

AN ACT to legalize the assessment of Hyde county, Dakota Territory, for the year 1884, and to authorize the board of county commissioners to equalize the same.

AN ACT to legalize a certain ordinance of the town of Wahpeton providing for the establishment of water works and to legalize the issue of certain bonds issued thereunder.

AN ACT to authorize the county commissioners of Ramsey county, to fund the outstanding indebtedness of said county.

AN ACT to authorize the county commissioners of Ramsey county, Territory of Dakota, to issue bonds to build roads and bridges in the county.

AN ACT to amend section 1, chapter 62, of the special laws of 1881.

AN ACT authorizing the board of county commissioners of Custer county to levy a ten mill tax for county general fund.

AN ACT authorizing the county of Morton to issue bonds for the purpose of procuring ground and erecting court house and jail for the county of Morton.

AN ACT authorizing the board of county commissioners of Day and Hyde counties to fund the outstanding indebtedness thereof.

MEMORIAL to Congress praying for the passage of the Mexican war pension bill now pending in the U. S. house of representatives.

AN ACT legalizing the incorporation of the village of Valley Springs, Minnehaha county, Dakota Territory, and the official acts of the officers of said village; also for fixing the time of holding village elections for said village.

AN Act authorizing the county commissioners of Richland county to issue bonds of said county for the purpose of paying certain indebtedness thereof.

AN ACT providing for the construction of a court house in Edmunds county, Dakota Territory.

AN ACT to vacate the town site of Belmont, in the county of Traill, Territory of Dakota.

AN ACT authorizing the board of county commissioners of Dickey county to fund the outstanding indebtedness thereof.

MEMORIAL to congress praying that Gen'l Grant be placed on the retired list.

AN ACT to amend an act entitled "An act to incorporate the city of Bismarck," approved February 14, 1875.

AN ACT to amend an act entitled "An act to incorporate the village o Flandreau," passed at the eleventh session of the Legislative Assembly of the Territory of Dakota.

AN ACT to amend the charter of the village of Minto, Walsh county, Dakota Territory.

AN ACT to amend the charter of the city of Elk Point, Union county.

AN ACT to amend the charter of the city of Lisbon, and for other purposes.

AN ACT to amend the charter of the village of Egan, Moody county, Dakota.

AN ACT to incorporate the city of DeSmet.

AN ACT establishing independent school district of Flandreau

AN ACT to incorporate the city of Spearfish.

AN ACT to establish a board of education for the town or city of Alexandria, Hanson county, Dakota

AN ACT providing for a school board for the city of Lisbon, and for other purposes

AN ACT incorporating the village of Woonsocket, Dakota Territory.

AN ACT to provide for a charter for the city of Pembina, Dakota Territory.

AN ACT to incorporate the city of Groton, Dakota Territory.

AN ACT to incorporate the city of Salem, of the county of McCook, Territory of Dakota.

AN ACT to incorporate the city of Big Stone City, Grant county, Dakota, and to create an independent school district.

AN ACT to incorporate the town of Bridgewater, county of McCook, Territory of Dakota.

AN ACT to incorporate the city of Frankfort.

AN ACT amending the charter of the city of Man ian.

AN ACT to incorporate the village of Webster.

AN ACT to incorporate the city of Alexandria.

AN ACT to incorporate the city of Clark.

AN ACT to incorporate the city of Watertown, in Codington county.

AN ACT authorizing the board of county commissioners of Grand Forks county, D. T., to fund the outstanding indebtedness of said county.

AN ACT authorizing the county of Foster to issue bonds for the building of a court house, and for other purposes.

AN ACT authorizing the commissioners of Grant county to fund the outstanding indebtedness thereof.

AN ACT to enable the school districts of the counties of Barnes and Griggs to fund their indebtedness.

JOINT resolution and memorial to the Congress of the United States relating to the reduction of the prices of public lands within the railway grants of this Territory.

AN ACT providing for the erection and construction of a court house and jail for the county of Brookings, Dakota Territory.

AN ACT to allow the school township of Ordway, in Brown county, to issue bonds to fund outstanding indebtedness.

AN ACT in relation to the bonds and coupons issued by the township of Elk Point, Union county, Dakota.

AN ACT to change the name of Elgin, in Cass county, to Ayr.

AN ACT to vacate certain portions of the town site of Elk Point, Dakota Territory.

AN ACT to authorize the county commissioners of McCook county to fund the outstanding indebtedness of said county, and for other purposes.

JOINT resolution and memorial to Congress praying for the passage of the bill pending to name Lieut. A. W. Greeley assistant chief of the United States signal service.

MEMORIAL to the Congress of the United States praying for the granting of civil and criminal jurisdiction to the probate courts of the Territory of Dakota.

AN ACT providing for the issue of bonds for the erection of court house and jail for county of Wells, and other purposes.

AN ACT to repeal chapter thirty-seven of the special and private laws of 1881, relating to the pay of county commissioners in Stutsman county.

AN ACT to change the name of the Saint James Protestant Episcopal church of Jamestown, Dakota.

AN ACT to provide for the removal and location of the county seat of Bon Homme county.

AN ACT establishing civil townships in Traill county, Territory of Dakota.

AN ACT to authorize the " Lenham elevator and lumber company" a corporation, to change its name.

JOINT resolution asking for the opening of the Sisseton and Wahpeton Indian reservations.

AN ACT to change the name of the township of Logan, tonwship 103, range 64, Aurora county.

AN ACT authorizing the board of trustees of the town of Plankinton, Aurora county, to fund the outstanding indebtedness thereof.

AN ACT to legalize the acts of the board of county commissioners of Dickey county, D. T., in building a court house.

AN ACT authorizing the city of Bismarck, Dakota Territory, to issue bonds for the purpose of retiring and refunding bonds heretofore issued for building and furnishing a school house.

AN ACT to establish an independent school district, to be designated as Independent School District No. 2, Turner county, Dakota.

AN ACT to change the name of the village of Nordland, in Kingsbury county, Dakota, to that of Arlington.

AN ACT to amend an act establishing Independent School District No. 1, of Turner county, Dakota.

AN ACT to establish the Independent School District of Bridgewater, and to provide for the organization and government of the same.

AN ACT providing for the erection and construction of a court house and jail for the county of Hyde, Territory of Dakota.

AN ACT to establish the Independent School District of Grand View, in the county of Douglas, Territory of Dakota, and for other purposes.

AN ACT to authorize the board of county commissioners of Union county to fund the outstanding indebtedness thereof.

AN ACT authorizing the county commissioners of Edmunds county, Dakota Territory, to fund the outstanding indebtedness of said county.

AN ACT for the relief of Milton C. Conners.

AN ACT to fund the indebtedness of Fort Ransom school township of Ransom county, Dakota.

AN ACT authorizing the board of county commissioners of Custer county to fund the outstanding indebtedness thereof.

AN ACT to amend an act entitled " An act to incorporate the city of Canton."

AN ACT establishing Independent School District No. 1, of Hutchinson county, D. T.

AN ACT to amend the charter of the city of Yankton, Dakota Territory, approved March 9, 1883.

1885—38

AN ACT to amend "An act to incorporate the city of Mitchell."

AN ACT to incorporate the village of Webster.

AN ACT to incorporate the village of Howard, Miner county, Dakota Territory, and to repeal former acts of incorporation.

AN ACT to incorporate the city of Fairbank.

AN ACT to incorporate the city of Sioux Falls.

AN ACT to amend the charter of the city of Casselton.

AN ACT to incorporate the city of Milbank.

AN ACT to incorporate the city of Madison, Dakota.

AN ACT to amend sections 25 and 26 of article 2 of the city charter of Jamestown, Dakota.

AN ACT to amend sections 2 and 6 of chapter 1 of the city of Grafton.

AN ACT incorporating the city of Mayville, Traill county, D. T.

AN ACT for the incorporation of the city of Scotland.

AN ACT to incorporate the village of Volga, Brookings county, Dakota Territory.

AN ACT granting a charter to the city of Columbia.

AN ACT providing for a charter for the city of Wahpeton.

AN ACT to change the name of the town of Victoria, in the county of McLean, Territory of Dakota, to Coal Harbor.

AN ACT to change the names of Edward C. Hitchcock and Louise Jane Hitchcock to Edward C. Brelsford and Louise Jane Brelsford.

AN ACT to legalize the assessment of Butte county, Dakota Territory, for the year A. D. 1883.

AN ACT to legalize the acts of the voters of school township No. 2, of Towner county, Dakota Territory.

AN ACT authorizing the city of Bismarck to issue bonds.

AN ACT to authorize the county commissioners of Nelson county to fund the outstanding indebtedness thereof.

AN ACT to vacate Cherry street in the town of Menno, Hutchinson county, Dakota Territory.

AN ACT to provide for the bonding of the outstanding indebtedness of Marion school township in Turner county.

MEMORIAL for an appropriation to improve the navigation of the water-way or route between Big Stone Lake and the Red River of the North and for other purposes.

AN ACT to vacate that part of Helmsworth and McLean's addition to the city of Mandan, lying south of the main track of the Northern Pacific railroad.

AN ACT authorizing and empowering the county commissioners of Cavalier county, Dakota, to fund the outstanding indebtedness of said county.

AN ACT entitled an act to authorize the purchase of a poor farm for Walsh county.

AN ACT to amend an act entitled "An act to fund the indebtedness of the counties of Moody, Brookings, Burleigh and Grand Forks," passed at the thirteenth session of the Legislative Assembly of the Territory of Dakota, held in 18 9.

AN ACT to authorize the village of Egan to issue bonds.

AN ACT to change the boundaries of Crystal and Park townships in the county of Pembina.

AN ACT providing for Winona county to assume a portion of the indebtedness of Emmons county.

AN ACT to establish independent school district of Canova, Miner county, Dakota.

AN ACT supplemental to an act entitled "An act to enable the school districts of the counties of Barnes and Griggs to fund their indebtedness."

AN ACT to establish independent school district of Howard, Miner county, Dakota.

AN ACT to authorize a special election in the county of Steele.

AN ACT authorizing and directing the county commissioners of Lawrence county to settle with and release the sureties upon the official bond of Robert Neill, formerly treasurer of said county, upon certain conditions.

AN ACT to fund the indebtedness of Codington county, Dakota.

AN ACT to amend "An act providing a board of education for the city of Jamestown, Dakota Territory, and regulating the management of the public schools therein."

AN ACT to establish independent school district No. 2, in Bon Homme county, Dakota Territory.

AN ACT to amend council bill 244, that certain townships shall assume the bonded indebtedness as if they were still within the limits of Burleigh county

AN ACT to vacate certain portions of Cooper's addition to the city of Grafton, Walsh county, Dakota Territory, and for other purposes.

AN ACT to legalize certain acts of the county commissioners of Spink county, Dakota.

An act establishing the city of Springfield, Bon Homme county,
    Dakota Territory, as an independent school district, to be
    designated as independent school district of Springfield,
    Bon Homme county, Dakota.

An act granting authority to the board of county commissioners
    of Eddy county to issue bonds to meet the current expenses
    of said county and to furnish its county offices as required
    by law.

An act to amend an act to create the office of district attorney for
    the several counties of Dakota Territory, and for other pur-
    poses.

An act to authorize the county commissioners of Benson county
    to issue bonds to fund their outstanding indebtedness, and
    for other purposes

An act to vacate North Tyndall, in the county of Bon Homme,
    Dakota.

A act to legalize the assessment of taxes in Roberts county, for
    the year 1883.

An act to create a joint school township in the counties of Griggs
    and Steele.

An act authorizing the county of Fall River to construct a county
    bridge over the Cheyenne river, and to issue bonds therefor.

An act providing for the erection and construction of a court
    house and jail for the county of Clark, Territory of Dakota.

An act authorizing the board of county commissioners of McPher
    son county to fund the outstanding indebtedness thereof.

An act authorizing the county commissioners of Roberts county
    to fund the outstanding indebtedness thereof.

An act establishing Independent School District No. 1, Traill
    county, Dakota Territory.

An act to authorize the board of county commissioners of Sargent
    county, Dakota Ter.itory, to issue bonds to fund the debt
    of the same.

An act to authorize the commissioners of Deuel county to fund
    the outstanding indebtedness thereof.

Joint resolution and memorial relative to the pine lands in Min-
    nesota.

An act to establish independent school district No. 1 of Douglas
    county, Dakota Territory, and for other purposes.

Memorial protesting against the removal of the Deadwood land
    office.

An act to establish a portion of the school township of Denver
    in Kingsbury county, Dakota Territory, also a portion of

the school townships of Windsor and Bangor, in Brookings county, Dakota Territory, as an independent school district number one (1) of Kingsbury county, Dakota Territory.

AN ACT to provide for a special election in McHenry county for the election of county officers and the temporary location of the county seat thereof.

AN ACT to amend an act entitled "An act to annex certain territory to the Vermillion City school district, and for other purposes."

AN ACT authorizing the board of county commissioners of Aurora county to fund the outstanding indebtedness thereof.

AN ACT supplementary to an act entitled "An act to legalize a certain ordinance of the town of Wahpeton, providing for the establishment of water works and to legalize the issue of certain bonds issued thereunder."

AN ACT to authorize the trustees of the city of Groton, Brown county, to extend the time for the collection of taxes of the year 1884.

JOINT resolution of the Council and House of Representativ s of the Legislative Assembly of the Territory of Dakota to provide compensation to the chief clerk of the Council of the Legislative Session of 1874-75 for completing the Council Journal.

AN ACT to vacate a certain portion of the town of Sterling, situated in county of Burleigh, and Territory of Dakota.

AN ACT to authorize school district number 52 of Deuel county, to issue bonds to build a school house.

AN ACT to create certain territory now within the school township of Brightwood, Richland county, Dakota Territory, as an independent school district, number one (1) Richland county, Dakota Territory.

AN ACT to amend chapter 17 of the special and private laws for 1881.

AN ACT to establish the Plankinton independent school district in Aurora county.

AN ACT to authorize Montrose and Grant school townships, McCook county, to issue bonds to fund their outstanding indebtedness.

AN ACT to legalize school tax levied by the Andover school township number nine (9) in Day county, July 12, 1884.

AN ACT to legalize the organization of New Salem civil township, Morton county, Dakota Territory.

AN ACT to establish independent school district number twenty (20) of Hanson county, Dakota Territory.

1885—39

AN ACT authorizing the county of Stark to issue bonds for the purpose of erecting a court house and jail for the county of Stark.

AN ACT authorizing Union township of Edmunds county, to issue bonds for the purpose of paying off the outstanding indebtedness.

AN ACT to authorize Andover school township number nine (9) in Day county, to issue bonds to build school houses.

AN ACT to provide for the bonding of the outstanding indebtedness of Big Stone school township in Grant county, Territory of Dakota.

AN ACT establishing independent school district of Walcott, Richland county, Dakota Territory.

AN ACT to change the name of the village of Marshall in the county of Ransom, Territory of Dakota, to that of Englevale.

AN ACT to amend Council Bill number 79 of the special laws passed at the Legislative Assembly of 1883, approved February 21st, 1883.

AN ACT establishing independent school district of Gilman, Lake county, Dakota.

AN ACT authorizing and empowering the county commissioners of Towner county, Dakota, to fund the outstanding indebtedness of said county.

AN ACT to provide for funding the indebtedness of Sully county, Dakota.

AN ACT to amend section 4 of an act entitled "An act providing for the erection of a court house and jail for Walsh county, Dakota."

AN ACT to empower school district No. 78 of Walsh county, D. T., to issue bonds for school purposes.

AN ACT to provide for the building of a court house and jail in Brown county, Dakota Territory.

AN ACT to provide for the issue of bonds in aid of the construction of a court house and jail for the county of Walsh.

AN ACT to vacate certain portions of Matthews and Scobey's addition to the city of Brookings, Brookings county, Dakota Territory.

AN ACT establishing the independent school district of Woonsocket, Sanborn county, Dakota Territory.

AN ACT to change the name of certain churches in Bon Homme county, Dakota.

AN ACT authorizing the board of county commissioners of Cass county to issue bonds for the purpose of funding the indebtedness of the road and bridge fund.

AN ACT authorizing the board of county commissioners of Cass county, Dakota, to issue bonds for finishing and furnishing the court house.

AN ACT to authorize Lawrence county to issue bonds for the purpose of erecting a jail and providing for the payment of the same.

AN ACT legalizing the acts of John P. Belding, late acting sheriff of Lawrence county, and for other purposes.

AN ACT authorizing the board of county commissioners of Stutsman county to fund its outstanding road and bridge indebtedness.

AN ACT to extend and connect certain streets in the town of Madison, Lake county, Dakota

AN ACT to amend and supplementary to an act entitled "An act to provide for building a court house and jail in Hamlin county," passed at the sixteenth session of the Legislative Assembly of the Territory of Dakota, and known as Council bill No. 134.

AN ACT entitled an act to provide a special election in Rolette county for the election of county officers and locating the county seat.

AN ACT authorizing the board of county commissioners of Grand Forks county to offer a reward for the apprehension and conviction of a murderer.

AN ACT to vacate certain portions of the townsite of Oriska.

AN ACT to authorize school district No. 18, Cass county, to issue bonds to build a school house.

AN Act establishing independent school district No. 4, Lake County, Dakota.

AN ACT to amend section 1 of chapter 44 of the special laws of 1883.

AN ACT authorizing the boards of county commissioners of Lake and Kingsbury counties to fund the outstanding indebtedness thereof.

AN ACT to amend an act providing for a board of education for the city of Fargo, and regulating the management of the public schools therein.

AN ACT establishing school district No. 3, of Walsh county, Dakota as an independent school district.

AN ACT establishing independent school district No. 3, Lake county, Dakota.

AN ACT to provide for building a court house and jail in Hamlin county and for other purposes.

INDEX.

APPEALS—Bond not required in certain cases......................... 8
    Appeals—in contested elections... 97

APPEARANCE—Time to be specified in summons, when............... 206

APPLICATION for new trial—how made... 175

APPORTIONMENT—Legislative.. 8
    Apportionment of delegates to Constitutional convention............. 52
APPRAISAL—Of property exempt—how made............ 98

APPROPRIATION—For Agricultural Societies, how divided............ 4
    For printing reports of regents of agricultural college............. 7
    For Dakota Hospital for the Insane................................. 11
    For North Dakota Hospital for the Insane......... 12
    For university of Dakota.. 12
    For university of North Dakota..... 12
    For penitentiary at Sioux Falls..................................... 13
    For normal school at Madison.. 13
    For school of mines... 13
    For agricultural college—Brookings........... 14
    For territorial library—purchase of codes, etc...................... 14
    For blanks for Governor's office.................................... 14
    For printing report of grain commissioners.......................... 14
    For penitentiary at Bismarck.. 14
    For legislative furniture, heating, etc.............................. 17
    For purchase of laws for members of legislature 18
    For expense of certain contest cases,................................ 19

1885—40

Lightning Source UK Ltd.
Milton Keynes UK
UKHW011033051118
331794UK00012B/1123/P